STORIES I NEVER TOLD
THE SPEAKER

Stories
I Never Told
the Speaker

The Chaotic Adventures
of a Capitol Hill Aide

Marshall L. Lynam

Dallas: Three Forks Press, 1998

THREE FORKS PRESS
P.O. BOX 823461
DALLAS, TEXAS 75382

LIBRARY OF CONGRESS CATALOG CARD NO. 97-061458

ISBN: 0-9637629-7-4

PRINTED IN THE UNITED STATES OF AMERICA

FIRST EDITION

To EDDIE, my wife and my love

who collaborated with me

in three outstanding

previous works—

Marsha Ann

Charles Lee

and Sharon Kaye

thus inspiring these five superb sequels—

Michael Justin

Jennifer Ann

Tiffany Elizabeth

Marshall Joseph

and Maryann Evelyn

Contents

Author's Note

Reflections of a Lucky Man

If I'm not the luckiest guy on earth, please consider me at least a runner-up. For most of my life I've worked in what I consider two of the most enjoyable and exciting jobs on earth—in the old days as a newspaper reporter and then, for more than a quarter century, as a Capitol Hill staffer.

In this book I'd like to share a few of the funny, touching and occasionally historic things these jobs have allowed me to do, or at least to see. These little stories are true. Most repose in my own memory, sometimes reinforced by musty old papers from tattered cardboard boxes my wife Eddie has tried for years to persuade me to throw away. Other stories on these pages come from trusted friends who were involved in whatever drama or mischief was afoot. Quotations have been re-created to reflect the substance and tone of the conversations.

Most people in this book are my friends, and their names and descriptions are real. But in a few cases, to prevent friends from being embarrassed or compromised, I have given them alternate identities.

My lifelong streak of good luck, however, started long before I began either of my careers. It started, in fact, with my parents. Genes don't come any tougher or more durable than the ones I inherited.

My father, Lee Lynam, was as resilient as a front wheel spring on his 1930 Model A Ford. He never failed to bounce back—back from the challenges of life as a kid on a dirt-poor Texas farm, as a doughboy gassed and left for dead on a battlefield in France, as a car dealer bankrupted by the Depression, as an oil field roughneck overtaken by age, and as an aircraft mechanic for the Navy in World War II. Yet through all these personal ordeals, never once did he waver in his unshakable pride in the United States of

America. He was, above all, an unashamed patriot. Neighbors knew better, for example, than to joke about his flagpole.

In the tiny front yard of the home in Bishop, Texas, where he and my Mother spent their final years, Daddy erected a flagpole imposing enough to serve an Army fort. And in a way, I'm responsible.

A few years after coming to work in Washington, I sent him a flag that had been flown over the Capitol of the United States on his birthday. My boss, Congressman Jim Wright, was kind enough to write an accompanying letter warmly praising his service to our country. In the last few years of Daddy's life, this letter and this flag were his proudest possessions.

On holidays, he would go out in the yard just before dawn and, standing alone in the dewy grass, await the first rays of sunrise. Then, with a pride as deep as any ever stirred by a full-dress parade at West Point, he would ceremoniously raise the flag, hobble back a few steps and snap a crisp salute. On one of his last birthdays, he limped on his game leg to the breakfast table. In his hand he clutched the flag.

"Where are you going with the flag?" asked my Mother.

"Going to put it up," he said.

"On your birthday?"

"Yes."

"That's silly, Lee. People don't put up the flag on their birthday."

Daddy took a sip of coffee, but said nothing.

"You're supposed to put up the flag on national holidays, like Memorial Day and the Fourth of July," Mother pointed out.

He grunted.

"What would you say," Mother asked, "if I put up the flag on my birthday?"

Daddy thought for a minute. "It's not *your* flag," he said, shuffling out toward the flagpole.

Years later, as Mother related this story to me, she smiled understandingly. To her, coping with a headstrong Lee Lynam was a personal obligation as compelling as the duty she felt to look after family members and friends when they became too sick or incapacitated to care for themselves.

Day after day for nearly four years, this quiet Texas housewife provided loving and selfless full-time care for her mother, who suffered a stroke at age 84 and was never again able to speak, feed herself or leave her bed. Moving her into the front bedroom of our home, Mother cared for this withered, gentle soul for the rest of her life. In addition to her regular household duties, Mother cooked special food for her mother, fed her spoonful by spoonful, kept her sick bed spotless and even administered occasional hypodermic shots to ease her pain. In later years, she gave similarly tireless care to other family members and friends. Never on earth did there live a kinder, more selfless person than our Mother. May Lynam's devotion to others and reverence for life extended even to ants.

In the 1950s, my brother Jimmy was an F-86 crew chief at a U.S. Air Force Base in Germany. Once he wrote home using an envelope which, unaccountably, happened to contain a tiny sugar ant. As Mother sat at the kitchen table, reading this treasured letter from one of her beloved sons, the ant, still perky after its transatlantic flight, crawled out of the envelope.

"What did you do with it?" I asked.

"It came from Jimmy, so I gave some sugar to the poor little thing and put it out in the back yard," Mother said.

Our Dad died in 1969 and Mother in 1982, but they would be as proud as I am today of Jimmy and our sister Gwen. Both are truly remarkable people. Jimmy and his wife Marie now live in Fort Worth, not far from their daughter Penny and son Butch, or Jimmy Wayne. Marie, a delightful and energetic retired school teacher, now devotes full-time to Grandchildren 101. Jimmy, having completed a distinguished Air Force Reserve career as a Chief Master Sergeant, the highest possible enlisted rank, now is a Deputy Sheriff. But when it comes to sheer personal achievement, Jimmy and I both stand in awe of our younger, red-headed sister.

Like many young couples, Gwen and her husband Richard had to work hard to provide for their two small children, Joy and Ricky, in the early years of their marriage. Short on money and busy wiping noses and changing diapers, Gwen got a late start toward her dream of becoming a professional educator. Not until her second child was four years old could she devote the time necessary to attain her bachelor's degree. With her duties as wife and mother still getting top priority, she somehow managed to juggle a number of outside jobs through the years along with her unrelenting pursuit first of her master's degree and then of her doctorate. Demonstrating skill and understanding in each task she undertook, she advanced quickly through the ranks of academia. Only fifteen years after the day she won her bachelor's degree from Texas A&I in 1966, Dr. Gwendolyn Tilley, Ph.D., became Vice President of Instruction at San Jacinto Junior College, an institution with 10,000 students in Houston suburb of Pasadena.

And if middle-aged husbands are supposed to buy snazzy sports cars in fond hope of recapturing their youth, Gwen's husband Richard Tilley didn't fit the mold. As he neared the end of an admirable career in petrochemical engineering, he sweet-talked Gwen into letting him buy not a sexy red Porsche coupe but an eighteen-wheel diesel truck. Finally having realized his long-suppressed dream of thundering along the highway at the wheel of a massive tractor and semi, he even got Gwen to take one trip in this monstrous machine. For years, from their home in Pasadena, Richard contracted for hauling jobs all across the nation. As their truck roared along the interstates, it was perhaps the only Peterbilt rig in America driven by a petrochemical expert who at least once carried with him an attractive Ph.D. to share coffee and help with the maps.

Grateful for the sturdy genes God gave me, I was understandably diligent in my search for a spouse who had been similarly blessed. While working as a projectionist at a movie theater in Kingsville, I met a very pretty, vivacious girl named Eddie Forrest. She worked in the box-office, and I shamelessly used to lure her up to the projection room now and then for a little smooching.

In fact, as the daughter of an old-time locomotive engineer as tough and level-headed as my own father, Eddie looked like an ideal candidate for wifehood, except for one thing. I wasn't sure she always exercised sound judgment. My suspicions were confirmed when she agreed to marry me in the full knowledge that the $14 in my pocket was all the money I had in the world. In retrospect, however, her judgment may have been better than I thought. To date our marriage has lasted 48 years.

Our first child was a delightful little girl named Marsha Ann, who inherited both her mother's attractiveness and her superb culinary skills. Today she is the mother of three children—Michael, Jennifer and Tiffany—and operates a small catering business in the idyllic little Shenandoah valley town of Strasburg, Virginia. Next came our son Charles, whose turbulent years as a teenager made life interesting for Eddie, for me and once even for the sheriff of Arkadelphia, Arkansas. (See Chapters 8 and 9.) These days Charles lives with his wife Sandy and two children— Marshall and Maryann—in Leakey, Texas. Our youngest daughter, Sharon Kaye, is a warm and soft-spoken person who loves every little animal that God put on earth. Before moving to her present home in Bradenton, Florida, she lived in Virginia Beach, Virginia, and operated a unique business called Dirty Dog Bathers, Inc. You'd never guess what service the company rendered.

In addition to family members, no human has ever been luckier than I in the matter of friends. From my newspaper days I cherish the memory of working with guys like Gene Gordon and Carl Freund, whom you will meet in Chapter 1, and Madeline Williams, a female reporter who often beat us men in what was supposed to be our private domain.

Her late husband, Mack Williams, was the fastest rewrite man and the best friend a fellow ever had. Others, too, have gone wherever ink-stained newspaper wretches go. I think about such greats as George Dolan, Bill Haworth, Jim Vachule, John Mort, Joe Titus, Jack Gordon and Sam Hunter. I like to think that these days they may be talking shop with an earlier bunch of reporters named Matthew, Mark, Luke and John.

On Jim Wright's staff, too, served some of the finest people on earth—people in Washington like Kathy Mitchell, who kept Jim Wright organized, and Anne Page, who did her best to keep me organized also, with occasional instances of success. Then too there was John Mack, Jim Greer and his late wife Peggy, plus the Fort Worth crew—Jimmie Lee Bodiford, Larry Shannon, Norma Richson and Orabeth McMullen. Three others—Craig Raupe, Joe Shosid and Carlos Moore—you will meet inside the book.

In the following chapters also you will get a glimpse of three of the very best friends I ever had—George Troutman, Dayle Henington and Seth Kantor. Dayle and his pretty wife Juli use San Antonio as home base these days as they flit around the country visiting friends. George and his vivacious and tireless wife Dottie live near Upper Marlboro, Maryland, on a beautiful estate nearly large enough to qualify for statehood. My friendship with Seth, a superb journalist, began back in our days on the old *Fort Worth Press* and grew even stronger as we worked together in Washington. Seth died unexpectedly in 1993. His wife Ann remains one of our closest friends.

In 1989, after nearly three decades as a Capitol Hill staffer, I was lucky enough to be retained as a Congressional consultant for two prestigious hometown organizations. One was Dallas/Fort Worth International Airport. Through the years as DFW improved its facilities and grew in traffic volume to become the second busiest airport in the world, I have been privileged to work with a succession of great DFW executive and staff people—Oris Dunham, Vernell Sturns, Jeff Fegan, Kevin Cox and Joe Dealey and Clarees Vesey, to name only a few.

For eight years I have also represented Fort Worth's own Tandy Corporation which, along with its other enterprises, commands attention on Capitol Hill by virtue of sometimes appearing to have a Radio Shack store on every corner in America. As a pioneer in the field Tandy probably has done more than any company in America to popularize the personal computer. Fortunately John Roach and Ron Parrish, my bosses at Tandy, never bothered to ask how much I knew about computers. So I may have neglected to mention that my data processing sophistication was limited to my old-time Underwood manual typewriter. Having used computers for eight years, of course, I can see they are clearly more efficient. On the other hand, my Underwood never ate seven hours of work if I happened to punch the wrong keys at 2 o'clock in the morning.

On such occasions I have always telephoned my oldest grandson, Michael Williams, a computer wizard. So often did I roust him out of bed seeking help that he finally gave up his apartment and moved into our basement. Now all he has to do is come upstairs. To him I owe thanks for retrieving several large sections of this book from the electronic gizzard of my computer.

For research help, my thanks also go to Glenda B. Stevens, archivist for the Jim Wright papers at Texas Christian University. She cheerfully dug through countless folders to locate documents I hazily remembered but needed to see again. Similar thanks are due to Charlcia Bullard, reference librarian for the *Fort Worth Star-Telegram*, for allowing me to refresh my memory from old clippings in her files.

For other bits of background and information I am indebted to such friends as Graham Purcell, Donnald K. Anderson, Don Kennard, Kathy Mitchell, Anne Page, Joe Shosid, Bill Newbold, Phil Duncan, Carl Freund, Wayne Franke, Eugene L. (Gene) Krizek, Norman Sherman, Jack Russ and Major General Roger P. Scheer, USAF (Ret.).

In closing, there is one other good friend I would like to mention. His name is Jim Wright. Look carefully in this book and you may find some further reference to him.

MARSHALL LYNAM
Washington, D.C.
June, 1997

Foreword

By Jim Wright

Everybody who knows Marshall Lynam will expect this book to be chock-full of hilarious human stories about a lot of the great, near-great and obscure but fascinating folks he's come to know in his eventful life. They won't be disappointed. Others who've not yet heard of Marshall Lynam are in for a treat—a treasure of fascinating true tales, fun to read and never before told in print.

Marshall has worked, managed and written for daily newspapers, presidential candidates, the Speaker of the House and the world's second busiest airport. First as a nineteen-year-old waist gunner on a B-17 and later as a representative of our government, the author has traveled over much of the world and met dozens of world leaders. He was my Chief of Staff during the years I served as House Majority Leader and Speaker.

During his years as a newsman and top congressional aide, Marshall Lynam has been close enough to the levers of power to tell us what's written inside Ted Kennedy's shoes and what refreshments Billy Graham orders on a private airplane. He has seen four-star generals weep, presidents get tangled up in their telephones, congressional leaders trip on their egos and fall flat on their dignities. With it all, Marshall is never mean. He spots the humor in every situation, whether being chased down a hallway by a notorious Texas gunman or being dropped by parachute into the depths of Biscayne Bay. (He writes of the latter experience that it was great fun but he enjoyed most the part where he came back up to the surface.)

Marshall can find something funny in a royal wedding, a lynch mob carrying a noose with his name on it, or a dose of castor oil. Always intrigued with the vagaries and charming foibles of human personality, he tells each story with the practiced skill of a born raconteur. He makes us see the human side of characters we've only read about in headlines.

Not that the scores of episodes told in these pages are all frivolous. Far from it. Here Marshall covers the deeply personal side of stories that shook the earth and changed the world—from the historic meeting in Jerusalem between Menachem Begin and Anwar Sadat that reversed the course of centuries and led to the historic peace between Egypt and Israel, to a fateful visit with Mikhail Gorbachev in Moscow that presaged the end of the Cold War. He was there—and makes you feel you, too, were there.

This book is not a partisan polemic nor an appeal for any particular ideology. It is a collection of warmly human stories told by a warmly human guy gifted with the eye of a marksman, the ear of a father confessor, and the pen of a poet.

When Hurricane Beulah smote the coastal lands along the Gulf of Mexico in 1967, leaving a path of human wreckage on both sides of our international border, President Johnson declared an "open border policy." Rescue crews in helicopters lifted stranded families away from the cruel floodwaters and carried them to safety, not stopping to ask their nationality. At the height of that disaster, Marshall and I, along with a small group of other congressmen and newsmen, visited a place called Camp Ringold where military barracks had been converted into a refugee camp to house and feed several thousand victims of the flood. We watched as bedraggled, storm-tossed kids, cleaned up and in dry clothes, got their first meal in two days.

En route back to Washington by plane, a reporter came up to Marshall asking help. He said he'd written most of his story but couldn't seem to compose a simple single sentence that would capture the essence of what he he'd seen. Marshall slipped a page into his portable typewriter and immediately hammered out the following: "Happiness is a little Mexican boy with oatmeal on his face."

In every situation, he instinctively discovers the human side.

When I first met Marshall those many years ago, he was a lanky, long-legged young fellow with a disarmingly cherubic face, perceptive as a radar beam but down to earth as pair of resoled cowboy boots. After a quarter century of working closely with him on presidential visits, legislative schedules, high negotiations with heads of state and down-to-earth sessions with troubled constituents, I appreciate him as a gentleman, a skilled workman, a marvelously gifted writer and a cherished friend.

Read this book, and you'll understand why.

1

A Tale About Tincy

One day long ago in Fort Worth, Texas, I had a couple of unusual experiences. First a thug named Tincy Eggleston threatened to kill me. A few minutes later I stumbled into a Congressman's office to use the phone and wound up working for him for 27 years. I survived both occurrences.

To begin with, there was Tincy Eggleston. If this notorious hoodlum were still alive, the nicety-nicety people in today's P.C. world probably would describe him as a hit person, which would serve him right, since the whole idea of gender neutrality would have infuriated him. Tincy would be a hero, however, to today's mossback conservatives who want to privatize every government function except that of the 82nd Airborne. As a pioneer in the field of privatization, Tincy pushed the envelope even beyond what Adam Smith had in mind. For the right money, Tincy bragged that he could provide a free-enterprise service of a sort ordinarily carried out only on court orders in the Texas Prison System execution chamber in Huntsville. Tincy's methods were different, but the results were the same, and there was far less paperwork and no lawyers at all.

Appropriately enough, Tincy even looked like a hit man—or at least what most of us imagined a professional hired gun ought to look like. A wiry, coiled steel spring of a man in his late 40's, he had eyes like fixed bayonets—cold, piercing, merciless. Amid the mayhem of the Fort Worth underworld, Tincy also dealt in such ancillary services as hijackings, gambling turf wars and shakedowns. His enterprises often were chronicled under big black headlines in Texas newspapers.

These activities understandably aroused the interest of various branches of the Texas constabulary. Once Tincy was being driven to Dallas for questioning about one of his jobs. Bored by the long drive, he unexpectedly struck up a conversation with Carl Freund, a newspaper reporter sitting in the front seat alongside the beefy Dallas deputy sheriff who was driving. Philosophizing about his craft, Tincy warned Carl to be especially wary of getting robbed by novice bandits.

"Those damn amateurs are liable to get scared and kill you," Tincy said. "On the other hand, you take guys like Cecil Green and me. We know our business. We just want your money. We would never get nervous and kill you, because then it would be a lot of trouble to go to court."

Carl nodded understandingly.

"But if somebody slipped me five thousand bucks and wanted you dead, that would be another matter, you understand," Tincy explained.

It's hard to imagine today, but Fort Worth in the 1950's was sort of like Chicago in the 1920's, with a couple of obvious differences. One was that Al Capone surely must have had a classier, more sophisticated bunch of hoodlums. The other was that Fort Worth's gang battles were fought not mainly over control of bootlegging, as Chicago's were, but rather over control of lucrative gambling territories.

In Fort Worth the violence started with a car bombing in 1950. Nelson Harris, a local gambler, his wife and their unborn child were killed. After that, with disturbing regularity, thugs representing various factions began shooting each other, blowing each other up, and stuffing each other down abandoned wells.

In those days I was a reporter for a brash little newspaper called *The Fort Worth Press*. Usually I was assigned to cover humdrum offices in the Federal Courthouse rather than gang murders. When the City Desk was short-handed, though, I was thrown into the breach—as I was the day an innovative assassin craftily buried a box of dynamite in front of the roadside country mailbox near Fort Worth. Having strung detonating wires to a clump of trees nearby, the killer hid and waited until Herbert (The Cat) Noble drove up to check his mail. Then, when the hit man touched the two wires together, Noble abruptly lost the last of the nine lives to which his nickname theoretically entitled him.

On another occasion, I was dispatched to a house near Lake Worth occupied by a gambler named Frank Cates. Somebody planted a bomb under the floor directly beneath Cates's telephone, then went to a nearby phone booth, rang his number and asked, "Is that you, Frank?" It was. Blooey.

Incredibly, Cates survived the blast. When police arrived, he looked like he had been through a meat grinder and his clothing was shredded, but he was busily counting a pile of still-smoking money. The money didn't help him much, however. Two months later a mysterious assailant walked up to his car and killed him with a shotgun blast.

The Fort Worth Press, which breathlessly described such activities in lurid detail each day, was an incredible institution. Forever teetering on the edge of bankruptcy, the paper was such a penny-pincher that reporters had to turn in the stub of a copy pencil to get a new one. To make a phone call to New York took prior approval from the City Desk. And once when a reporter rode with sheriff's deputies to a crime scene out in the suburbs and then asked how to get home, the City Desk told him to hitchhike.

Worst of all, in the sweltering summers of Fort Worth, *The Press* had the only major downtown building without refrigerated air conditioning. Instead we had washed-air coolers on the roof. During the winter these would get clogged with dirt. When the water was turned on in late spring, the blowers would hurl tiny mudballs through the city room. So it was a goshawful place to work, right?

Wrong. For the young crew in the newsroom, it was wonderful. One sports writer doubled at night as a honkytonk piano player. A retired circus performer worked as a rim man on the copy desk, and one day he strung a tightrope up among the ceiling lights and gamboled aerially over the City Desk.

The city staff was boisterous, savvy and ambitious. Most of us had seen combat in World War II. One guy left a leg on Guadalcanal. *The Press* had virtually no sacred cows, perhaps because it got so little advertising from local merchants there was hardly anybody capable of bringing economic pressure on us. If you could get a story, you could print it. We loved the challenge of trying to beat the pants off the big, rich *Fort Worth Star-*

Telegram, the morning and afternoon papers which dominated the area with a circulation five times our own and a news staff to match. I once was sent out on a late-breaking murder story in an office building downtown and found myself opposed by four reporters from the *Star-Telegram*. On *The Press*, we were impoverished in everything but esprit de corps.

My desk adjoined that of Carl Freund, the county courthouse reporter. I always suspected Carl of possessing some mysterious physical property enabling him to absorb news through his pores, or something. Still active today as a private news gatherer for Fort Worth commercial interests, Carl can ferret out more information in less time than anybody I ever knew. In *The Press'* heyday of the Fifties, he was a walking encyclopedia on the gang wars. But Carl was out of the office on that spring morning in 1955 when City Editor Dave Hall motioned me over to his desk.

"Tincy Eggleston's testifying today before the federal grand jury that's looking into gambling," he said. "Go over there and see what he'll tell you. Take Gene and get a piece of art."

From the photo department I picked up my pal Gene Gordon, a young red-headed cameraman with whom I often worked. He grabbed his cumbersome old Speed Graphic and we headed for the Federal Courthouse Building. Knowing Tincy's reputation only too well, Gene asked: "How are we going to do this?"

"I think Tincy will talk to us if we approach him right," I said. Modesty prevented my saying so, but I was certain that my moon-faced boyish innocence would charm the socks off even a thug like Tincy Eggleston.

We found him sitting alone in a second-floor hallway just outside the grand jury room. Donning what I believed to be my most benign, pure-hearted expression, I walked up to Tincy and stuck out my right hand.

"Good morning, Mr. Eggleston," I said, certain that he seldom had been addressed in that fashion.

Tincy ignored my proffered handshake and scowled.

"My name is Marshall Lynam. My friend Gene Gordon and I work for *The Press*," I bubbled in what I hoped was childlike purity.

Tincy scowled again. His eyes narrowed.

"If you're not too busy at the moment, we thought we'd like to talk with you for a few minutes," I said.

Tincy stared squarely at me—stony, silent and unblinking.

"May I sit down and talk with you?" I said, motioning toward the bench.

Tincy said not a word, but kept those carbon-steel eyes fixed on me. I felt my collar tightening. Finally his lip curled and I could see his message coming.

"Listen, you *son of a bitch*," he hissed. "Hell, no, I ain't going to talk to you. And let me tell you something else. If you try to take my picture, *I'll kill you.*"

Up to that time, I never knew anybody could talk in italics, but Tincy did.

His menacing eyes followed us intently as Gene and I moved down the hall toward the stairway. "What now?" Gene asked.

"I've got to call the City Desk," I said. "Is there a pay phone around here?"

"Don't see any. All these offices seem to be locked up. Maybe there's an office open upstairs."

There was. On the next floor up, the door to Room 327 was standing wide open. Neither Gene nor I knew it at the time, but this was the office of Fort Worth's newly-elected Congressman, Jim Wright. He wasn't in at the moment, but I had seen him around town a couple of times—a personable young fellow with a shock of red hair and trademark eyebrows whose overhang provided as much shade as your average carport. In Texas he already was known as a political giant-killer. The previous year, he had confounded the Fort Worth political establishment by beating an incumbent Congressman personally hand-picked by the most powerful man in town.

Even though Jim Wright was clearly brainy and ambitious, we never dreamed in 1955 he was destined to achieve the most powerful legislative office in the world. In our frantic quest for a telephone, we had bumbled into the office of the man who would be Speaker of the House of Representatives in the historic 100th Congress of the United States.

And I certainly would have scoffed at the notion that I, of all people, would find myself standing at this man's side in his dealings over the years with three Presidents in the White House, Menachem Begin in Jerusalem, Anwar Sadat in Cairo, Margaret Thatcher in 10 Downing Street, and Mikhail Gorbachev in the Kremlin.

When Gene and I popped into Jim Wright's office that day, a gracious lady on his staff was busy talking to a group of his constituents, but paused long enough to give us permission to use the telephone.

I called Mary Crutcher, Assistant City Editor at *The Press*.

"Tincy says if we try to take his picture, he'll kill us. What should we do?"

"Where did you talk to him?"

"On a bench outside the grand jury room."

"Was anybody else around?"

"Just Gene and me. What should we do?"

Mary hesitated. "Hold the line. I'd better talk to Dave about this."

For several minutes Mary left the line, apparently discussing the matter in some detail with Dave Hall, the City Editor. Finally she came back on the line. "Dave said he doesn't want to decide this by himself. We're going in to talk it over with Humphrey."

Walter R. Humphrey was the big cheese himself—Editor of *The Fort Worth Press*. The whole staff knew Mr. Humphrey must have the most important job on the paper, because in his closed-door private sanctum purred the only window air conditioner in the news department.

The conference with Humphrey went on and on. All around Gene and me, visitors were talking to Jim Wright's staff about Social Security and stuff like that. I kind of felt guilty for keeping the phone tied up for so long. Finally I heard somebody pick up on the other end.

"Go ahead and take the picture," Mary ordered. "Humphrey says Tincy can't talk to us like that."

I swallowed hard.

"What'd she say?" Gene asked.

"She says that Humphrey is not the least bit afraid of Tincy, and we should go ahead and take his picture."

"A truly courageous man," Gene observed.

After thanking the Wright people for letting us use their phone, Gene and I stepped out into the third floor.

"What we've got to do," I intoned, is to analyze this situation very carefully and then formulate some kind of sophisticated strategic plan to enable us to retain both our jobs and our lives."

"You mean take the picture and run like hell?"

"Precisely what I had in mind."

Down the west stairs to the grand jury hallway marched Gene and I, young and willing candidates for martyrdom to the lunacy of American journalism. Just ahead we could see Tincy, still sitting alone on the bench. Resolutely we strode forward, eyes straight ahead, fixed on our escape route—the east stairway, approximately 150 feet away. Gene was trying to be nonchalant as he lugged the clunky Speed Graphic, roughly the size of a shoebox, in his left hand, facing Tincy.

At the precise moment we came abreast of Tincy, Gene hit the shutter button. A brilliant flash filled the hallway. Even if momentarily blinded, Tincy sprang from bench like hungry Rottweiler. The chase was on.

Never before had I realized how much noise a frantic three-man chase can generate in a marble corridor. The hallway reverberated with our frantic footfalls and Tincy's vengeful cries of rage. In the bedlam as we galloped toward the stairs, office doors popped open. So did the mouths of astonished federal employees.

"Why are those guys running?" a court clerk asked J.R. (Red) Wright as we barreled past one office door. Wright was a crusty old U.S. Marshal who shared a surname but no kinship to our Congressional telephone benefactor.

Having seen Gene clinging dearly to his camera as Tincy furiously pursued us, the aging lawman laughingly admitted later that he instantly figured out what was happening. But he said he saw no reason to intervene, since it looked as if Gene and I were likely to get outside the Federal Building before Tincy murdered us.

In answer to the baffled clerk, Marshal Wright said, "Oh, you know how crazy those newspaper guys are. They've probably got a deadline."

Gene was younger than I, but handicapped by the camera. With my long legs in warp speed, I reached the stairway about the same time he did. We leaped down the stairs, several steps at a bounce. Tincy was still right behind us, panting and cursing.

Not until we got out the east door of the Federal Building did Tincy give up. Still scowling and cursing, he returned to await his appearance before the grand jury. Breathless but elated at having escaped, Gene and I stood for a moment on the sidewalk in the comforting sunshine. Suddenly we both broke into hysterical laughter. When we got back to the paper, we were still giggling. But we talked it over and finally decided it wasn't necessary to go in and congratulate our Editor on the sheer guts it took for him to demonstrate that Tincy simply couldn't talk to us like that.

That afternoon I gingerly ventured back into the Federal Building and was relieved to find that Tincy had finished his testimony and left—for what turned out to be the last time.

On August 31, 1955, his body was found in an abandoned well six miles north of Fort Worth. A killer whose identity is still unknown today had blasted a three-inch hole in the base of Tincy's skull. Gene and I were never even questioned as suspects.

2

The Red-Headed Stranger from Weatherford, Texas

When Jim Wright called me at home one Sunday morning late in 1961, I was a little puzzled. Without saying what was on his mind, he asked if I could meet him that afternoon for a cup of coffee.

The more I thought about his call, the more curious it seemed. It had been a long time since the Tincy Eggleston caper, so surely he wasn't calling to chew me out for getting his office mixed up in such a ridiculous episode. Besides, since he was not in his office that day, I wasn't sure the Congressman himself even knew what happened. I had talked to him several times since then, but somehow the subject of Tincy Eggleston never came up.

What's more, in the intervening years my whole life had changed. I left *The Fort Worth Press* in 1958, spent a year as managing editor of a little afternoon daily in East Texas, then returned to Fort Worth to work, of all places, in the newsroom of my old arch-enemy, the *Star-Telegram*.

Life had changed even more dramatically for Jim Wright. No longer was he merely the red-headed stranger from Weatherford, Texas, noted only for pulling an astonishing political upset in 1954. Nor was he any longer an obscure novice lawmaker on Capitol Hill. After three terms in Congress, he had proved he could bring home the bacon for the voters of Fort Worth.

Moreover, his legislative skills were beginning to catch the eye of the House leadership. In December, 1961, Jim Wright was clearly a young lawmaker on his way up.

Earlier that same year, he had stunned the conservative Texas political establishment by finishing near the top in a spectacular off-year election to fill the Senate seat vacated by Lyndon B. Johnson when he became Vice President. To everybody's surprise, this special Senate election attracted an outlandish field of 71 candidates. Some were nutty enough to be ideally suited for something like an old Mack Sennett slapstick comedy—maybe Keystone Kongress, or perhaps Kandidates R Us.

In this wild race, Jim Wright came in a close third, narrowly missing a chance to offer a runoff challenge to the ultimate winner, Republican John Tower. Even so, Jim Wright's strong showing in this race stirred a groundswell of support for him to run for Governor of Texas in 1962.

When the phone jangled that Sunday, I was sleepily browsing through the weekend papers. His entire conversation with me lasted hardly more than a minute.

"Who was that on the phone?" asked my wife, Eddie.

"Jim Wright," I said.

"Jim Wright the Congressman? What did he want?"

"He didn't say. He just said he wanted to talk to me."

Eddie knew the *Star-Telegram* had pulled me in the previous day to cover a Jim Wright press conference. "You made a mistake in the story," she concluded.

"I didn't make a mistake in the damn story. He said he had decided not to run for Governor, and that's what I wrote."

"Why else would Jim Wright want to see you?" Eddie asked with a certain degree of logic.

Over coffee at a nearby cafe that afternoon, the Congressman astonished me by inviting me to join his Congressional staff in Washington. He said he needed somebody to help with writing and press work, and that he had admired my work as a reporter. He said he believed I would make a valuable addition to his team. Even though flattered and intrigued by this offer out of the blue, I realized that for Eddie and me, this would be a tough call.

On the one hand, she and I loved Fort Worth. The kids were doing well in school, and I had a great job on the *Star-Telegram*. My bosses in the newsroom had enough confidence to give me some great assignments. In recent months I had done what turned out to be an award-winning story on the dramatic landing of a crippled airliner, a state legislative investigation, a one-on-one interview with Vice President Johnson, the funeral of Speaker Sam Rayburn, a travel piece that took me to Mexico, and even an East Coast missile launching.

Moreover, compared to *The Press*, working on the *Star-Telegram* was fat city. In 102-degree Texas summers, the news staff luxuriated in real, honest-to-goodness air-conditioning. Reporters got expense money and could rent cars if needed. What's more, we didn't even have to turn in our pencil stub to get a new one.

Even so, Jim Wright's offer was exciting. Washington—and especially Capitol Hill—held a professional fascination for most reporters. While I might wind up as only a spear carrier on Jim Wright's staff, at least I would be able to see from the inside how Congress really worked. And who knows where the job would lead? Jim Wright obviously was hard-driving and ambitious.

Never would I have imagined that I would spend more than a quarter of a century on Capitol Hill at the right hand of this man, first as his Administrative Assistant and then, when he became Speaker, as his Chief of Staff. Had I any inkling of the interesting, chaotic and often hilarious adventures that loomed ahead for me, I surely would have wanted to ask Jim Wright several important questions.

I would have inquired, for example, whether he would eventually forgive me for disclosing the secret of Ted Kennedy's shoes.

Also I would have wanted to know—a purely hypothetical question, you understand—whether he would ever consider taking a bunch of high-ranking old geezers from the Kremlin into a rip-roaring Texas honkytonk.

Additionally, it would have been useful for me to know how my Congressional career path would be affected in the off chance that my son happened to ram the *U.S.S. Sumter* into an oil tanker in Chesapeake Bay.

But of course I had no way of foretelling what events might lie in the future if I joined his staff. I should have known, however, that life would hardly be placid working for the young whippersnapper who slapped Amon G. Carter in the chops at the height of his political power—and managed to get away with it.

As one of Texas's most influential figures, Mr. Carter was Publisher of the *Fort Worth Star-Telegram* and Grand Poobah of Everything Else in Town, Amen. In 1946, just after World War II, Mr. Carter had chosen and orchestrated the election of a man he considered his own personal Congressman, a war veteran and lawyer named Wingate Lucas. Later, as a reporter, I covered Wingate. He was a decent and friendly fellow, but not exactly a shining star in the Congressional firmament.

Then, in 1954, this young upstart named Jim Wright suddenly stepped onto the Fort Worth's political scene—an unlikely challenger from an unlikely place. From the charming but drowsy little city of Weatherford, 24 miles west of Fort Worth, emerged this latter-day prairie populist with impressive talent and a personal agenda to match. At 31, Jim Wright was trim, quick and muscular. From his school days he held a hatful of Golden Gloves awards, and in World War II he earned a Distinguished Flying Cross as a B-24 combat flier in the South Pacific.

Almost invariably people found him outgoing and likable, but close friends knew that he possessed a volcanic Irish temper as well. Usually he kept this under the same rigid control Alan Greenspan exercises today on the prime rate. On rare occasions, though, Jim Wright's temper flared up like the eruption of Vesuvius—as it once did at an American Legion breakfast in Weatherford. A loud-mouthed fellow Legionnaire, who may have had several stiff eye-openers before breakfast, made three mistakes. The first was being unable to fathom the difference between a populist and a communist. The second was to apply the latter appellation to Jim Wright. The third (and worst) was to throw a haymaker at him. Ducking, the former Golden Glover responded with a fast-forward series of lefts and rights which reduced his antagonist to the threat level of a bag of dirty laundry. Old-timers in Weatherford still cackle over the episode.

As a voracious reader with a quick, analytical mind, Jim Wright consumed information like kids gulped Big Macs. In high school and college he steeped himself in history, economics and government, and later, as a lay minister, demonstrated that he knew more about the Bible than your average seminary student.

In marching to his destiny as a giant-killer, young Jim Wright brought all the necessary credentials. His name, for example, was a political natural—easy to remember, ideal for political sloganeering (the Wright slant, the Wright man for the job, etc.). Most important of all, he developed a speaking talent capable of persuading Lucifer to give up his pitchfork.

A moderate Democrat (liberal by Fort Worth standards), Jim Wright defined national political issues in Texas horse-sense terms that impressed even the leathery-faced old curmudgeons who sat, spitting and whittling, outside the pool hall. And when he smiled, giddy little old ladies melted and ran down into their shoes.

He had sharpened his political skills with a term as a state legislator, as Mayor of Weatherford and as President of the Texas League of Municipalities. Now, in 1954, he had the effrontery to take on Wingate Lucas, the fair-haired favorite of the Fort Worth Establishment, Amon G. Carter, Prop.

In Texas Congressional elections, these were the *tantamount* days—the days when the newspapers invariably pointed out that victory in the Democratic primary was tantamount to election in November. While the election of Dwight D. Eisenhower in 1952 signaled the beginning of a new era for Republicans in Texas, local and Congressional races in 1954 were still strictly Democratic shows. The standing joke was that Republicans held their state convention in a phone booth.

Faced with this smart-aleck upstart from Weatherford, it didn't take Mr. Carter long to roll out his most potent political weapon—his newspaper. With both morning and afternoon editions, the *Star-Telegram* in those days provided almost legendary news coverage of Fort Worth and the far reaches of West Texas. And its editors knew only too well where Mr. Carter's political preference lay. When Jim Wright's poor-boy Congressional campaign showed signs of gaining momentum, the *Star-Telegram* brushed it aside with a few snippy little stories back among the hemorrhoid ads.

And then, only days before the crucial Democratic primary election, Mr. Carter made a grave political error. In a *Star-Telegram* front-page editorial, he attacked Jim Wright, accusing him of refusing to spell out his position on important national issues. This triggered a monumental political event. Suddenly the focus of the campaign shifted. Jim Wright was no longer running against Wingate Lucas, the man whose name was listed on the ballot. He was running against a Higher Authority. He was running against the string puller, the ventriloquist himself. He was running against Amon G. Carter.

Infuriated by the editorial, Jim Wright struck what turned out to be the campaign's decisive blow. He dashed off "An Open Letter to Mr. Amon G. Carter" that was destined to shake the political foundations of the city. Defiantly he plunked down $974.40 out of his savings account to buy the biggest damn ad that amount would buy. To everybody's astonishment, Mr. Carter allowed the *Star-Telegram* to accept the ad. Whether he did this in a spirit of fairness, or merely to avoid the added embarrassment of having this in-your-face challenge published in the scrappy little *Fort Worth Press*, nobody will ever know.

"You have at last met a man, Mr. Carter, who is not afraid of you...who will not bow his knee to you...and come running like a simpering pup at your beck and call," Jim Wright's letter proclaimed. He charged the publisher with ignoring his clear-cut statements on crucial national issues like taxes, spending and the cold war. He asserted that one of his campaign speeches had been censored by Mr. Carter's television station and that the publisher had deliberately ordered the *Star-Telegram* to pooh-pooh the growing strength of his campaign.

"Is this how you have controlled Fort Worth so long?" Jim Wright demanded. "By printing only that which you wanted people to read? By refusing to quote a man in your paper when he does take a stand and then running a front-page editorial saying he has not taken any stand?"

Today it's hard to appreciate the guts it took to throw down such a challenge to Amon Carter and the political establishment in the Fort Worth of the 1950's. In those days the crusty old publisher wielded such immense political power it was virtually unthinkable for him to be kicked in the political shins by this obstreperous interloper from Weatherford.

As the political and economic godfather of Fort Worth, Mr. Carter dominated not only the city's most powerful newspaper but also was board chairman of its leading television and radio stations. Nor did his influence stop at the Texas border. He was a founder and the largest stockholder of American Airlines. In his great biography, *Amon*, Jerry Flemmons wrote that at the time of his death in 1955, Mr. Carter was responsible for bringing to Fort Worth companies which employed half the population of the city.

At his Shady Oak Farm and in the Fort Worth Club, where Mr. Carter entertained dignitaries who dropped into town to pay homage to him, the guest books bristled with names like Calvin Coolidge, Jack Dempsey, Charles Lindbergh, Will Rogers, Franklin D. Roosevelt, Sally Rand, Babe Ruth, the Mellons, Whitneys, Doolittle, Rickenbacker, Durante, Nimitz and Luce.

Flemmons recounts how, in 1941, with Pearl Harbor still smoldering after the Japanese attack, Mr. Carter wrote a long letter to President Roosevelt, giving instructions on how to the run the war:

"The disaster at Pearl Harbor, as tough as it is, may be a blessing in disguise. It certainly unified the country overnight. [You] silence those [expletive] isolationist and America First sons of bitches, Lindburg, [sic] Wheeler, Bennett, Clark, Nye and Fish. If they open their mouths again they ought to be put in concentration camps. From now on, all sabotage of any nature should be answered with a sharp bayonet or a good old Texas Forty-Five."

This, then, was the man Jim Wright challenged—a shrewd and powerful sagebrush Goliath who had no tolerance for latter-day Davids. Challenging Mr. Carter with an advertisement in his own newspaper was seen as a silly, foolhardy thing for Jim Wright to do. There was only one good thing you could say about it. It worked.

From then on, the race was not between Wright and Lucas, but Wright and Carter. The ad captured the imagination of the townspeople. Many who thought Wright's act was crazy nevertheless admired his guts. On election day, Jim Wright won with 60 per cent of the votes. Even today, old-timers in Fort Worth talk wistfully about the election that dethroned Amon Carter and changed forever the political complexion of the city.

In June, 1955, only five months after Jim Wright took office, Mr. Carter died at the age of 75. By the time Jim Wright offered me a job six years later, the ink-stained wretches at the *Star-Telegram* had become so impressed with Jim Wright's record in Washington that all had been forgiven. What's more, the late publisher's son, an incredibly nice guy named Amon G. Carter, Jr., became one of Jim Wright's closest friends. Before Amon Jr.'s own death in 1982, he headed, of all things, the Congressman's local support group, the Wright Appreciation Committee.

So close had the two men become, in fact, that at Jim Wright's request, Amon Jr. granted me a leave of absence so I could return to the *Star-Telegram* if I didn't like working on the Congressman's staff in Washington. In the face of a no-lose proposition like that, the temptation was too great. I agreed to give the job a try. Eddie, who was so proud of our modest little GI home in Fort Worth, threatened not to accompany me. But later, after the kids finished the school year, she reluctantly did.

So it was, on a bright Sunday morning in January, 1962, I landed at Washington National Airport, grabbed my bags and stepped outside the terminal. There, just across the Potomac, loomed the stately Washington Monument and the imposing white dome of the Capitol. Then, crossing Memorial Bridge toward downtown Washington, I saw the horses.

On either side of the bridge, then as now, two gilded equestrian statues sparkled in the sun. The massive horses in these statues face east, toward the downtown area.   Thus when visitors approach the city from the west, they are confronted by a greeting unique to the Nation's Capital—two big, prominent, glistening horses behinds. I began to wonder what kind of people I would meet in Washington.

3

Revenge of the Green Hornet

A few years ago, browsing in a book store, I picked up a bestseller entitled simply, *Chaos*. Its author, James Gleick, introduced "chaos theory" as a new science which might show, as I understand it, that when you accidentally drop your car key, there is a solid scientific reason why the key bounces straight down the nearest storm sewer. In short, the book seeks to demonstrate—pay attention, now—that *apparent disorder is meaningful*. When I read this, I was delighted. What a blessed relief this will be, I thought, to Paul Willis.

Dr. Paul Willis was the first person I met when I landed, alone and somewhat intimidated, in Washington to join Jim Wright's staff. On his own, without anybody having asked, Paul met me at the airport, welcomed me to the city and drove me to the Capitol. From that time until now, I see him as the genuine article—the embodiment of both a gentleman and an intellectual. He even sounded like a scholar, using the phrase "in terms of" and stuff like that. He held a doctorate in political science and, in what I imagine was a less stressful time in his life, was a professor at Drake University. Exactly how he came to be in a town as frenzied as Washington I don't know. For a true disciple of orderliness, quiet reflection and deep thought, Paul struck me as being somewhat out of his element in the pandemonium of Capitol Hill.

When I went to work for Jim Wright, Paul was the Congressman's top staff person—Administrative Assistant or AA, in Hill jargon. His desk, with a banker's lamp glowing discreetly over whatever Congressional document he was perusing, sat in one of the less hazardous spots in our jam-packed little room on the third floor of the Longworth House Office Building. Day after day Paul must have struggled to keep coherent thought from being washed away by the swirl of chaos and tumult of our Congressional office.

"You tell the Congressman we're sick and tired of being insulted by that jerk Fidel Castro—you hear?" says a visitor, looming over Wanda, the receptionist.

"Good morning," breaks in another fellow, interrupting the first. "My son wants an appointment to West Point. Is it too late to get him in for the September term?"

Two phones are ringing. On one, a woman calling from Fort Worth demands, "Have you heard anything yet about Henry's Social Security?" On the other line, a little girl working on her school lessons wants Congressman Wright to tell her the names of the nine justices of the Supreme Court.

Through the swarm of visitors weaves a breathless Congressional page. "The Majority Leader wants Mr. Wright to come right away to a press conference in the Rayburn Room," he gasps.

Two desks away, Julie hisses to a fellow staffer who is furiously pounding the keys on her typewriter. "Dammit, Marie, don't you have that speech draft finished yet? Twice already the boss has asked for it."

"Is this where I pick up tickets for the White House tour?" asks a harried fellow whose wife and six kids cluster in the doorway. "How should I know?   I'm from Western Union, trying to pick up a telegram," the other guy replies.

"What happened to those Medicare letters? The boss needs them—now," cries Anne, bursting out of the Congressman's private office.

"Excuse me, please," says a kid from the House Post Office, elbowing his way through the office to dump off yet another armload of letters. It is the fifth mail delivery of the day.

"How much longer is Congress going to keep doling out foreign aid to those deadbeats in Europe?" demands a fat man methodically placing colored pamphlets on everybody's desk.

Amid piles of newspapers back in one corner, a legislative staffer shouts into the phone, arguing with a reporter. "I can't help what you're hearing, Joe—I'm telling you that TFX research appropriation is in good shape."

A distraught TCU student is calling from Texas. "How long before we hear something from the Philippines about my brother's emergency furlough? Dad's still in intensive care."

A well-dressed woman politely approaches a typist. "Excuse me, but I understand you can get me one of the flags they fly over the Capitol."

"Where's your boss?" cries a frenzied clerk from the Public Works Committee. "The chairman needs him for a quorum."

"Don't ask me. If I don't get corrections over to the Capitol in the next five minutes, Jim's remarks will be all screwed up in tomorrow's *Record*," exclaims a legislative staffer.

"Hey, Kathy," I call across the room. "Pick up line 4. It's that guy calling again about Jim Wright talking Friday at the Rotary Club."

An office intern bursts in. "The copy machine broke down. What am I supposed to do with these letters the boss wants to go out this afternoon?"

Whew.

As a newspaper reporter I hadn't realized what an bewildering range of requests were routinely handled in those days by the more active Congressional offices. If House and Senate members of that era had done nothing but make laws, serving in Congress would have been a snap. The real problem lay in the dozens of Congressional fringe services that many offices rendered to enhance their popularity with the voters.

The tempo of work in any given office, I found, usually reflected the character and temperament of the member it served. If Congressman Dulltool were a ho-hum fellow, content only to vote and vegetate, he wasn't bothered by a deluge of letters, phone calls or visits from constituents. If, on the other hand, you served on the staff of an irredeemable workaholic like Jim Wright, the pace ranged between the frantic and the impossible. It soon dawned on me that my boss was a guy born in a hurry with flaming red hair and an ambition to match. Over the years the red hair thinned but the ambition did not.

He devoutly believed that his Constitutional title— *Representative* of the 12th District of Texas—meant exactly what it said. One day I made the mistake of telling him that I suspected a Fort Worth war veteran was not, in fact, entitled to the pension he was requesting. "All right, Marshall," he said. "All the poor guy wants is a chance to present his arguments to those bureaucrats in the Veterans Administration. If I don't help him get that chance, who will?"

With this clear charter, our office staff responded not only to the thousands of inquiries we received each month on legislative matters, but also to the countless plain, everyday citizens pleading for help in their dealings with government agencies. Back home people knew Jim Wright and his staff were their voice in Washington—taking their side in problems with the federal bureaucracy, selecting good kids for nominations to the military academies, sending out flags that had flown over the Capitol, arranging White House tours and straightening out Mrs. Murphy's problems with the Social Security Administration.

Even in those days, of course, only a few Congressional offices were as busy as ours, and today there are fewer still. As quaint as it may sound in the me-first 1990's, Jim Wright really felt it was not merely an option but a duty to go to bat for people who ran into problems with government agencies. Once I saw him get the Secretary of the Navy personally on the phone to demand an immediate flight home for a sailor on Guam who had been refused Navy transportation when his father died in Fort Worth.

Coming aboard in 1962 as a writer and press secretary, I became the eighth member of Jim Wright's Washington staff. Having grown up in the newspaper business, where bedlam and deadline pressure were part of the job, I was used to a frantic level of activity. So was Kathy Mitchell, a pretty, absolutely unflappable woman who joined Jim Wright when she was 19 and worked with competence and unswerving loyalty as his personal secretary and Executive Assistant until she retired. But the person who suffered most from chaotic environment and the monumental work load in our office, I believe, was Paul Willis. As an academic, he was accustomed to a job where one had time to think.

What worried Paul most, I suspect, was the unbelievable volume of mail we received, mostly from constituents in the Fort Worth area. It wasn't unusual, even then, to receive two hundred letters a day. And Jim Wright demanded that every letter receive a prompt, responsive answer.

Legislative mail was the hardest to handle, because it covered such an incredible array of subjects—taxes, foreign affairs, defense, civil rights, transportation, criminal justice, and on and on. In the 87th Congress, 20,316 pieces of legislation were introduced. During that period (1961-62), the House was in session for a total of 304 days. Thus any member silly enough to try to read all these proposals would have found an average of 66 new bills or resolutions on his desk or bedside table every day the House met.

When a constituent wrote about a bill, sometimes it took considerable detective work just to find what piece of legislation the writer was talking about, not to mention drafting a responsive reply based on the Congressman's feelings about it. Word-processing computers were still just a dream, and sometimes even diligent staff members simply found themselves swamped by the mail. Take what happened to our friend Grayson Chase, a likable, free-spirited Congressman from the Midwest who occupied the office next door.

One day I needed a new ribbon for my manual typewriter, and there was none in our storeroom. Knowing that Congressman Chase occasionally pecked out his own letters on a typewriter like mine, I popped over to ask Marie, his receptionist, if I could borrow a ribbon.

"The Congressman's back in the district today, but let's take a look," she said. When she opened the door to his private office, I blinked.

There, squarely in the middle of the floor, was the biggest pile of mail I had ever seen, except once when I visited a post office during the Christmas rush. Thousands of letters, packages, newspapers and mailing tubes were stacked in a waist-high jumble. Obviously untouched since its delivery, the mountain of mail would have filled a small truck.

"Looks like you have a few letters," I mumbled in the type of embarrassment one might feel at finding a friend had a crazy aunt locked in the attic.

"Yes," Marie said, casually skirting the stack of mail to get to the cabinet where she believed might be a typewriter ribbon.

"The Congressman won't let us open any of this until we finish the mail we already have."

"I see," I said, deciding not to pursue the matter. I thanked Marie for the ribbon and returned to our office, quietly thankful that our staff, at least, that had no such horrendous backlog. I would have been even more thankful if I had not discovered two drawers of unanswered mail squirreled away in the desk of Joanna, a legislative assistant who resigned unexpectedly a week or so later.

Personally, I never hid any mail. I'm not devious enough for that. If letters were too silly to answer or I simply didn't have time, I felt it was far more conscientious to stack them in plain sight on the corner of my desk. Then, if anybody complained about a missing letter, I could usually find it. If not, I eventually would get so sick of looking at them I could muster the courage to throw them away. But I considered that only a minor sin, at least compared to what I did with one of Jim Wright's newsletters.

Every couple of weeks, the Congressman prepared a one-page report called *The Wright Slant*, giving his assessment of issues before Congress. Several thousand copies were printed on the Gestetner, an ancient duplicating machine known more familiarly to the staff as the Green Hornet. It acquired this nickname because, for a reason still not completely clear to me, Jim Wright wanted all his newsletters printed in a garish green ink. However distinctive its color, this ink was a bilious goo that the Gestetner roundly resented having thrust into its innards and which it regularly regurgitated over walls, chairs, file cabinets and any humanoid silly enough to try to operate it, which in this case was me. If my experience with this machine had a silver lining, it probably was the fact that on St. Patrick's Day, I didn't need to wear a green tie.

Despite all the stories you hear about the perversity of machines, I don't believe they can really take reprisals against humans. But if scientists someday discover that machines do indeed have this power, I can tell them the exact day the Green Hornet extracted its revenge from me.

Soon after I joined the staff, Jim Wright signed off on a newsletter I had helped him prepare. He instructed me to go ahead and send it out to constituents who had asked to be placed on our mailing list.

"You don't have to run off any envelopes," said a fellow staffer, genuinely trying to be helpful. "We printed an extra set last week, and they're in those boxes stacked out in the hall." So when I finished running off the newsletter on this accursed machine, I notified the House Folding Room, which in those days folded and stuffed such mailings and got them to the post office.

In an hour or so, a workman wheeled up a cart and loaded the newly-printed green newsletters. Then, at my direction, he picked up the boxes in the hall—about a dozen big boxes, all filled with envelopes addressed to people in Jim Wright's district. At least I thought that's who they were addressed to.

The first call, as I remember, came only a day or so later from the editor of a newspaper in Temple, Texas.

"Why did Congressman Wright send me thirteen copies of his newsletter?" he asked in a reasonably civil voice.

"You got thirteen copies of it?" I said. "The post office must have gone bananas."

"It's not a post office mix-up. They're all addressed to me," he said.

"Oh," I said.

As it turned out, the boxes I sent to the folding room did not contain one envelope addressed to each constituent on our newsletter list. Instead the boxes contained envelopes carefully prepared for an entirely different purpose—the mailing of progress reports on Texas's Trinity River canal project. In the boxes were thirteen complete sets of envelopes for every newspaper, radio and television station in Texas.

Jim Wright should have fired me, but he didn't—possibly because he needed me to help write apologetic letters responding to dozens of angry editorials condemning our little old newsletter. Texas newspapers and broadcasting stations, quivering with elation at having caught us green-handed, inveighed loudly about this clear-cut abuse of the Congressional frank. But would you believe it? Not a single one of those ingrate editorial writers had the courtesy to thank me for providing such a splendid example of government waste. But actually, the joke was on them. They never found out about my world-class blunder involving a letter to a Korean war veteran in Fort Worth.

Today, with the larger staffs and gee-whiz computers in most Congressional offices, it may be easier to keep track of correspondence. Maybe it also was easy in my days, but somehow I never mastered the technique. To me, the most nettlesome problem was what we called "case mail."

Say, for example, that Mrs. Flossie Schwartz wrote to the Congressman complaining about a mix-up in her Social Security. This would be a "case," and we promptly responded over the Congressman's signature, assuring Mrs. Schwartz he would investigate her problem immediately. Then we bucked Mrs. Schwartz's incoming letter to Social Security headquarters, which usually straightened out the trouble promptly and sent a letter to the Congressman saying so. This reply from Social Security we sent to Mrs. Schwartz, along with a warm and fuzzy cover letter from the Congressman saying how delighted he was to have been able to resolve this problem for her.

Those of us on the staff never tried to leave a false impression, but it simply couldn't be helped if Mrs. Schwartz imagined that the moment the Congressman received her complaint, he dropped everything else, personally summoned to his office the head cheese of the whole blamed Social Security Administration, angrily chewed him out and ordered him to solve Mrs. Schwartz's problem by nightfall. But whatever the method, Mrs. Schwartz's problem really did get solved and, chances are, she would remember, on election day, how the Congressman helped her.

One case like this sounds simple enough, but our office often was working on hundreds of them at the same time. As the press person, I wasn't called on to handle many, and it's a good thing. Try as I might to keep them all straight, I occasionally misplaced a file. Then, when the response arrived from the federal agency, sometimes I couldn't figure out what prompted the constituent to write in the first place. One day, for instance, a letter arrived from the Army responding to one of my inquiries. The letter read like this:

Dear Congressman:

Thank you for your recent inquiry regarding Mr. Jerome K. Dinglehoofer of 1624 Perrywinkle Street in Fort Worth, Texas.

After a search of Army records we have found that Mr. Dinglehoofer, at that time a Staff Sergeant, received a medical discharge from the U.S. Army on July 18, 1951, as a result of advanced syphilis.

> *Sincerely,*
> *Troy G. Buttondown,*
> *Maj., USA*
> *Office of Legislative Liaison*
> *Department of the Army*

For days I tried to find a copy of the original incoming letter, but to no avail. I wanted to get off the Army's response to the constituent as soon as possible. But even more I was personally curious. What type of inquiry, for Pete's sake, would prompt a response like this? After rummaging through desk drawers, file cabinets and even waste baskets in a vain attempt to find a copy of the original incoming letter, I appealed for help from Kathy, the Congressman's personal secretary.

"What should I do?" I asked.

"Keep looking for the incoming letter. It's probably here somewhere."

"I've already looked everywhere, Kathy. The damn thing is just not here."

"Maybe somebody else on the staff has it."

"I've asked everybody. Nobody will admit having a case file on a guy named Dinglehoofer. I think I'll just throw away the Army letter and forget about the whole thing."

"No, you ought not to do that."

"Well, the Army letter has Mr. Dinglehoofer's name and address. I suppose I could just mail it to him with cover letter apologizing for having lost the file."

Kathy looked up, startled. "Oh, no—I really wouldn't do that," she said.

But I did. Against Kathy's advice, I sent it directly to Mr. Dinglehoofer.

Then, a few days later, I found the original incoming letter. It had been put in the file of another case, and it read like this:

Dear Congressman:

I wonder if you can help a group of ladies at our church with our Christmas project. Each year at Christmas time we pick out a deserving family to whom we can bring gifts and good cheer during the holiday season.   This year we are thinking about helping a Mr. Jerome K. Dinglehoofer and his family, who live in Fort Worth at 1624 Perrywinkle.   We believe he is a disabled veteran. Could you please check on this for us?

Sincerely,
Mrs. Clara Sophengopher
Chairwoman, Ladies Society

"Oh, no!" cried Kathy, when I finally told her what I had done. "I told you we shouldn't send that Army letter to that poor man," she said.

"Well, do you think it would have been better to send it instead to the church ladies?" I growled.

"No, of course not."

"And don't you suppose Mr. Dinglehoofer knew the reason he was being discharged?" I demanded.

"Yes, I suppose he did," Kathy said softly. "But he probably never expected to be reminded of it in a nice Christmas letter from his Congressman."

In retrospect, I can understand why life was so difficult for my friend Paul Willis. I am sure my office endeavors added to Paul's burden, even though I really didn't mean for them to. At any rate, not long after this episode, he told Jim Wright he had decided to return to teaching. As his words were recounted to me, Paul said to the Congressman:

"Jim, in each of us there are two persons—the activist and the contemplative. Working in this office, there is simply no time for the contemplative."

In Room 1327 of the Longworth House Office Building in the year 1962, he was damn sure right.

4

Haunted by Ted Kennedy's Shoes

L ooking back on the whole thing, I probably should have apologized to Senator Ted Kennedy, and I did consider it a couple of times. He used to drop by occasionally to see Jim Wright, and I could easily have buttonholed him for a moment. But to tell the truth, I never knew how the Senator might react if I told him I was the fellow involved in matter of the shoes. So I just kept quiet.

It all started with Mitch Elderson, but I can't really blame him. He was just trying to do me a favor, and he didn't do that for many people. Fat because he was forever eating and melancholy for reasons he never disclosed, Mitch was one of my bosses in the city room of the *Fort Worth Star-Telegram* back in the early 1960's.

In his prime I'm sure Mitch was a crackerjack newspaperman. But when I knew him he was just whiling away his few remaining years before retirement. Occasionally he would fill in as City Editor. This meant he was responsible for directing the efforts of about 20 or so reporters like myself in gathering and writing the news in the Fort Worth area. What made this so strange is that Mitch detested news. He hated for anything to happen— especially anything people would be interested in reading about.

On slow news days, Mitch tolerated his job responsibilities pretty well. In the early afternoon as the morning paper reporters straggled in to work, he would quietly pass out ho-hum assignment slips. After that, he would just sit and vegetate, hands clasped Buddha-like on the City Desk. Of course the phones were always ringing, but usually other guys on the desk would answer them. Only in the most unusual circumstances did his desk mates intrude on Mitch's ritual reveries.

When the reporters came in from their beats, Mitch would take a perfunctory look at their stories and wordlessly pass them over to the Copy Desk to be given headlines and dummied into the paper. Then he would pick up his hat and go home. He was the only City Editor I ever knew who hated news.

One night just before deadline for the four-star edition, the Miss Texas contestant from Fort Worth beat out dozens of other shapely and talented girls and won the statewide title. This was a big deal for hometown folks, easily worthy of a Page One story and the obligatory bathing suit picture. When the Associated Press bulletin came in from Galveston, Mitch's brow wadded up like a K-Mart throw rug. "Umm," he grumphed. "Might have known it. Nothing else would do her. She just had to go down there and win."

Despite his idiosyncrasies—or perhaps because of them—I really liked Mitch, and he always treated me well. For one thing, he knew I enjoyed national politics. Like thousands of other reporters across the nation, I yearned for a piece of the action in the escalating presidential campaign of 1960—the classic battle between John F. Kennedy and Richard M. Nixon.

One day late in September, as the campaign was moving into high gear, I saw Mitch peer over his glasses in my direction. He motioned for me to come over to the City Desk.

"Would you like to go out to Arlington State College?" he asked.

"What's happening out there?"

"Teddy Kennedy is supposed to be making a talk. We're going to have to cover it, I guess," he sighed.

"Teddy Kennedy is making a campaign speech at a state college? Won't the Nixon-Lodge people raise hell about that?"

"I surely hope not," Mitch murmured.

It wasn't a Pulitzer Prize type of assignment, but I was pleased with this chance to get a first-hand look at a younger brother of the man who might soon be President. In Texas, as in virtually every part of the country, each day was bringing new momentum to the race between the brainy, tousled-headed Massachusetts

Senator and the buttoned-down political pro who had dutifully served eight years as Eisenhower's Vice President. And because Senate Majority Leader Lyndon B. Johnson of Texas was on the ticket as Kennedy's running mate, the campaign already had become the biggest day-to-day story in our state.

Only two weeks before, John Kennedy had made a crucial appearance before the Greater Houston Ministerial Association. He presented a shrewd, head-on challenge to the myth that, because of presumed loyalty to the Vatican, no Catholic should ever be entrusted with the Presidency. With his straight-forward speech and forthright answers, he won the respect if not the support of many distrustful Protestant clergymen.

This was important, because even with Lyndon Johnson as his running mate, the fate of Texas's 24 electoral votes was still very much in doubt.

That summer, prior to John Kennedy's nomination at the Democratic convention in Los Angeles, I had read that his younger brother Teddy was busily rounding up Kennedy delegates in several Western states. I was eager to see this 28-year-old political wire-puller who, with another brother, Robert, 34, stood at either elbow of the 43-year-old Massachusetts Senator who aspired to be the 35th President of the United States.

When photographer Wilburn Davis and I arrived at Arlington State College, at first we couldn't find any sign of Ted Kennedy. At the administration office, the staff professed to know nothing about plans for any such visit. Then, as we wandered around the front of the Student Center, we nearly bumped into our quarry.

Lean and dynamic in those days, Ted Kennedy had just whooshed up in a gleaming white convertible. Handsome in a gray suit with a PT-109 clasp on his tie, he was welcomed and applauded by several hundred ASC students and faculty members. After working the crowd, he began looking around for a speaker's stand—or at least something to stand on.

Finding nothing, he began speaking from a spot in the roadway near the car. Then, frustrated because he could see the faces of only the few people nearest him, he stopped for a moment, shucked off his coat and then his shoes, and climbed up on the hood of the shiny convertible.

This was exactly the type of spontaneous, decisive action his youthful listeners were expecting to see—and they loved it. And his political appeal was squarely aimed at them.

"We need the help of all of you here—we need the young people and their ideas,"   Kennedy cried. The crowded nodded and clapped and whistled.

But not all his listeners were focused exclusively on political concerns. "Isn't he wonderful?" one coed sighed dreamily.

Her female companion, likewise transfixed by the exciting young man on the car hood, could gurgle only three words: "Yes—just wonderful!"

Before his enraptured audience, Kennedy ticked off a litany of what he called Republican failures to lead the nation—the stoning of U.S. officials in Latin America, protest rioting in Japan which forced President Eisenhower to cancel his scheduled visit, and the upsurge of communism in Cuba.

It was a fine speech. The only trouble was, from a reporter's standpoint, it was devoid of any new news. Every issue Ted Kennedy raised was old hat—a collection of worn-out old topics explored time and again in national utterances by either John Kennedy, Lyndon Johnson, or both.

This is the ultimate anguish for a reporter—to have several pages of quotes—all old, dull or uninteresting. Back at the office that day, I must have ripped a dozen false starts out of my old Underwood manual, feverishly trying to come up with a substantive lead that contained something new, exciting or different about Teddy's speech. Finally, with my copy deadline looming and Mitch casting anxious glances in my direction, I decided in desperation to give up on substance and fall back on froth and cuteness:

SHOELESS KENNEDY CAMPAIGNS ACROSS AREA FOR BIG BROTHER

By Marshall Lynam

Some politicians take off their coats and loosen their ties before lighting into the opposition.

But Ted Kennedy, 28-year-old brother of Senator John F.

Kennedy, did better than that while stumping for the Democrats in the Fort Worth area Friday.

He took off his shoes, too.

It happened at Arlington State College. Arriving there at noon, young Kennedy found there was no speaker's stand.

Unhesitatingly shucking his shoes as well as his coat, he climbed up on the hood of a gleaming white convertible.

Moving back and forth in his stocking feet across the groaning hood, he lit into the Republicans for assertedly letting America's prestige drop in the eyes of the world...

From this point on, I devoted 16 paragraphs to a conscientious report on the tired old issues Teddy recycled in his speech. Near the end of the story, however, I did include this unfortunate one-sentence observation:

Before Ted put this shoes back on, a nosy reporter looked inside and found they were imported British models.

After handing in my story to Mitch, I never gave it another thought. I was very much aware that the products of my literary efforts, like those of all newspaper reporters, are used mainly for wrapping fish and lining the bottoms of bird cages. I had no reason to think I would ever hear of this story again. I was wrong. In 1966 the story, like a ghostly boomerang which had been circling in the Bermuda Triangle for six years, came sailing back to haunt me.

Over these intervening years, of course, tumultuous events had occurred. John F. Kennedy won the 1960 Presidential election by a hairbreadth popular vote margin (with the help of Texas). Two years later Ted was elected by Massachusetts voters to fill his brother John's former seat in the Senate. President Kennedy was killed by a madman in Dallas in 1963. And now, in 1966, the third brother, Robert, was serving his second year as a Senator from New York—destined to be killed by yet another madman in 1968.

The passing years also had wrought significant changes in my own life. After leaving the *Star-Telegram* in 1962 to work as a Congressional staffer, my viewpoint on newspapers had broadened considerably. As a reporter, I used to think politicians were just chronic bellyachers in their complaints about news stories. But in four years as a staffer on the Hill, I learned that elected officials sometimes had legitimate reasons for accusing reporters of being incompetent, careless, or just plain mean. My heart was still in the newsroom, but I had seen many instances where my boss, Jim Wright, had what I thought was a justifiable beef about a story.

In the office we subscribed to a clipping service which provided us with a copy of every newspaper story in Texas that mentioned Jim Wright. When one of these packages of clippings came in, inevitably he would find one or two stories that infuriated him. One night, an hour or so after the rest of the staff had gone home, the phone rang on my desk.

"Marshall, have you seen this scurrilous damn story on the Trinity canal?" Jim Wright demanded.

"I'm not sure which story you mean. I'll be right in," I said.

As I opened the door to his office he was hunched over his desk, rereading the offending story. As I got closer, I could see his face was crimson. Suddenly he slammed the clipping down on his desk so hard it sent other clippings fluttering into the air like maddened butterflies.

"Who is this stupid jackass Harold Weston? He makes up a bunch of phony statistics and claims that our Trinity project is a just a big boondoggle!" he thundered.

I picked up the clipping and glanced at the byline. "Oh—it's that guy from the *Herald*," I said. "He damn well knows better than this. He came by here and I gave him the Corps of Engineers study with the accurate cost-benefit figures."

"You gave him the accurate figures and then he goes ahead anyway and writes tripe like this?"

"I'm afraid so."

"Why do newspaper reporters do things like this, Marshall?" he asked, almost pleading. "We work our butts off for a project that will benefit all of Texas, and then we have to put up with crap like this."

By this time he was beginning to calm down. His face was no longer flushed, and he leaned back in his chair, idly toying with a ballpoint pen.

"I just don't understand what makes these fellows tick," he sighed. "Do you know, Marshall, I even remember a story years ago about Ted Kennedy. He came down to make a speech, and while he was there, some rattle-brained idiot from the *Star-*

Telegram looked inside his shoes—*looked inside his shoes*, mind you—and then wrote in the paper about them being imported from England."

I gulped, unsure whether or not he was baiting me. After all, if he read the story, hadn't he seen my name on it? But then, who pays any attention to bylines? From his expression I decided he was not merely taunting me. He was dead serious. And then, fumbling for something appropriate to say, I took the coward's way out.

"Is nothing sacred to them?" I croaked.

Over the next few weeks, every time I recalled this conversation, I smiled—not because I had kept Jim Wright in the dark, for that to me that was not a smiling matter. What actually made me smile was my own cowardice—cowardice so blatant it was funny. Then, while still trying to decide whether my hypocrisy was funny or sad, one day I got a call from a friend and fellow Hill staffer, Janet Howard.

Janet was an attractive, politically savvy young woman from Brownwood, Texas, who worked for one of our Senators, Ralph Yarborough. She told me this was the birthday of Tom Wilson, a mutual friend on the Hill. She invited me to join a bunch of Senate people gathering after work for a couple of shooters to help Tom celebrate.

I arrived at the little cocktail lounge in Plaza Hotel about 6:30, and the party was well underway. Rather than offend Tom by refusing to toast him on his birthday, I knocked off a couple of vodka martinis and soon felt considerably better about Tom, his birthday, the Constitution of the United States, my case of athlete's foot, and practically everything else. In this spirit of goodwill and camaraderie, I introduced myself to a fellow I didn't recognize who was sitting at our table.

He gave me his name, and I asked him where he worked.

"I'm Administrative Assistant to Senator Ted Kennedy," he said.

Feeling a twinge akin to the Twilight Zone, I managed to gurgle something about being pleased to meet him. At this point I urgently needed another vodka, so I invited my new acquaintance to join me.

By the time the drinks came I had regained my composure and was actually enjoying my conversation with the fellow. He had a great sense of humor, we swapped a couple of laughs about recent antics on the Hill. The vodka was making me even more intelligent and amusing than usual.

"Those of us who work in the House don't usually share secrets with you wizards from the House of Lords," I laughed, "but I'm going to tell you a funny little story."

And I did.

At least I thought it was funny.

He didn't.

"You son of a bitch," he said, getting up from the table.

At first I thought he was going to hit me.

"I'm sorry," I said, clumsily standing up. "I just thought you'd get a kick out of it. I didn't mean to make you mad."

"No, no," he protested. "You don't understand. I'm not mad."

"You're not?"

"No—of course not. I was just surprised. You just cleared up a mystery that's been bugging me for six years."

"I did?"

"Yes," he said, explaining that he had been working with Teddy in the 1960 campaign. About a month before the election—approximately when Teddy might have been returning to Massachusetts from Texas—the two of them were rushing downtown to a big campaign rally in Boston Common.

"We were running down the street, late as usual, when all of a sudden Teddy reaches out and grabs me. 'Wait a minute,' he said. He looked down at my feet, mad as hell, and said, 'Are those imported shoes?' "

By this time everybody around our table in the cocktail lounge was listening, unable to make sense out of what my new friend was saying. I could have explained, but I didn't.

"Anyhow," he continued, "I held up one of my shoes for him to see. I said, 'Yeah, Teddy, these are brand new Italian models. Just got 'em. Really proud of 'em. Don't you like the little tassels?' "

Teddy, it developed, did not like the tassels. Nor the Italian shoes. Nor shoes from England. Nor any damn shoes from any damn place other than those from Massachusetts shoe factories like those in Lynn and Lowell and Salem. Teddy's furious words, as recalled by his staffer, were these:

"You silly jerk! Don't you know that you never go to a political rally wearing imported shoes?"

I never did apologize to Senator Kennedy. If I had, I could have told him how to avoid any future problems like this. Just by making sure a speech contains a tiny smidgen of news that a hard-working reporter can use for a lead.

5

The Cable Man Comethh

Cable television came to the Washington suburb of Arlington, Virginia, in the 1970's, and the brick home Eddie and I had just bought on Lee Highway happened to be in one of the first neighborhoods to be wired up. Not long afterward, during one of Jim Wright's daily breakfast meetings in the Capitol with his staff, I mentioned how delighted I was with this new toy.

"It's great," I bragged. "Besides the 24-hour news, we get all those marvelous old movies with Jimmy Stewart and Spencer Tracy and Katherine Hepburn. And watching the House proceedings on C-Span—it's better than a seat in the gallery."

Obviously interested, Jim Wright looked up from his scrambled eggs. "That does sound good," he said. "I'd like to get that service myself. Could you check on it for me?"

"Sure," I said. "They're wiring up the neighborhoods one at a time. I'm not sure when they're scheduled to get to your area over near Columbia Pike. Let me check it out for you."

By chance, at a recent reception on the Hill, I had been introduced to the boss of the cable company. I looked up his card and gave him a call. He was delighted to hear that the Congressman was interested in becoming a customer. He promised to check immediately on when his neighborhood would be wired. About an hour later, he called back.

"I'm sorry, Marshall," he said, "but it looks as if Mr. Wright's neighborhood won't be wired for at least a year or so."

As a good staff man, I saw that my duty was clear. "That's an awful shame," I said slowly. "Jim Wright doesn't miss very many sessions of the House. But if he were sick or something, it would really be important for him to be able to tune in C-Span to keep an eye on floor proceedings.

"And of course," I added, warming to my pitch, "it's absolutely essential for him to keep on top of what's happening around the world, and the great coverage on CNN would be just the ticket. And then too, his wife Betty—do you know Betty?— she really loves old classic movies."

On the other end of the line, the cable boss was quiet for a moment. "I think I understand," he said finally. "Let me see what I can do."

What he did I am not sure, but it worked. Within a week or so the Congressman was happily wired up as a subscriber to cable television. Of course I saw no point in burdening Jim Wright with the exact nature of my little talk with the cable company's head man, because I thought the story was over. I was wrong.

One Saturday morning a year or so later, Jim Wright answered a knock on his front door. There stood a well-groomed, businesslike young man carrying a sheath of papers.

"Good morning, sir," he said. "I'm with the cable television company. We wiring your neighborhood, and I wondered if you would like to sign up for our service."

At this point you need to understand one thing about Jim Wright. He almost had rather take a Texas horsewhipping than to be compelled to say "No" to any request from a friend, or even a stranger. Maybe a small part of this is a politician's professional need to be liked. But with Jim Wright it's deeper than that. After 27 years I'm convinced that an earnest desire to help people is embedded deep within his very bones. As he looked at the young man standing at his door, he was characteristically solicitous.

"Well, I really would like to sign up for your cable service," he said. "But I'm afraid I already have it."

The young salesman studied this older fellow in the rumpled smoking jacket and smiled patronizingly. "Sir," he asked gently, "why would you believe that you already have service?"

"Well, it was installed a year or so ago. And I really want to congratulate you and your company on the service. Betty and I find it very interesting and enjoyable."

Obviously trying to be patient, the young man decided to lay it on the line: "Sir, there is no way you could already have service."

"There isn't?"

"No, sir, I'm afraid there's not. You see, we are just beginning to wire this neighborhood, so there's no way you could already have it."

Jim Wright arched his imposing eyebrows and looked thoughtful. "Well," he said slowly, "I *think* we have it."

"Why would you think that, sir?" the young man asked. There was a touch of quiet pity in his voice.

"Well, we get CNN, and we get C-Span. And we like to watch American Movie Classics."

"On your television?" the young man asked incredulously.
Jim Wright nodded. "But look," he said. "You obviously are working very hard to sell this service. If it would help you, why don't you just let me sign up again."

"No, sir," the young man replied, shaking his head as he walked away. "Not if you think you already have it."

Even today, after all these years, I still savor an imaginary scene in which the dedicated young salesman delights his pals with the hilarious story of his encounter with the old geezer who was under the delusion that he already had cable TV.

When the Congressman recounted this conversation to me, I had only one regret. I wish Jim Wright had told the young man, "Yes—as a matter of fact, I like your cable coverage of the House of Representatives proceedings so much that sometimes I appear on C-Span myself."

6

The Lettuce
Cigarette Caper

Jim Wright used to smoke three packs of Winstons a day. Like millions of other Americans, he tried time and again to quit. Unable to do so, he wistfully hoped somebody could at least come up with a safe cigarette.

That, of course, was not the main reason his good friend Congressman Graham Purcell invited him to speak at a big dinner in Wichita Falls, Texas. It was a good reason, all right, but not the main one.

The main reason was that many people regarded Jim Wright as the best orator in the House, and Graham needed a real stem-winding speaker to draw a crowd for the dinner he was planning.

The dinner had two purposes—to raise funds for Graham's re-election campaign, and to welcome an innovative new company to Wichita Falls, the largest city in Graham's Congressional district.

The new company was unique. When the U.S. Surgeon General warned in 1964 that cigarettes could cause lung cancer and all manner of other bad things, the company envisioned a great new business opportunity. It would manufacture and market an entirely new type of cigarette—a safe cigarette. Instead of tobacco, its cigarettes would be made of, er, uh, lettuce.

A lettuce cigarette?

Sure, why not? Practically every kid in Jim Wright's day used to sneak out behind the barn and smoke such odd things as corn silk or cedar bark. Nobody ever heard of those killing anybody. Besides, Graham presumed that the new company had done its homework and determined that lettuce was considerably less toxic than tobacco.

Jim Wright readily accepted the invitation because Graham Purcell was his good friend and he wanted to help him in any way he could. And while he undoubtedly would have welcomed a safe cigarette, he certainly never gave much thought to smoking lettuce.

After all, it was quite a stretch to imagine a smoker walking up to a cigarette counter and saying, "A pack of king-size Romaines, please."

Graham probably did not dwell at length on the subject, either. If people wanted to try to sell lettuce cigarettes, that was fine with him. He smoked cigars, anyway.

When Jim Wright invited my wife Eddie and me to fly up to the dinner in Wichita Falls with him, I wondered if this company had, in fact, come up with a genuinely safe, decent-tasting cigarette.   If so, there should be no shortage of potential customers. Many people were addicted, then as now, because they grew up in a world where virtually everybody smoked.

It seemed to be such a simple pleasure. Besides, kids saw it as the sophisticated, grown-up thing to do.

In grammar school days, we used to snitch a cigarette, crawl under a bridge and light up. We would get a mouthful of smoke, blow it through a white handkerchief, and giggle about the yucky brown stain it left. Some men actually prided themselves on the nicotine and tar stains left on their fingers by years of holding lighted cigarettes. It probably never occurred to them that their lungs were about the same color.

Down deep, though, we probably knew they were deadly because we used to laugh and call them coffin nails. But we preferred not to think about it.

On the day of the dinner, Jim Wright, Eddie and I climbed into a little four-seat chartered airplane at Meacham Field in Fort Worth. No sooner had we taken off for Wichita Falls than Jim Wright lighted up his last Winston and wadded up the empty package. I knew what was coming, so I fished in my coat pocket for the Marlboros I smoked occasionally. The box contained only three cigarettes.

Within 10 minutes Jim Wright turned to me. "Marshall, do you have a cigarette?"

I handed him my Marlboros. "Take these," I said. "I don't need one right now."

Those three cigarettes lasted until just before we landed in Wichita Falls, where Graham had a car waiting. Arriving at the convention hall, we found that waiters already were busily serving the food. Jim Wright was whisked immediately to his spot at the head table. Knowing he soon would nervously start rummaging through his pockets in a futile quest for a cigarette, I left Eddie at our table and started searching the building for a cigarette machine. There was none, and no stores were open nearby.

On the dais fifty feet away there already were signs of impending trouble. While most of the audience probably noticed only that Jim Wright was graciously making small talk with the fellow seated beside him at the head table, I detected something else. In a ritual I had seen many times, he already had begun now and then to reach up and pat his shirt pocket, subconsciously hoping to detect a pack of cigarettes he had overlooked. It was clearly time for desperation measures.

I turned to the eight people seated at our table. "Excuse me, folks," I said, "but do any of you happen to have any cigarettes?"

"None of us smoke," one lady sniffed. All the rest gravely shook their heads. From their expressions I could see they thought it was I who wanted a smoke. *Humph!* they were thinking. *If he wants to kill himself, at least he ought to buy his own damn cigarettes.*

As the evening's program got under way, I could see Jim Wright squirming in his chair. I was sympathetic, but there was nothing I could do. At this point, even if I had found a supply of cigarettes, it would have been impossible to make a discreet delivery to him on the dais. For a while I had hoped he might be able to bum a cigarette from one of his seatmates at the head table, but nobody up there was smoking. And then, out of the blue, came the answer to a smoker's prayer—or so I thought.

Two pretty little girls, dressed in red, white and blue uniforms, approached the head table. In their arms they carried, of all things, what appeared to be cartons of cigarettes. Eureka! I thought. Of course! The lettuce cigarette company! Handing out samples! Jim Wright is saved!

Smiling sweetly, the little girls handed a carton of this new kind of cigarette to each dignitary at the head table. They didn't know what to do with them.

Just ask yourself: You are a civic leader—a guest at an elegant dinner. You are seated in plain view of five hundred of your fellow citizens. They are watching your every move. Suddenly you are handed an exciting new hometown product—a carton of lettuce cigarettes. For Pete's sake, what do you do with it?

Most head table guests coped with the problem pretty well. They waved the cartons aloft, smiled enthusiastically and clapped their hands to show their support for this great new Wichita Falls enterprise. Then they gratefully deposited the doggoned things under their seats. All except Jim Wright.

Like a hungry bear, he ripped open the carton and dug out one of the packages—an act which instantaneously captured the attention of everybody in the hall. He was the only person at the head table who seemed interested.

He was oblivious to the fact that the program had resumed. When the master of ceremonies noticed from the podium that every eye in the house was on Jim Wright, the emcee stopped talking and started watching, too. And why not? After all, what could be more beneficial to the new hometown product than to have it demonstrated in public by this most distinguished guest?

So intent on reaching his prize was Jim Wright that he failed to recognize, even now, that he held the rapt attention of the entire audience. Eagerly he tore open the package, snatched out a cigarette, and lighted up. As the smoke whooshed down into his lungs, a look of astonishment crossed his face and he emitted a loud, agonized gasp.

Echoing through the hall, the tortured wheeze was one you might hear from a fireman fleeing from a smoke-filled building, or perhaps a burning lettuce warehouse. Raw and rasping, it was the outcry of a man fighting for breath. Head down, shoulders heaving, coughing violently. I was thunderstruck.

I've killed him, I thought. I've killed my boss. I could have saved him if I had only found him some nice, tarry Winstons.

But then, in only a few seconds, it was all over. Jim Wright stopped coughing, wiped his eyes, regained his composure and gamely waved a hand to signal that he was OK.

Stunned, people in the audience didn't know at first whether to laugh or call an ambulance. But then, grateful that their keynote speaker had survived this unexpected field test of the city's newest product, the guests enthusiastically applauded his courage, pluck and resilience.

But it wasn't the gasping and the coughing that worried me. Jim Wright would soon get over that. But he was, above all, a man of towering pride and dignity. When he arose to make tonight's main speech, what on earth would he say to these people about their miserable lettuce cigarettes? But I need not have worried. As usual, my boss came through like a polished diplomat.

As he moved to the podium, he had fully recovered from the experience. From the looks on people's faces they were sheepishly awaiting Jim Wright's verdict on their product. Smiling, Jim Wright admitted to the audience that it might take people a while to get accustomed to lettuce cigarettes.

"But I'll tell you one thing," he said. "I'd rather smoke a lettuce cigarette than eat a tobacco salad."

The audience laughed and applauded. They liked Jim Wright. But I never heard any more about lettuce cigarettes.

In the interest of full disclosure, I should report that Jim Wright no longer smokes cigarettes of any kind. He gave up lettuce cigarettes that very night. Later, in 1978, he quit the tobacco kind, cold turkey. Then, in 1991, doctors discovered a small malignant tumor at the base of his tongue. He underwent surgery and four weeks of radiation treatment at M.D. Anderson cancer center in Houston. In the past six years he has suffered no recurrence and his doctors are optimistic about the future. He urges people to avoid smoking cigarettes. Even lettuce cigarettes. *Especially* lettuce cigarettes.

Except for Jim Wright, I never met a Congressman I admired more than Graham Purcell. Over the years we became good friends, and I worked as a volunteer in several of his campaigns. I'd like to tell you about some of his political experiences—and mine, too.

To me, Graham always brought to mind old-time cowboy star Gary Cooper. Rawboned and leathery, he looked to me as if he might have just moseyed in from the OK Corral—quiet and tough but not hankerin' for no trouble.

Born and raised in the prairie country around Archer City, he entered the Army just after Pearl Harbor and fought in Tunisia and Italy as an infantry captain. Far from the cartoon version of a loud-mouthed, back-slapping politician, Graham was friendly but reserved, almost shy. He spoke sparingly, but when he did it was with an imperious voice deeper than a Panhandle water well.

In politics he made his mark first as a no-nonsense District Judge. Whenever he pronounced sentence on a drunk driver or a thief, his words rumbled through the courtroom with the same awesome finality many of us are fearful we may hear from Saint Peter upon our arrival at the Pearly Gates.

The respect Graham won as a judge paved the way for his victory in a special election to Congress in 1962 from the 13th District of Texas. It was a race to succeed the incumbent, Frank Ikard, who was retiring. In a runoff Graham beat Bailey Meissner, one of five Republicans originally in the race, by a margin of 2 to 1. In his district, which lay in the sprawling ranch and farm country northwest of Fort Worth, most voters shared Graham's politics as a conservative to moderate Democrat.

In Congress, he was appointed to the House Agriculture Committee and worked his way up to Chairman of the Livestock and Grains Subcommittee—a position important to the farmers and ranchers he served back home. Yet when it came to elections, Graham seemed to be snake-bit. In six consecutive elections, he drew a new opponent every time.

In 1964 he faced a particularly uncertain race because the Texas Legislature had just redistricted the state and given him a chunk of Dallas County. Voters here were far more conservative than those he served in the area around Wichita Falls, and Graham didn't really know what to expect from these Dallas folks.

Since I knew Jim Wright considered Graham a good friend and an exceptionally able member of Congress, I asked if I could use my vacation time to work as a volunteer in his campaign. In less time than it takes for the driver behind you to honk when the light turns green, Jim Wright said yes, by all means. He knew that for Graham it might be a tough fight against a determined and well-heeled Republican opponent.

In his campaign in North Dallas, Graham allowed me to try out what, in 1964, was a wild idea. Since most people in that growing and affluent area had never even heard of Graham Purcell, I suggested that we send each of our prospective new voters a personalized letter, zeroing in on the precise hot button that would energize him or her on election day.

To do this we organized a boiler room where teams of Purcell volunteers conducted thousands of personal telephone interviews with individual voters. Each was asked to select, from a prepared list, the issue he or she considered America's gravest national problem. Based on these interviews, Graham's people then cranked out by computer to each voter a carefully-crafted letter, addressing the particular issue which that voter regarded as most important—and, moreover, telling the voter how Graham planned to handle that issue.

Today such amateurish efforts would seem laughable, but they didn't in 1964. Even with the conservative areas of Dallas in the district, Graham won that election by a margin of 3 to 1 over Republican George Corse. (Campaign motto: Corse, of course.)

Once again in 1966 I volunteered to spend my vacation time helping Graham. This time I found out that folks out in West Texas sometimes don't get too picky about election matters.

Four days before the Tuesday general election, I was at our campaign headquarters in Wichita Falls when Graham unexpectedly received an important invitation. He was asked to speak that day before the city's top-level movers and shakers— bankers, lawyers and assorted fat-cats—at a downtown civic club luncheon. This was an opportunity too good to pass up. Trouble was, Graham was scheduled that day to lead a Vote-for-Purcell motorcade out through the dusty hinterlands west of Wichita Falls. He asked me if I would substitute for him on the trip.

Unable to imagine anything more exciting than accompanying a group of ladies in funny little campaign hats handing out Purcell circulars in a bunch of remote little West Texas towns where dogs slept on the courthouse steps, I said certainly.

Once we got rolling through the little towns, though, I was kind of ashamed of my thoughts. True, the ladies wore funny hats and the towns were tiny, unsophisticated and sleepy. But in these little towns, in the barber shops and the courthouses, lived real, honest-to-goodness people. True, they had never dined at *Lion D'or* on Connecticut Avenue, and they wouldn't have known Madeleine Albright from Dear Abby—but they were people I'd doggoned sure trust with my wife, my books or even that yellowed copy of my 1943 orders to report to Fort Sam Houston. Better still, these people were solid supporters of Graham Purcell— money, marbles and chalk, as Texas politicians used to say.

It was late afternoon when our motorcade reached the tiny Stonewall County seat of Aspermont. As we pulled up to the courthouse on the town square, I was tired, bedraggled and sweaty. For a moment I toyed with the idea of staying in the car. But the ladies, still perky and enthusiastic after 130 miles, shamed me by storming this last courthouse like the Marines going up Mount Suribachi. Led by Mrs. Purcell, they enthusiastically carried our campaign into every cranny of the courthouse.

As I stood waiting in a hallway, one of Stonewall County's top officials, who shall remain forever nameless, approached me and introduced himself. He was a portly guy in the unmistakable uniform of an old Texas political pro—white shirt, damp around the armpits, a tie hanging forlornly from an unbuttoned collar, and a frayed blue vest. His expression indicated clearly he was carrying some sort of heavy burden. He edged me into a nearby corner.

"You work for Graham?" he whispered.

"Yes, I'm helping him with the campaign," I said.

He looked at me closely. "Has Graham got an opponent this year?" he asked.

The question startled me. "Yes—of course," I said. "That's the reason for this motorcade. Graham's got a very serious Republican opponent. He's spending a lot of money trying to beat us, too."

My friend looked troubled. "We've got a problem," he said.

"What kind of problem?"

"We haven't got the other fellow's name on the ballot," he said.

I was stunned. This was a Friday afternoon before the election Tuesday. In Texas in 1966, voting machines were used mainly in big cities. Like scores of other rural counties, Stonewall used paper ballots.

"Wait a minute," I said. "Are you telling me you really haven't got Buddy Norwood's name on the ballot?"

"Is that the fellow's name—Buddy Norwood?"

"Actually it's D.C. Norwood, and he puts Buddy in parenthesis. How on earth could you leave his name off the ballot?"

"Weren't expecting Graham to have an opponent, I guess. I don't know how it happened. What do you think we ought to do?"

"You better have the ballots reprinted—right now," I said.

"Can't do that. The people over in the newspaper office say they can't get new ballots printed before Tuesday. What should we do?"

"This is terrible. This could really hurt Graham," I said. "You'd better get some clerks together right away and have them print Norwood's name on all the ballots as clearly and legibly as they can."

"You really think they would notice, then?"

"That Norwood's name doesn't appear on the ballot? You're damned right they'd notice. Somewhere in the county there must be at least one Republican, and he for doggoned sure would notice that his man's name is missing."

"I guess you're right," he mumbled.

"Don't you see?" I demanded. "You're liable to get every single ballot in the county invalidated. And this election could be close. Graham's going to need every last vote he can scare up."

"OK," he promised. "I'll see what I can do."

Still shaken, I climbed back into the car. As we started to pull away from the courthouse, my friend came waddling down the courthouse steps, waving at me.

I rolled down the window and he stuck his head in the car.

"You going to see Graham tonight?" he asked.

I nodded.

"Tell him the absentee ballots already are in—and all counted!" he said, winking.

Just prior to the election, Norwood's name was added to the ballot with a rubber stamp. But then, on election night, we learned that *both* Graham's and Norwood's names were left off the ballot in Baylor County, another of the 19 counties in the district. At any rate, Graham won this election 4 to 3.

He went on to win two other elections, in 1968 and 1970, before being defeated in 1972—the year our Democratic nominee for President, George S. McGovern, carried only Massachusetts and the District of Columbia.

Today Graham is doing what he likes to do best—presiding over a courtroom.   As a visiting District Judge, he serves on temporary assignments in various cities around the state. I'm glad he's enjoying life, but I wish he were back on the Hill.

7

LBJ: Small Glimpses of a Large Man

The first time Lyndon B. Johnson ever spoke to me was, appropriately enough, from the heavens.

Not from very high in the heavens, it's true. Even so, he sure got my attention.

The year was 1948, and the country was still sorting itself out after World War II. I was going to college under the GI Bill. Even though I had heard of this young Hill Country school teacher who had managed to get himself elected to Congress in 1937, Lyndon B. Johnson was still not a name that quickened the pulse of voters, even in Texas.

Nobody had any idea what tumultuous years lay ahead for Johnson, and how his fate would be bound tightly to that of the nation. And certainly I had no inkling that over the years to come, my own life would brush here and there along the fringes of the historic career of this man whose memory even today seems to inspire both love and hate in abundant measure.

Between 1961 and 1971, first as a newspaper reporter and later on the staff of Jim Wright, I was lucky enough to be in the right place on many occasions to catch a few first-hand glimpses and to form a few personal opinions about this endlessly fascinating fellow from the hardscrabble country northwest of San Antonio.

To me, Lyndon B. Johnson will always rank as the most incredibly complex man God ever made—a walking, talking bundle of contradictions. He could be as mean as a Texas rattlesnake and as kind as a Salvation Army captain on Thanksgiving. He could be as quick-tempered as a scalded Bengal tiger and as patient as your neighborhood undertaker. His ego was roughly the size of Jupiter and sometimes—just sometimes, I emphasize—you got a momentary feeling that his heart was about the same size.

My first exposure to this unusual man came one quiet afternoon as I sat at my typewriter in the tiny, cluttered office of *The Bishop News*, the weekly serving my home town in the blackland coastal plain of Texas. As a college student, I was working part-time as a reporter—unpaid, but that was OK. After all, there was seldom much excitement in Bishop—except occasionally in the *News* office itself.

From time to time while the paper was being printed, our cantankerous old flatbed press would run amuck. This ancient machine printed newspapers, one at a time, by means of huge platform which careened to and fro. Bolted onto this wildly oscillating platform were the massive steel forms filled with the slugs of molten lead belched out by the Linotype machine, which itself gave the appearance of a rather large octopus in the midst of a fit.

Occasionally while the press was running, the vibration would work loose the bolts holding the page forms on the moving platform. At that point the page forms would career into the air like an F-18 being launched from the *U.S.S. Nimitz*.

When that happened there were only three things to do— make sure nobody was hurt, clean up the mess, and begin to reset all the type. But on this particular day, our flatbed press was on good behavior.

I was sitting at my desk, talking with the editor, W.E. Newton, and a wonderful honest-to-goodness reporter, Edna May Tubbs, when a thunderous sound enveloped Bishop's entire one-block business district.

"HELLO, THIS IS YOUR FRIEND, LYNDON JOHNSON!" an amplified voice boomed from the sky.

The entire editorial staff of our paper—all three of us—ran outside. There, hovering whup, whup, whup over Main Street, was the first helicopter I had ever seen in flight.

Bishop, Texas, population 997, was agog. Townspeople swarmed from the barber shop, from Moerbe's Grocery, from both drug stores and even from the bench where Ben Davis and his pals used to sit in front of the pool hall. They ran into the middle of Main Street and gazed up in awe. In a minute or so, the helicopter wheeled on its course to the next little town in its statewide tour—but not before its ambitious passenger, Congressman Lyndon Baines Johnson, made a feverish mid-air pitch for votes in the Democratic primary. He was running against former Governor Coke Stevenson for the U.S. Senate, a race he was destined to win—but only by a hotly-contested 87 votes in a runoff election.

In retrospect, I can see that day was marked by several momentous events. First, Bishop and a lot of other little towns across South Texas got a foretaste of what campaigning might be like in the new postwar world of American politics. Second, a reporter named Lynam got a pretty decent little story for *The Bishop News*. And third, people from the barber shop, the grocery store and the pool hall heard a name they would be hearing for a long time to come. Lyndon B. Johnson was on his way.

My first real meetings with Johnson didn't come until 1961— the year he became Vice President. Again I was in the role of a reporter—this time for the *Fort Worth Star-Telegram*. It was during this period that I noticed a characteristic common to all prominent politicians—an abiding (and usually justified) distrust of the press.

When Johnson came to Fort Worth to speak to a group of U.S. immigrants gathered proudly for their naturalization ceremony in the U.S. Courthouse, I asked for and was granted a private interview. I've forgotten what the story was, but I do remember that his press secretary, George Reedy, stood uncomfortably close to me and took far more notes of Johnson's utterances than I did.

If I had asked, I'm sure George would have said he had to stand next to me and take notes because Johnson might say something profound on which he would get inquiries from other reporters.

But his presence there sent me a far clearer message: If you screw up the Vice President's comments, you SOB, I'll have the notes to prove you're a liar.

Later, while covering the Vice President on a trip to Wichita Falls, I witnessed one of his classic performances. At the airport, as Johnson walked from the plane, a local radio reporter intercepted him, thrust a microphone into his face, and asked some inane question. Johnson brushed aside the question, telling the radio reporter he had nothing to say on that subject. The reporter then asked the same question again, in slightly different words.

Johnson, who towered at six feet three, stopped, looked down at the fellow, and then abruptly reached out and entwined him octopus-style in his long arms. He pulled the astonished reporter so close their faces were only inches apart. I was standing close enough to hear.

"Son," Johnson hissed, staring unblinkingly at his hapless prisoner, "did you hear what I said?"

The poor radio man fled in terror, thoroughly intimidated. And that brings me to *Lynam's Theory* about Johnson's vaunted skill in convincing the unconvincable. The question was, how was Lyndon Johnson, in one-on-one conversations, almost invariably able to bring around opponents, so quickly and deftly, to his own viewpoint? My personal, two-premise theory is this:

Premise 1: American politics, in Johnson's time even more so than today, was predominately a man's game.

Premise 2: Most American males are uncomfortable to the point of frantic embarrassment when they are physically embraced or touched in any way but a handshake by another man. My private belief is that Johnson recognized this early on and, whether consciously or not, perfected the technique. Most men in the United States, unlike those in Italy and elsewhere, had rather be beaten with a blacksnake whip than be embraced in public—or even in private—by another hairy-legged man. Even though homosexual male-to-male affection today gets a small measure of grudging acceptance from the public, this was not the case in Johnson's day.

Conclusion: A man who is ready to back up physically is also ready to back up psychologically. In other words, if a towering, forceful Texan suddenly wraps his long arms around you, hugs you

as he would a woman and brings his face down close enough to kiss
you, you are so surprised and panic-stricken that you have only
one overriding thought: How do I get loose from this son of a
bitch? If escaping requires telling him "Yes" to whatever the hell
he wants, tell him "Yes!"

While persuasiveness was his trademark, Johnson also could be
downright cruel. One incident was described to me by a friend of
30 years—a retired U.S. Air Force colonel who flew as an escort
officer on a Johnson trip to space installations around the United
States. My friend swears he saw Johnson, then Vice President,
throw a Cutty Sark and soda into the face of an Air Force steward.
The reason? The sergeant had failed to use a freshly-opened
bottle of soda in mixing the drink.

Yet this is the same Lyndon B. Johnson who personally saw
to it that a full-dress military funeral in Arlington National
Cemetery was given to a Texas soldier killed in action in World
War II—after the soldier's hometown cemetery refused him burial
because he was of Mexican descent.

At least Johnson was even-handed with his anger. He would
turn on friends as readily as enemies. One good friend in the press
was the late Seth Kantor, a wonderful buddy of mine who worked
as Washington correspondent in the 1960s for a number of
Scripps-Howard papers, including *The Fort Worth Press*. After a
briefing on plans for a controversial new fighter plane called the
TFX, Johnson quietly drew Kantor aside and tipped him that the
fantastically lucrative contract would go to General Dynamics in
Fort Worth—a news beat of monumental proportions in Texas.

Yet from time to time, Johnson would get furious, even with
him. Once Kantor wrote a page one story reporting the incredible
fact that Johnson, then Vice President of the United States, not
only had his home telephone listed in the Washington directory,
but that he often answered it himself. A few days later, probably
after hundreds of strangers had swilled a few beers and then decided
to give ol' Lyndon a call, Johnson ran into Kantor at the weekly
Texas Congressional delegation luncheon. Johnson's eyes
narrowed piercingly as he loomed over Kantor. "I sure want to
thank you for putting my telephone number in the paper, Seth,"
he hissed.

Not even Johnson's good friend Jim Wright was immune.
One evening in 1961 the Fort Worth Chamber of Commerce was

holding its elegant annual dinner in the Texas Hotel. A surprise guest was Vice President Johnson. As Fort Worth's Congressman and Johnson's good friend, Jim Wright went to the podium and gave him a lavish introduction.

Later that evening, in a private hotel suite upstairs, a handful of privileged local politicos was invited to gather with the Vice President to watch a video tape of his speech. On the tape, just as Johnson was warming to the subject of his speech, Jim Wright could be seen in the background, lighting a cigarette and glancing for a split second away from the podium. "Well, Jim," Johnson growled, "I see that as soon as you finished introducing me, you quit listening."

After succeeding to the Presidency, Johnson brought into the White House staff a delightful young woman named Delores Stacks. Attractive, articulate and politically savvy, Delores had worked in Johnson campaigns in Houston and had a wide acquaintance among Texas movers and shakers.

So valuable did she become in Texas political matters that she was usually among the staffers who accompanied the President when he went home to his ranch in the Texas Hill Country. As a good friend, Delores once told me a surprising thing. Despite Johnson's unsurpassed skills of persuasion over the telephone, he never really took a minute to understand the mechanics of how the blamed thing worked. Especially troublesome to him were the sophisticated phones set aside for the President's use, with their rows of blinking lights and assorted bells and whistles and doodads. Often Johnson punched the wrong button and cut himself off, she said, leading him to curse and pound the phone with his fist.

At the LBJ ranch in Texas, one of Delores's jobs was to screen calls from Texans who described themselves as old school chums, long-lost cousins, good friends of good friends, and business moguls with urgent messages. They all had one thing in common—it was crucial that they talk to the President—right now.

Once Delores fielded a call from Austin, the state capital. On the line was a fat cat businessman who claimed to be a lifelong friend of the President. Delores recounted the story this way:

"Lemme talk to LBJ, honey," the fellow blustered. "I've got somethin' real important to tell him. Ol' Lyndon and I go back a long way together, and he'll be real interested in what I've got to say."

Delores recognized his name as that of a man who had attended a barbecue at the LBJ Ranch, but she knew that the President didn't want to take any calls. Just as she was about to say how sorry she was that the President wasn't available, she was dumbfounded to hear the President's voice on the line. Apparently he had picked up the phone, under the impression that he could talk to Delores without being heard by the guy calling from Austin.

"Tell him I've gone to California," Johnson whispered.

Delores swallowed hard and said, "I'm awfully sorry you missed the President, sir, but he has gone to California."

The fellow in Austin obviously recognized Johnson's voice, but was intimidated enough not to say so. "Well, uh, honey..." he stammered. "It's really important that I talk to him."

"Tell him I won't be back for a week and probably not then," came the Johnson's voice again.

"The President won't be back for a week and probably not then," Delores repeated dutifully.

"Well, uh...Well OK, then, honey," said the Austin executive, accepting ignominious defeat.

Delores also told me the story of another Presidential phone call—a call that will always remain memorable to her. It came after one of the most shattering experiences of her life—learning that she had breast cancer.

Johnson was devastated at the news. To him, Delores was more than a trusted White House staffer, she was a dear friend. And, as President of the United States, he simply did not intend to put up with anything like this.

"Get me the Mayo Clinic on the phone—the head man," he ordered.

After the call went through, Delores remembers the President giving the head doctor at Mayo some very specific orders: "One of my most important staff members has the cancer. I'm going to send her up to you. You cure her—you understand?"

The boss at Mayo assured Johnson that he did indeed understand, and if Delores came there, Mayo's doctors would do their best. But he reminded the President that perhaps the world's foremost cancer treatment center was located in his own home state—the M.D. Anderson Hospital in Houston.

The President nodded his acknowledgment into the telephone. "All right, then," he said. "I'll send her down there. I'll make *them* cure her."

He did, too. At least Delores was, in fact, completely cured. Moreover, she apparently liked Houston doctors pretty well. She married one.

In politics, Johnson was such a crafty manipulator of people that it's sometimes easy to write him off as a person without feeling...to conclude that he was immune from the everyday emotions and human longings that the rest of us have. True, most of the time he kept any such feelings well concealed. But on rare occasions there was a chink in the armor and a tiny signal seeped out, as it did one day in October, 1971.

This was a year when Jim Wright, steadily advancing in stature and seniority in the House, had become chairman of an important subcommittee of the House Public Works Committee. Johnson, feeling his Presidential leadership fatally compromised by the national agony of Vietnam, had declined to seek re-election to the White House in 1968 and had gone home to Texas, devoting most of his time to the LBJ Library in Austin. He still loved the telephone, though.

One day in the summer of 1971 he telephoned Jim Wright. They had a long conversation touching on a multitude of subjects—how each other's families were doing, how things were going on the Hill, and of course the performance of Johnson's successor, President Richard M. Nixon. Then, near the end of the conversation, Johnson said: "Jim, I'd like to have you come down here and see me."

Jim Wright accepted this as the kind of perfunctory invitation that any two friends might routinely extend to each other in closing out a conversation. He gave Johnson the kind of answer he thought he expected—that he would sure try to come down, one of these days.

A month or so later, Johnson called again. Once more he and Jim Wright exchanged political tidbits and touched all the usual bases. Before hanging up, Johnson repeated his invitation to come down and see him, and Jim Wright repeated his perfunctory answer that he would really like to do that one day.

Then, as the leaves of the stately oak trees on the Capitol grounds began to take on a tinge of autumn, Johnson called again. This time he was more direct.

"Jim, I've asked you twice now to come down and see me," Johnson said. "Is there some reason that you don't want to come?"

Surprised, Jim Wright immediately offered amends. "To tell the truth, Mr. President, I thought you were just being courteous in inviting me down. If you really need to see me—of course, I'll come down right away."

After promising to call back soon to work out an agreeable date, Jim Wright hung up the phone, frankly puzzled. What on earth could Lyndon B. Johnson want to see him about? He turned the question over and over in his mind, but came to no conclusion.

Back when Johnson was President, Jim Wright asked for White House help on several occasions. Sometimes he got it, sometimes not. On one big-ticket item, he received virtually no help at all. This was the massive Trinity River project, which envisioned construction of a shipping canal from the Gulf of Mexico to Fort Worth and Dallas—at that time an area second only to Mexico City as the most populous place in the world without access to a navigable waterway.

While in the White House Johnson had been reluctant to support such a costly and controversial project for his home state. Could Johnson's call now have any bearing on the Trinity? On the future of the sprawling General Dynamics aircraft plant in Fort Worth? On Jim Wright's political future? If not any of these, what?

On October 25, 1971, Jim Wright flew to Austin. Because he still had no idea what Johnson wanted, he took along me and two Public Works Committee staffers, Jack O'Hara and Betty Hay.

Assuming that Johnson would want to talk privately over lunch with Jim Wright about whatever mysterious subject he had in mind, I suggested that Betty, Jack and I would grab a quick sandwich downtown and then stand by at the LBJ Library in case the Congressman wanted us.

But when our cab arrived at the library, Lady Bird intercepted us on the portico and insisted that all us—not just Jim Wright—

come in for lunch. I glanced at the Congressman and he nodded his OK.

Gracious as always, Lady Bird gave us a brief tour of the library and then took us to their private apartment upstairs. The former President was there, relaxed in a sport shirt and khakis. We had a nice lunch, but I don't remember what it was because I was searching so intently for a clue as to what this trip was all about.

The luncheon conversation yielded not the slightest hint. Lady Bird and the former President then escorted us into the living room. Johnson pulled out a copy of his recently-published book, *The Vantage Point*, and told how he arranged an assembly line of staffers to help him with the autographing of several thousand books—one staffer to open the book and put it in place for signing, another to take it away.

Then, relaxing on a couch, Johnson began reminiscing—about life in the Hill Country...how he fought to bring electricity and roads to those impoverished rural families...about his pride in having worked in Congress and in the Presidency for education and for civil rights and to help people climb out of poverty. It was an eloquent story, and as it went on and on, I began to get the first faint glimmer on why Jim Wright had been summoned here.

At one point Johnson turned to Lady Bird. In quiet, solemn tones he told us how proud he was of her, how grateful he was that she had shared his life, and how, because of her, his life was complete. I should have tried to write down exactly what he said, because his words came across with an eloquence and a sincerity I felt not many people had heard before.

For two and half hours, the former President talked. By the time he finished, and everybody stood to shake hands and express appreciation for a good lunch and a fine visit, even a cynical old newspaperman like me had gained a new appreciation of this unbelievably complicated man.

Fifteen months before his death on January 22, 1973, the 36th President of the United States had summoned his friend Jim Wright down from Washington—not because of an urgent political need, but because of a far more fundamental human need. Lyndon B. Johnson was lonesome.

8

Jim Wright
Ventures
Into the Galaxy

Early in our marriage, my wife Eddie and I were blessed with three children. Two were lovely little girls, Marsha and Sharon. Neither of them ever got jailed by an Arkansas sheriff, made a Congressman wish he were dead, or touched off panic aboard a U.S. Navy warship at sea. And then there was our son, Charles.

Don't get me wrong. I couldn't be prouder of Charles. Today he is a skilled carpenter and respected church and community leader. Several times a week, even after an exhausting day of work, he serves as a nighttime volunteer driver for the local Emergency Medical Service. A year or so ago, a woman bought a big newspaper ad to publicly thank him for saving her life. Charles and his devoted family live in a house they themselves built with their own hands, plank by plank, beside the shimmering Frio River in a little hamlet in the Texas Hill Country. Their home is so full of love and warmth and serenity I suspect that the guardian angel currently assigned to Charles must be a calmer, more sedate replacement for the madcap, frolicsome spirit who sat on his shoulder in his youth.

I'm not saying, mind you, that Charles was a bad boy. It wasn't a question of malice. It was just that he was adventurous by nature and, in his youth, had the judgment of a turnip. Wherever he went, pandemonium erupted. Whatever he did,

chaos ensued.   Once while scrounging along the shore of the
Potomac River above Washington, he nailed together a few
waterlogged boards as a raft.   Then he pushed off, alone, down the
sprawling, turbulent river.   As he was exulting over his voyage
past Georgetown and the Kennedy Center, the churning current
tore apart the pitiful little raft.   Charles managed to cling to a
plank and somehow reached shore.   His misadventures on dry
ground were equally hairy.

When he got a job as a construction helper on a high-rise
apartment project in Virginia, several floors of the building
collapsed.   Charles didn't cause it, of course, except perhaps by his
mere presence in the same neighborhood.   After those episodes, in
what his mother and I naively thought was a positive
development,   Charles turned his attention to automobiles.

Hoping he had inherited the superb nuts-and-bolts mechanical
craftsmanship of his grandfathers, we bought Charles a second-
hand Ford van to tinker with.   After poking around under the
hood and in the mysterious, oily recesses under the chassis, he
concluded that the vehicle needed a number of replacement parts.
Within a week he scrounged up a similar model van that had been
virtually demolished in an accident.   With the help of a few young
friends, Charles managed to tow this greasy, weather-beaten hulk
into the spotless concrete driveway we shared with our next-door
neighbor in the prim suburban neighborhood of Arlington,
Virginia.

Then, for more convenience in scavenging replacement parts
from the wreck's grimy underside, Charles and his cohorts turned
it upside down.   From its long-deceased engine, syrupy black sludge
oozed down our pristine driveway.   These acts had what the State
Department would describe as a destabilizing influence on our
relationship with the neighbors.   They seemed to feel that the
wrecked, overturned van perhaps would be better suited to a
location in a far corner of   Joe's Junkyard than to our
scrupulously neat, well-manicured neighborhood.   Some nearby
residents took their concerns to such worthies as the police and
the zoning authorities.   But our closest neighbor, a gentlemanly
old fellow who loved our kids, suffered in anguished silence.   Only
years later did he admit his distress at having the cannibalized van,
its rotting tires jutting skyward like a piteous plea for mercy,
adorning our driveway.   "I just bit my lip," he said.

Later, when my own beloved conveyance, a 1964 Mustang, developed peculiar rumblings in the transmission, my wife admitted under questioning that Charles had sneaked it out several times to participate in drag races. And once, just before leaving with another teenager to drive his van to Texas, Charles emphatically assured me three times to me that, yes, he had his driver's license securely in his pocket. "Don't you trust me, Dad?" he protested.

Several days later, in my office in the Capitol, I received a call from the sheriff in Arkadelphia, Arkansas. Did I know Charles L. Lynam? He was under arrest for driving without a license. It took three hours on the telephone to spring him from the Arkadelphia stir by getting Virginia authorities to wire confirmation that yes, somewhere on earth, there did indeed exist a valid driver's license bearing the name of Charles L. Lynam. In light of all these episodes, Eddie and I surely should have known better than to give Charles our old 1962 Ford Galaxy.

But the old car had seen its best days, and since we were planning to get a new car, we figured, once again, Charles would enjoy tinkering with it. We were right. Only a few days after we gave him possession of the Galaxy, I came home to discover he had removed its seats—all its seats. Where the driver's seat had been, our son had placed a wooden box.

If you've never seen a car whose complete interior has been replaced by a box retrieved from the trash bin behind the Safeway store, it's an eerie sensation. Charles couldn't understand why I was so perturbed.

"Are you out of your mind?" I demanded. "Why on earth would you do such an idiotic thing?"

"Oh, it'll be all right, Dad," he said. "I'm going to put in a new interior. You'll like it. You'll see."

But, just as I expected, four weeks later the interior of the Galaxy was still untouched and bare, except for a few wisps of shredded upholstery dangling like crazed stalactites from the ceiling. The new interior Charles had blithely promised consisted of a tattered stadium cushion on top of the driver's steering box. The neighbors snickered, but that wasn't the worst part. The worst part was the next Saturday afternoon when the phone rang.

"Marshall, this is Jim," came the Congressman's voice. "I just landed here at Dulles, and I can't reach anybody at my house. Can you run out here and pick me up?"

"Sure," I said confidently. And then, only after hanging up, did I remember that my Mustang was in the garage for a brake job. It wouldn't be ready until Monday. Our new car wouldn't be delivered for a week. I thought about borrowing a car, but knowing that our neighbors had seen the results of Charles's handiwork on our Galaxy, I decided not to ask. I could have rented a car, but that would have taken an hour or so. Jim Wright was a man not celebrated for his patience, and he was waiting at the airport. I could visualize him, restlessly drumming his fingers on the arm of his chair and casting anxious glances at his watch. I turned on Charles like a tiger.

"Now what am I supposed to do?" I hissed. "Jim Wright is expecting me to pick him up at Dulles, and thanks to you, I don't have a car."

"Oh, you can take the Galaxy, Dad," Charles said reassuringly.

"Sure," I bellowed. "I'll just drive out there and say, 'Hop in, Congressman. There's no seats, but I'm sure you won't mind sitting on the floor.' "

"I can put seats in, Dad."

"Don't give me that stuff. It would take you a week to put those seats back in—if you could do it at all."

Clearly unintimidated, Charles looked at me evenly. "I'm telling you I can put some seats in the car."

I didn't really believe it, but I had no choice.

"Give me 10 minutes," he said.

I'm glad I didn't watch what happened next. Apparently our resourceful son went down to the basement and uncovered a massive overstuffed chair which Eddie had long since ordered out of our living room. Somehow he wrestled this monstrous piece of furniture out the back door and into the Galaxy, placing it squarely in the center of the car's devastated interior.

"Now, for you, I'll get a straight-back chair out of the kitchen," he said.

"Never mind," I growled, glancing anxiously at my watch. "I'll sit on your damned box."

When I found Jim Wright in the Dulles waiting room, I tried to prepare him.

"I want to apologize for the car I'm driving today. It's the only one I could get on short notice, and I'm not sure you're even going to want to ride in it."

"I'm sure it'll be all right. I've ridden in your Mustang before."

"That's the problem. My Mustang's in the shop. I had to come in our old Galaxy."

"What's wrong with that?"

"It really doesn't look so good."

"Don't be silly, Marshall," he said. "You know I don't stand on formality. Besides, I'm in kind of a hurry. I've got to pick up some reports from my desk down at the Capitol."

"You're going to the Capitol?" I asked weakly.

"Got to," he said, picking up his suitcase.

Now I really had a problem. It had been my plan to sneak him along some remote route to his home in suburban Virginia. Now he needed to go directly to the Capitol—a trip which would expose my increasingly well-known Congressional leader to public guffaws along one of the busiest routes in Washington—along the George Washington Parkway and across the 14th Street Bridge to the Southwest Freeway. I wanted to throw up.

When I opened the door to the car, Jim Wright glanced inside and then turned to me as if to say something, but didn't. As resigned as a person climbing into a dentist's chair for a root canal, he stepped inside the Galaxy and eased himself gingerly into the mammoth chair. Still he said nothing.

At this point I had no idea what to say, but I felt compelled to say at least something. Finally, knowing that he had a son about Charles's age, I tried to pass off the chair as merely one of the indignities that fathers must suffer.

"Charles is going to put in a new interior," I said.

"I see," he said.

On the drive back to town, I kept as far as possible from other traffic. But as cars passed us, it was obvious that my fears were well grounded. People's reactions came in two separate and distinct stages. At their first glance in our direction, they looked startled—clearly unprepared to see a faded 1962 Galaxy, its passenger compartment bare except for random strips of ceiling upholstery gently undulating over a sickly green chair almost the size of a throne.

More surprising still, passersby could see, immersed in this monstrous chair's billowy cushions, a rather distinguished, bushy-browed man in a nattily tailored suit, staring grim and unblinking at the highway straight ahead. Some of them surely recognized him as someone seen occasionally on the 7 o'clock news. I took comfort in the hope than they could not remember his name.

After their initial shock, people in passing cars would go into a second stage of reaction. Now certain what they actually were seeing, they burst into convulsions of laughter, pounding their steering wheels and dashboards in wild exhibitions of glee. In their mirth, some honked and waved, particularly as we negotiated the crowded 14th Street Bridge. Somber and unblinking, Jim Wright stared relentlessly at the road ahead, hoping, I suppose, that by sheer will power, he could shorten it.

After years of dealing with members of Congress, staffers and constituents on the Hill, I felt pretty smug about being able to discern people's true feelings. Even if a fellow were saying one thing, there were often subtle signs he actually felt quite differently. Now, as I drove toward the Capitol, I glanced in the rearview mirror. Sure enough, my skills allowed me to read Jim Wright's expression very clearly. It said: *I wish I were dead.*

Actually, I suppose, we were pretty lucky that there were no lives lost that day. Since people in passing cars were already in virtually uncontrollable spasms of glee at the scene in the Galaxy, it's a good thing they couldn't see the rest of the car's interior. If they had seen, for example, that the driver's seat consisted of a Safeway box, they might have lost control of their vehicles, with possibly fatal results.

The trip finally ended in the most secluded parking spot I could find at the Capitol. If Jim Wright minded my letting him off some distance from where his colleagues were likely to be, he didn't complain.

Never in all the years since then has Jim Wright ever given any hint that he remembers that awful day. Even though I am sure he has tried to put the episode out of his mind, I suspect it may have been a factor in his decision to run for Majority Leader. The Majority Leader of the United State House of Representatives is, of course, provided with a driver and own government car—one whose interior has been professionally installed.

But however chaotic that trip from Dulles, it stands as a paragon of orderliness compared to the day the United States Navy happened to put Charles in control an 8,000-ton warship in one of America's busiest waterways. I'll tell you about it in the next chapter.

9

The Day Murphy
Went to Lunch

In late 1972, Charles was one of the last batch of youngsters facing the draft in the Vietnam War. For kids his age, it was a tortuous time to be growing up. The 1960's had spawned a generation of youngsters who rejected old values and sought refuge in drugs, rock music and each other. And then came Vietnam, spilling the blood of 210,000 young Americans killed or wounded in combat, and corroding the spirits and patriotism of millions at home. Many saw military service as a cruel and useless exercise of what they believed to be an unfeeling and arrogant government.

Charles did not want to enter service. Yet he knew that I, as one of the World War II generation, would have virtually died of shame if he had turned tail and run off to Canada as did many kids his age. Even so, neither he nor I wanted him to have to slog through the rice paddies of Vietnam with those poor brave devils in the infantry.

So he started shopping around at the various recruiting offices. I tried to persuade him to join the Air Force. To his credit, Charles laughingly recognized this as misguided nostalgia growing out of my time in the old Army Air Force in 1944-45.

"I hate to tell you this, Dad," he said, "but they stopped making B-17's thirty years ago, and the Germans are on our side now."

But the Air Force blew its chance to make an airman out of Charles. Its recruiters refused to accept any enlistment less than four years. The Navy agreed to let him sign up for three, and early in 1973 Charles dutifully reported for boot camp at the Navy Recruit Training Center in Orlando, Florida.

From the very beginning, it was clear that he disliked every aspect of military life. In a letter home, he wrote, "They're teaching us how to handle rifles and do close-order drill and to march through puddles of water, but they're not teaching us much about ships and things like that." This, as it turned out, was an omission the Navy would come to regret.

Despite his aversion to military life, Charles did his job and kept his nose clean. When he finished boot camp, he was ordered to report for duty aboard the *U.S.S. Sumter*, an amphibious landing ship assigned to Squadron Eight, homeported at Little Creek, Virginia, on the outskirts of Norfolk. Built in the late 1960's, the *Sumter* was a far cry from the slow and cumbersome old LST's which I remembered.

Powered by six big diesel engines, the *Sumter* could cruise at 20 knots. At least that was the figure the Navy gave. Anyhow, at this point, the ship's speed was a moot question. For the first few months Charles was assigned to the crew, the ship remained tied up at her dock in Little Creek.

Because his fireman's rating made him part of the ship's engineering section, Charles was assigned to something called the "A" Gang, which sounded more like an Alabama penal road crew than a ship's maintenance unit. Even though Navy officers presumably were not aware of Charles's penchant for modifying vehicle interiors, they wisely kept him away from the big, sturdy chair reserved for the captain on the bridge of the *Sumter*. So, as far as I know, that chair is still in place, bolted securely to the deck, and the captain does not have to sit on a Safeway box.

But with the *Sumter* tied up at the dock week after endless week, the crew had little to do. This was tough on Charles. Cursed from birth with an excess of adrenaline, he was bored and restless. And since Little Creek was only a couple of hundred miles from our home in the suburbs of Washington, Charles would leap into his old beat-up van, gorge it with gasoline billed to my credit card, and pop up at home almost every weekend.

"When are you going to sail?" I always asked him.

"Don't know," was his inevitable answer. "They never tell us anything."

This went on for months. Actually I enjoyed toying with the idea of the experiences which might lie ahead for him. It was sort of vicarious adventure. In my Walter Mitty fantasies I have often dreamed of sailing to far-off exotic ports, full of mystery and intrigue and danger. Even though Charles was growing wearier by the week with the humdrum routine of shore duty, I knew he would be shipping out eventually to some exciting foreign port. I could hardly wait.

"Don't you have any idea where you'll go?" I would ask. "There's a lot of neat ports around the Mediterranean. During the war I remember some other guys and I got into Naples and—"

"Yes, I remember your Naples story, Dad," came the patient reply.

"Or maybe the ship will head south and you'll go through the Panama Canal. I've always wanted to see the canal. And then there's Hawaii. That's an interesting place. You might even get a chance to check out the hula girls," I chuckled, winking.

"Sure, Dad," Charles sighed. "Sure."

Then late one Friday afternoon my dream came true. Arriving from Little Creek, Charles pulled his van into our driveway and climbed out with a big smile on his face. "Great news, Dad!" he said. "We sail next week."

"Wonderful!" I cried. "Where to—Le Havre? Rio de Janeiro?"

Charles shifted uneasily. "I don't know how to tell you this. I'm afraid you're going to be disappointed."

"No, I won't. I'm just glad you're finally sailing. Where are you going?"

"Well, we're bringing the ship to Washington."

"Washington? Washington, D.C.? You're bringing your ship *here*?" I cried.

"Afraid so. We're putting the ship on public display down at the Navy Yard."

My romantic daydreams—my son, the swashbuckling, heroic sailor—were smashed. Instead of standing gallantly at his post on the *Sumter*'s heaving deck in the teeth of a fierce Atlantic gale, he would come chugging up the muddy Potomac to a dock in the Washington Navy Yard about a mile from my desk in the Capitol. I wanted him to go to Hong Kong or Capetown or somewhere. The Navy, for Pete's sake, was sending him home again. Only this time, instead of arriving in his disreputable van, he would be coming home in a vessel twice as long as a football field. There was, of course, some solace in knowing that every taxpayer in the United States would be sharing the cost of the fuel with me.

At first I was really disappointed that my son's first adventure at sea would be hardly more than just another trip home. And then, gradually, a wild idea began to hatch in my mind. But I wasn't sure Charles would buy it, so I sat him down for a talk.

"In my job I work with a lot of fellows in the Navy," I told him. "Several of them are very good friends of mine." These are the officers, I explained, who work in the Navy Legislative Affairs Offices in the House and Senate. Their job is to work closely with Congress on legislation and other matters important to the Navy. The Army, Air Force, Marines and Coast Guard also maintain such liaison offices on the Hill, for the fortunes of each of the military services are inextricably tied to the day-to-day actions of Congress. If an important committee chairman eats radishes for lunch, the Pentagon gets heartburn. True, the Constitution designates the President as the commander-in-chief of the armed services. But Congress holds the purse strings. It is up to the House and Senate to decide precisely how many dollars each of the services gets each year, and to a large degree how they can spend it. Does the Army need more tanks? Does the Navy want another nuclear aircraft carrier? Talk to Congress.

Moreover, Congressional offices send thousands of inquiries to the military services each year about individual service men and women. A soldier's mama in Muleshoe, Texas, wonders why the Army didn't give her baby boy the promotion to corporal he was expecting. So she dashes off a letter to her member of Congress, who immediately turns it over to the Army and demands a prompt answer, which the lawmaker can then forward to mama back in Muleshoe. With any luck, on election day mama will remember this little favor.

"So why are you giving me this civics lesson?" Charles wanted to know.

"Because some of the Navy liaison officers on the Hill have invited me time and time again to take another orientation cruise with them."

"Didn't you take a trip like that several years ago?"

"That's right. You've got a good memory. The Navy flew me and several other Congressional staff people out to visit the carrier *Independence* in the Atlantic."

"And now you're thinking about asking them to let you sail with us to Washington on the *Sumter*?"

I smiled. My son may not be much at decorating the interiors of autos, but he's no dummy. "Would you mind if I asked?" I said.

"It's OK with me."

"I promise not to try to countermand any orders they give you. In fact, once we're on the ship, I won't even get near you. I don't want your buddies razzing you about bringing your Daddy to take care of you."

To the Navy, the two most important committees in the House were Armed Services and Appropriations. Jim Wright served on neither of these panels, but he was a figure of increasing power in the House. Moreover, as a B-24 combat flier in World War II, he knew first-hand the importance of a strong defense establishment and had generally supported Navy authorization and appropriation bills. He and all of us of his staff had a good working relationship with Navy liaison officers, and they enthusiastically approved my request to hitch an eight-hour ride on the *Sumter*.

Clutching my authorization from the Secretary of the Navy, I reported to the Little Creek Amphibious Base shortly after dawn on May 11, 1973, and was promptly escorted aboard the *Sumter*. Even through dwarfed by carriers like the *John F. Kennedy*, the *Sumter* struck me as being one bigggg ship. She is 522 feet long, has a beam of 68 feet, is powered by those enormous diesels, and has a huge, 30-ton bow ramp for loading and unloading tanks and heavy equipment. On this particular morning, the crew roster called for 12 officers and 210 enlisted people—one of whom, Fireman Recruit Charles Lynam, was destined soon to star in a little drama that might have unnerved John Paul Jones himself.

Once on board, I made it a point to keep out of the way. If the captain had resented the Pentagon's cluttering up his ship with some tall, balding civilian from Congress just as he was busy preparing to sail, I would have understood. But the captain, an impressive young Commander who previously had served in a variety of important Navy posts ashore and at sea, could not have been more gracious. After a welcome and a brief chat, he assigned the ship's executive officer to make sure I had an interesting voyage.

After the ship dropped her lines, or whatever ships do when leaving port, the exec gave me a quick tour of the vessel and introduced me to a few members of the crew. On our rounds, we didn't happen to bump into Charles. I had no idea where he was assigned, and I didn't want to ask. Even if we had run across him, I had promised myself not to try to talk as long as any of his shipmates were around. The *Sumter* was going to be his home, and I didn't want anybody needling him about bringing his Dad along to nursemaid him.

From Little Creek the *Sumter* cruised northward into the lower reaches of Chesapeake Bay, one of the busiest waterways in the world. Immense ocean-going freighters and tankers churned to and from the bustling port of Baltimore on the bay's northern end. In this ponderous navigational revolving door, these mammoth vessels shared the crowded bay not only with each other, but with a beehive of recreational boats, any one of which seemed capable of materializing from almost any direction at almost any time. On a brilliant spring day like this, the Chesapeake teemed with power and sailboats. As their skippers savored the sunshine, sipped an occasional beer, and tediously picked their way through this maritime mixmaster, each was aware that a collision might reduce his boat to toothpicks and ruin his whole day. As I stood at the rail pondering this thought, my friend the executive officer asked if I'd join him for lunch.

When we arrived in the wardroom, a half dozen or so officers were already there, sipping fruit juice and chatting while the stewards finished preparing the tables. As the spotless silverware was being placed on the starched white tablecloths, the exec spoke to one of the stewards.

"Stevens, go up to the bridge and see if the captain is ready to come down for lunch," he said. The steward nodded and left the wardroom.

For the next few minutes the exec and I made small talk with the other officers. Learning that I worked on Capitol Hill, one or two officers expressed interest in pending bills, including some that I had never even heard of. But, as Congressional people sometimes do when they are not likely to be challenged, I graciously offered masterful assessments of their prospects for passage. As this was going on, the executive officer spotted Stevens, the steward.

"Is the captain ready to come down for lunch?"

The steward looked very uncomfortable. "I don't know, sir. I didn't ask him."

"You didn't ask him? Isn't that the reason I sent you up there?"

"Yes, sir," the steward replied edgily. "But they were having some kind of emergency on the bridge. The captain was furious. He was cursing and stamping his feet. I didn't figure I ought to ask him about lunch."

Stunned, the exec exchanged an anxious glance with the engineering officer. Slamming their fruit juice glasses on the table, they bolted out the door. They were gone about 20 minutes. When they returned, the exec apologized for having left me so abruptly. Naturally I was curious.

"Have some kind of problem on the bridge, did they?" I asked.

"No, sir. No problem at all. Everything is fine," said the exec.

This irritated me. "Look," I said. "I'm a guest, and I appreciate your hospitality. But it's obvious that you had some kind of problem. If you don't want to tell me about it, that's fine. But don't try to tell me that something didn't go wrong."

The exec nodded. "Well, we did have sort of a minor problem. We lost steering from the bridge."

"You lost steering from the bridge? You mean the fellow up there on the bridge couldn't guide the ship?"

"Yes, but that wasn't a serious problem."

"Sounds like a pretty serious problem to me."

"Not at all," said the exec. "On steering, like every other system on the ship, we have a backup system."

"A backup system?"

"Yes. In the event of just such a malfunction as this, we have a trained technician on duty in stern steering, ready to take control of the ship at a moment's notice."

"And that's what happened here—a trained technician took over?"

"Yes, sir."

We had an enjoyable lunch.   Since the exec clearly was uncomfortable discussing the flap on the bridge, I discreetly refrained from pursuing the matter—at least for the moment.   But I was really curious about the malfunction or screw-up or whatever it was that caused the captain to curse and stamp his feet, and I intended to try to find out more.   But by this time, the ship was approaching the mouth of the Potomac River.   The exec had gone on an errand, so I sauntered back up to my spot on the rail. There, by pure happenstance, I saw Charles, standing alone, on deck about 50 feet away.   I walked over.

"How's it going?" I asked.

"OK...now," he said.

"What do you mean—'now'?"

He motioned toward the stern of the ship.   "See that hatch back there?" he asked.   As I nodded, I began to feel uneasy.

An hour or so before, Charles explained, he was called to the ship's "A" Gang engineering office.   When he got there, a big fat petty officer gave him a three-word order: "Go relieve Murphy."

"I said, 'Who is Murphy?' " Charles related.   "He said, 'Never mind who Murphy is.   Just go back to the after hatch. You'll find him in a room three decks down.' "

Dutifully, Charles trudged back to the after hatch, still uncertain who Murphy was, where he could be found, and what he was supposed to relieve him of.

For some time, he wandered around in the labyrinthine passageways in the bowels of the ship.   The bulkheads quivered with the noise and vibration of the ship's two massive propellers flailing the water only a few feet away.   Finally, through sheer luck, Charles happened to open the right hatch.

It was a tiny room, filled with wheels and levers and switches—and, presumably, a fellow named Murphy.

As Charles recounted the story to me, it went like this:

"I thought you'd never get here," said Murphy, going out the hatch.

"Wait a minute," Charles shouted over the propeller noise. "What am I supposed to do?"

"You don't have to do anything."

"Nothing?   Are you sure?"

"Oh, well, if the phone rings, answer the phone.   But the phone's not going to ring.   I've been down here two years and the damn phone has never rung." With that, Murphy slammed the hatch and left.

Five minutes later the phone rang.

"Hello?" Charles said tentatively.

"After steering—take control!" commanded an authoritative voice.

In the tiny room a red light started flashing and a bell began clanging.

"Hello?" Charles shouted, trying to make himself heard over the bell and the propellers.

"We are going aft—you must take control now," said the authoritative voice.

"I don't know how to take control," Charles said.

"You don't know how to take control?"

"No, sir."

"Is this aft steering?" demanded the voice.

"I guess so. I'm not sure."

"You're not sure? Who is this?" demanded the voice, a bit shakier now.

"Fireman Recruit Charles Lynam," replied my son, probably feeling like he did the day his raft broke apart in the middle of the Potomac.

"Where is Murphy?"

"Murphy went to lunch."

It's only my speculation, but this is probably when the captain started cursing and stamping his feet.

In hardly more than a minute, half a dozen or so officers swarmed into the tiny room. Ignoring Charles, they began shouting orders and questions to each other. Even their frantic shouts were virtually drowned out by the ear-splitting shriek of the alarm bell, which was still clanging and which apparently nobody knew how to turn off. Overhead the red light continued to pulse, bathing the little room in rhythmic warnings of some type of impending cataclysmic event. In this surreal scene the officers furiously tried to figure out which knobs and wheels Murphy might turn if Murphy were not at lunch. At this point Charles got the impression that these officers were only slightly less mystified than he as to the purpose of these devices. Figuring that he personally could make no significant contributions toward helping the officers solve their dilemma, Charles quietly stepped out of the *U.S.S. Sumter*'s aft steering compartment, never, ever, to return.

Later that afternoon, the *Sumter*, fortunately still afloat and free of collision damage, docked uneventfully at the Navy Yard and Charles spent a few days at home with us. We looked at *The Washington Post* the next morning, but found no reports of supertankers or even rowboats being rammed by a U.S. warship in Chesapeake Bay.

It was about this time in Charles's Navy career that I began to accept the certainty that the mischievous guardian angel assigned to our son in his teenage years had surely been succeeded by a new, more responsible spirit. Otherwise the episode on the *Sumter* might not have ended as fortunately as it did for Charles, and incidentally, for the United States Navy.

Moreover, it was clear to me that Charles, now 21, had done a lot of growing up during his first year in the Navy—and so had his father. For one thing, I had belatedly come to realize how difficult the early 1970's were for young people—especially young men facing military duty in the Vietnam War. Torn between loyalty to their country and contempt for what many believed was an unjust war, many turned to drugs, rebelliousness and contempt even for their own families.

Despite his aversion to military life, Charles fulfilled his three-year commitment to the Navy, helping crew the *Sumter* on deployments to the Mediterranean and to the Caribbean.

It was a joyous day for Eddie and me when he completed his hitch and came home. One day a few weeks later, while Charles and I were driving to the store, we started talking about Vietnam.

"I want to ask you something," I said. "Did you like any part of your service in the Navy?"

"Not much," he said.

"Yet you didn't run off to Canada. You didn't try to shirk your duty to the country. You didn't go AWOL like some of your buddies, and didn't get into dope," I said. "I just want to tell you thanks—thanks for keeping your nose clean, and for doing your job."

"I didn't have any choice."

I frowned. "What do you mean?"

Charles looked squarely into my eyes. "I knew if I didn't, you would be ashamed of me," he said.

10

Politburo Podnuhs, Say Howdy to Billy Bob

I'm not sure Andrei Litvinov was a KGB agent, but a friend in the FBI told me that it was highly likely. All I know is that a few months after Jim Wright became Majority Leader, this personable, self-assured fellow showed up in the office and asked the receptionist if he could see me.

Since Jim Wright was always up to his ears in work, I tried to talk at least briefly with almost anybody who bothered to make a trip to the office.

Mr. Litvinov gave me a calling card identifying himself as Second Secretary of the Soviet Embassy. I got us a couple of cups of coffee and we sat in my office and talked for a few minutes, sizing each other up. Never before had I met an honest-to-goodness Communist, and I'll admit I was kind of fascinated by the guy.

And since I got all my defense secrets from the front page of *The Washington Post*, I saw no reason not to talk with him.

He was a man perhaps in his early forties, with a no-nonsense chin, sandy hair and alert blue eyes that I may have imagined as more restless than they really were. He stood maybe five feet eight and had the tough, wiry build of a Marine sergeant. His English was flawless and occasionally he displayed an inventively dry sense of humor. If he had any trouble understanding my Texas idiom, it didn't show.

We didn't spend much time that first day talking about the Cold War. Rather I recounted a little about life in Texas, and he described his life as a farm boy in the Soviet Union. He said his job at the embassy was to gain a better understanding of American government and policy, and that he'd like a chance to meet the Majority Leader some day. I told him Jim Wright was so busy that sometimes even his staff had trouble getting a minute with him, but we'd keep his request in mind.

After that, Mr. Litvinov dropped into the office now and then. Several of our women staffers found him charming and, I presume, somewhat handsome. In fact, if he had not been married, I think a couple of women might have been receptive to the idea of increasing their knowledge of the Soviet Union under his guidance, perhaps over a quiet cocktail. In all his visits, our conversations were more chatty than substantive.

Even so, my curiosity began to grow. I called a trusted longtime friend who at that time was in his second decade as an FBI special agent. I told him about my Communist acquaintance, who by that time we were calling Andy.

"Is my name likely to wind up in an FBI dossier because this guy drops in here to see us?" I asked.

"Probably," my FBI pal replied. "The Bureau keeps pretty close tabs on all those guys in high-level jobs down at the embassy."

"Do you think he is KGB?"

"I would guess that he is."

"Well, what should I do about it?"

"Nothing," my FBI friend said. "If it's nothing more than you say, I wouldn't worry about it."

Emboldened by this advice, I invited Andy and his wife to come out for cocktails one Sunday afternoon to our house in Arlington, Virginia. I told Andy I was also inviting another friend and his wife, but I didn't mention that the other friend was George Kopecky, a staff investigator with the House Public Works Committee who himself had spent years as an FBI special agent.

When Andy and his wife showed up that Sunday afternoon, they presented my wife Eddie and me with a delightful gift—a bottle of that Stolichnaya vodka. As I was pouring the drinks, I asked Andy whether he wanted his Stoly on the rocks or straight up.

"Actually I prefer scotch," he admitted.

The drinks stimulated the conversation, and before long George Kopecky happened to mention, as FBI veterans often do, an incident that occurred during his service with "the Bureau."

"The Bureau?" Andy inquired, showing hardly more than polite interest.

"The Federal Bureau of Investigation. I was a Special Agent," George said.

Andy looked at me, laughing. It was kind of embarrassing, because I suppose I had figured George's FBI affiliation would come up somewhat more delicately, if it came up at all.

At any rate, Andy appeared more amused than offended, and the conversation soon turned to a comparison between the governments of the United States and the Soviet Union. George pointed out that the three branches of our government serve as checks and balances on each other.

"That's all very well when your government makes a mistake," Andy responded. "But when my government makes a mistake..."

At this point he stopped abruptly. Then, grinning sheepishly, he said: "Of course, I am never supposed to admit to you that our government *can* make a mistake."

A few weeks later, I arranged for Andy to have lunch with Jim Wright. It was a delightful occasion, and no national secrets were compromised.

Shortly after that, Andy dropped out of sight. I'm not sure what happened to him. If he was sent back to the Soviet Union, I surely hope the KGB didn't punish him for spending so much time and getting so little information from Jim Wright and me.

After having dealt face-to-face with at least one real live Communist without spilling the beans as to the location of the Joint Chiefs of Staff latrine, I felt eminently qualified to handle my next encounter with minions of the Evil Empire.

In March, 1985, U.S. and Soviet negotiators were getting ready to open a new round of arms control talks in Geneva. In what probably was an effort to crank up a warm and fuzzy feeling with the citizenry of America in advance of these talks, Moscow decided to send a delegation of 35 high-level Communist Party bigwigs on a goodwill visit to the States.

Leading the group was a portly, moon-faced fellow whom Central Casting would surely have chosen for the role of a typical Kremlin commissar. His name was Vladimir Shcherbitsky, and besides being a Politburo member, he was the high muck-a-muck of the Communist Party in the Ukraine. Even through his political base lay outside Moscow, he was known to exercise respectable muscle in the Soviet leadership.

To satisfy diplomatic niceties, the Soviet visitors came to the U.S. in their role as parliamentarians. They all were, in fact, members of the USSR's national legislature, the Supreme Soviet. But their real power lay in their Communist Party positions which, in the diplomatic world, gave them no official status.

My own modest role in all this grew out of the fact that the Soviet delegation, after a day or so in Washington, was scheduled to visit three Texas cities, including Fort Worth. As House Majority Leader, Jim Wright would be a prominent host. Several other staffers and I would be needed to help.

In their first few days in the U.S., some of the Soviet heavyweights seemed surprised and maybe a little uncomfortable when they saw how many ordinary working slobs in the United States enjoyed attractive homes, shiny cars and color televisions. Even though nobody said so, you got the impression that most of the Soviet bigwigs grew up in pretty bleak surroundings. On the whole, they seemed to be fairly ordinary guys. Friendly but reserved, they seemed to be dazzled by the affluence of our country but reluctant to admit it. On occasion, a few of them would make a heroic effort to cope with our language.

In Austin, Congressman Jake Pickle treated the group to a lavish luncheon of Texas-style Mexican food. At my table a grandfatherly Soviet guest sampled a dish of refried beans.

"These are you say twice-cooked beans?" he asked.

I nodded politely, figuring that was close enough.

At Neiman Marcus in Dallas, there was a bit of clowning by Anatoly Dobrynin, the Soviet Ambassador to the United States who was accompanying the delegation on its U.S. tour. Stroking the arm of a model displaying an $85,000 Russian sable coat, Dobrynin pretended to be ready to buy it. "I am authorized, on behalf of the delegation—" he began.

One member of the delegation was not amused. His eyes swept around the ornate store and its tastefully restrained displays of lavish goods. "I think that only people who are wealthy come here," he said.

A still more somber note was struck by Shcherbitsky, the delegation leader, during an afternoon barbecue in a Dallas suburb. In an uncomfortable reminder that the whole world was shaken by the assassination of President John F. Kennedy in Dallas, Shcherbitsky recounted having been asked by his eight-year-old grandson: "Why are you going to Texas, where they kill people?"

The truth is, I myself was vaguely uneasy about the possibility of some unexpected incident marring this official Soviet visit Texas. Only too well did I recall November 22, 1963.

Ironically, that tragic day had begun as my boss' finest hour. Having represented the Fort Worth area in Congress for nine years, he had one of the highest privileges a lawmaker can have— the honor of hosting, on his own home turf, the President of the United States. The day began with a momentous public rally outside the Texas Hotel, followed by a fat-cat breakfast which drew hundreds of Texas movers and shakers. Even today I proudly remember that Mr. Kennedy called Fort Worth "Jim Wright's city" and assured the crowd of dignitaries that "no city in America is better represented in Congress than Fort Worth."

At that point Jim Wright probably could have gone flying on his own cloud. But the President invited him aboard *Air Force One* for the flight to Dallas. In the motorcade, the Congressman was only a few cars back when Lee Harvey Oswald opened fire.

When *Air Force One* brought Kennedy's body back to Washington that night, I was waiting at Andrews Air Force Base to pick up Jim Wright and drive him, numb and shaken, to his home. From the ramp beside the plane I witnessed the nightmarish scene that television seared into the memory of millions of Americans—the dried splatter of the President's blood still on Jackie's dress as she came down the steps...the

President's coffin being unloaded from the plane in the harsh, unearthly glare of television lights.

Even though more than 20 years had passed, I was still haunted by these memories as I worked on the Soviet delegation's Texas trip. While the Secret Service and state and local police agencies were taking every possible precaution to prevent trouble, there was always a chance some kook might try to harm the visitors. To have violence befall any member of such a high-level Soviet delegation in the United States might have had consequences too frightening to contemplate.

Fortunately, however, the physical security of the delegation was, I devoutly hoped, in more capable hands than mine. My primary job in Fort Worth was not to keep them from getting shot, but to keep them from being embarrassed. Jim Wright's other staffers and I had to try to steer the Soviets clear of any remark, any incident, at any place, intentional or not, that would humiliate the Soviet delegation and its host, the Majority Leader of the U.S. House of Representatives. That's the reason I got concerned when I heard about the visit to Billy Bob's.

Phil Duncan, then director of Jim Wright's office in Fort Worth, was briefing me on plans for the delegation's formal dinner at the Americana Hotel.

"What time do you figure the it will be over?" I asked.

"Maybe about 9:45 or 10," Phil replied.

"And then they'll be taken back to their rooms to get some rest?"

"No," Phil said. "The plan is to take 'em out to Billy Bob's."

"To Billy Bob's?" I exclaimed. "Are they crazy? Is somebody out of their mind? Who made this schedule, anyhow?"

"I don't know, but everybody has signed off on it."

"Including the Secret Service?"

"Including the Secret Service," Phil replied.

"And what are they going to do when some good ol' boy gets a bellyful of beer and calls 'em no-good Communist sumbitches and tells 'em to get the hell outta here? How's that going to look on the front page of *Pravda* and *The New York Times* and every other newspaper in the world? How's that going to make Jim Wright look?"

For those benighted souls who may have missed the listing in the Guinness Book of Records, please be informed that following its grand opening in 1981, Billy Bob's Texas was proclaimed the largest honkytonk not just in Texas, but in the world.

Named for its creator, a six-foot, seven-inch, 270-pound football player, rancher, rodeo performer and hell-raiser named Billy Bob Barnett, this incredible institution was launched in a 100,000-square-foot building once used as a cattle auction barn, located in what was then a dreary, run-down area—the Stockyards on Fort Worth's North Side.

In the late 1800's, the Stockyards was the heart of a thriving cattle industry. From here, great, bellowing herds were driven north along the Chisholm Trail. Then, in 1902, the giant Chicago meat packing companies, Swift and Armour, established plants in the city, opening an era of growth and prosperity in the Stockyards that lasted more than 50 years.

But by the time Billy Bob Barnett hatched his honkytonk idea, the glory days of the Stockyards had passed. The giant packing houses were closed, replaced by hundreds of smaller, more efficient feed lots and meat packing plants scattered across the Southwest. In the once-bustling Stockyards, thousands of people had no jobs and Fort Worth's surrounding North Side was mired in poverty. Winds stirring along deserted brick streets still picked up the pungent smell left behind by the herds, but the cattle were gone and so were most of the people.

Even so, Billy Bob Barnett and Spencer Taylor managed to round up a few courageous investors. They sank $5 million into transforming the one-time auction barn into a honkytonk whose sheer size still boggles the imagination.

Intrigued perhaps by the sheer audacity of the enterprise, the public loved it. On the club's opening night in 1981, the fire marshal allowed only the first 6,000 customers to enter. The rest took their places in lines outside, fretfully waiting to be admitted as some early arrivals began to depart.

And the lucky 6,000 customers who managed to squeeze through the front door decked out in their boots, blue jeans and cowboy hats—what did they find inside? Well, they found a total of 42 bars, 14,000 square feet of dance floors, a 500-seat rodeo arena for live bulldogging and steer wrestling, a 1,650-square-foot performing stage on wheels, several restaurants, a VIP club, 50 pinball machines, 27 pool tables, a Western wear store, plus places to get your boots shined, your picture taken, your caricature drawn and, perhaps, your fantasies fulfilled.

To this incredible institution came thousands of men and women, most in boots and jeans and a 10-gallon hats, to guzzle a few longneck bottles of Pearl, listen to Willie, Waylon and Loretta, dance the Texas Two-Step—and to raise a little hell, Texas style.

Even though patrons of Billy Bob's rarely punched each other in the jaw, peaceful conduct in a honkytonk flies in the face of a rich Texas tradition. Anybody familiar with the customs of the Lone Star State can tell you that roadhouse fist fights are as much a part of our sacred heritage as the Alamo.

After each participant has drunk enough beer to reach an acceptable state of belligerency, the fight is customarily touched off in one of two ways. The first requires that one participant must call the other a son of a bitch. This phrase in Texas is always interpreted literally, meaning that the other son of a bitch has denounced your mother as a dog. While this method is customarily reliable in jump-starting the punching match, a far more effective way is for one participant to challenge the other's patriotism.

Say, for example, that one participant is aware that the other's nephew sought a college deferment during the Vietnam war. It is not necessary for the nephew to have actually been granted a deferment. The request itself is sufficient. "What's that lily-livered Commie-lover of a nephew of yours doing nowadays?" one might idly inquire. This usually gets results far more expeditiously than the older, son-of-a-bitch method.

In my boyhood days, the knock-down, drag-out fights at Red's Place, our local saloon, were as much a part of South Texas life as Saturday night baths. We kids used to stand outside and listen for the telltale sound of wooden chairs being noisily pushed back from tables on the bare wooden floor. Inside we knew two guys were lurching unsteadily to their feet to try to clobber each other, and that in a moment one or both would come staggering outside with bloody noses or worse.

As a rule, women dared not venture into Red's Place. There was only one exception—a rotund, grandmotherly little Salvation Army lady who would march cheerily through its iniquitous swinging doors and move methodically along the bar and through the tables, shaking her tambourine to invite contributions. The guys in the boots and khakis, realizing that by their very presence in Red's Place they were deeply mired in sin, would self-consciously tip their sweaty hats to the Salvation Army lady and guiltily drop a quarter into her tambourine.

In later life, I was delighted to discover that in big cities like Washington, the watering holes and cocktail lounges were far more sophisticated. For one thing, they were so dark you needed a flashlight to discover, when the check came, that a shot of Jack Daniel's went for four dollars. But there were positive aspects, also. For one thing, the smell of stale beer was less pronounced than in Red's Place. But better still, these East Coast saloons were frequented not by corpulent little ladies in Salvation Army bonnets but rather by hypermammiferous young women in slinky, black, low-cut cocktail dresses. The presence of patrons like this, however, often short-circuited men's attention from really important subjects like patriotism and fist fights.

It was the memory of Red's Place that made me increasingly edgy as the Americana Hotel formal dinner for the Soviets dragged on and on. At one point I got on the telephone to Phil, who was standing by at Billy Bob's, awaiting our arrival.

"How do things look out there?" I asked.

"Got an awful big crowd tonight. The place is really jumping," Phil said.

"I was afraid of that. The longer it takes to get these guys out there, the more danger some drunk will start mouthing off about a bunch of dirty Commie bastards. I'm really worried."

Phil tried to reassure me. "Marshall, Billy Bob's got a plan that I think will keep anything from getting out of hand. Instead of taking the Soviets into the public areas out around the bars, he's going to bring the delegation into the rodeo arena. He's got ringside seats staked out for the whole bunch. The only thing is, the place is so crowded tonight Billy Bob is having a tough time keeping people out of the seats he's got reserved."

"Well, just try to make sure he hangs on to those seats. I'll let you know when we're on the way."

On and on went the after-dinner speeches. And then, to make things worse, I got word that the Soviets had asked to make a brief visit to the Amon Carter Museum of Western Art before going out to Billy Bob's. I kept looking at my watch and worrying about all those weekend cowboys guzzling all that beer and taking all those seats and looking for prospective sumbitches.

Finally, at long last, the Americana dinner ended. Finally we got the big delegation and its security people moved to the art museum. Mercifully, they did not tarry long, and at last the motorcade started toward Billy Bob's.

"We're on our way," I shouted to Phil over the telephone.

"The seats are gone. People somehow got into them. Billy Bob is doing his best to get them out," Phil said.

"Oh, shoot," I said, using a different vowel in the second word.

The ride out North Main to Billy Bob's seemed like the longest trip of my life. In my mind's eye I envisioned a confrontation between a surprised and angry Soviet delegation and a horde of bleary-eyed Texas rodeo fans who probably suspected that the Kremlin visitors might be Communists and what the hell were they doing here in Texas in the first place?

As we pulled up to the entrance of Billy Bob's I had convinced myself that life was over. Future historians would record that, with world peace hanging in the balance, the promising arms control talks originally scheduled for Geneva in 1985 were, alas, never held. Supported by civilized people everywhere, a righteously indignant Soviet Union abruptly canceled the crucial sessions because of the abject humiliation suffered by one of its prestigious goodwill delegations in an inexcusable international incident in a Fort Worth, Texas, honkytonk. Moreover, I was sure the full responsibility for jeopardizing world peace would be laid directly at the feet of one man—U.S. House Majority Leader Jim Wright. His brilliant Administrative Assistant, who was known to have triggered this debacle, was believed to have spent his remaining days as a wretched hermit on an obscure, windswept island in the Bay of Bengal, wherever that is.

And then came one of the most astonishing moments of my life. As the Kremlin delegation marched into Billy Bob's rodeo arena, several hundred good ol' boys and their women folk jumped up and started cheering, hoisting longneck beers in enthusiastic Texas honkytonk-style toasts. Again and again they whooped smilingly toward the visitors. Again and again they raised their beer bottles, motioning toward an inviting expanse of empty seats at ringside of the arena.

Understandably impressed by this friendly, cheering throng, the Soviets moved into these seats, nodding and grinning and soon hoisting their own beers to return the salute of their new-found Texas cowboy friends. The tableau would have warmed the hearts of people yearning for peace all over the world. Here were top-level officials from the Soviet Union, America's fierce arch-enemy of the Cold War, being welcomed in peace, respect and brotherhood by a beloved segment of the U.S. population—the good ol' boys of Texas. The whole thing gave me, as we say in Fort Worth, a lump in mah thoat.

When the enthusiastic greetings and salutes had died down, I found Phil and slapped him on the back. "Terrific! Wonderful!" I cried. "It was almost too good to believe—all that applause and cheering! The Russkies are on Cloud Nine. They'll never forget this. But how did you and Billy Bob manage to get these guys to salute a bunch of Communists?"

Phil smiled. "Well, it wasn't exactly what you'd call a salute," he said.

"But wasn't everybody standing and cheering and hoisting up their drinks to toast the delegation?"

"It was really more like they were saying thanks."

"Thanks? Thanks for what?"

"Thanks for all the free beer Billy Bob gave 'em."

"Free beer?"

"Yeah," Phil said. "That's the only way Billy Bob could clear out all those rodeo seats. He told the good old boys that if they'd get up and let the Soviets sit down, he'd give free beer to everybody. That's the reason they waved their beers and acted so happy to see the Russkies."

11

Notes on an Unraveling Red Sweater

It was 8 o'clock, and I was already 30 minutes late. A frosty black January night had settled over the Capitol, and most of the other offices had long since been locked up. I was perched on the arm of a couch in the Speaker's office, anxiously waiting for Jim Wright to finish.

He was sitting behind his desk, totally absorbed in a report we had received that day from the State Department. I kept glancing at the clock on the wall, hoping he would ask me why I was so fidgety. But he pored over the report again and again, pausing here and there to underline a passage.

"Have you read this" he said finally, looking up.

"Yes, sir," I said. "Fascinating stuff, isn't it?"

"Damn sure is," he said. "This guy is really interesting. But nobody seems sure whether or not he's for real. If he is, this could be the most important thing that's happened in the past 50 years."

He put aside the report and reached across the desk for his tattered black personal notebook—a volume which we staff members privately referred to as The Gutenberg, after the Bible of approximately the same age. Jim Wright seldom let this book out of his sight, guarding it as dearly as Linus does his security blanket.   Inviolate and treasured, the book may have been a hodgepodge, but it was *his* hodgepodge. It contained a calendar on which he frequently jotted notes, plus a number of yellowing newspaper clippings, a list of telephone numbers perhaps assigned personally by Alexander Graham Bell, a batch of long-forgotten business cards and, I always suspected, perhaps some letters his wife gave him to mail in 1978.

He thumbed through the calendar, scanning the next few months. "I'm trying to figure out the best date to do this," he said. "Why don't we check on April 10? That's a Friday, and the beginning of the Easter recess."

"Fine. I'll talk to the State Department and the Air Force tomorrow and see if April 10 works for them," I said, edging toward the door.

"You seem awful jumpy tonight," he observed.

"I'm sorry, Mr. Speaker," I said sheepishly. "It's just that I was supposed to meet Eddie at the Sheraton Grand for dinner at 7:30, and she's going to kill me."

Jim Wright laughed. "Tell her hello, and I'm sorry I made you late."

As it turned out, I escaped Eddie's wrath because when she reached the hotel dining room, she happened to bump into Wayne Franke, the friend with whom we were having dinner. By the time I arrived, they were enjoying a glass of wine at a window table with a spectacular view of the Capitol dome, floodlighted dramatically against the black wintry sky.

Wayne Franke, a good old Texas boy, was a lobbyist. He represented GTE Corporation in Austin, and flew up to Washington now and then to try to fend off whatever new and different indignities Congress was planning to foist upon his employer. We had been friends for many years, and as far as I know, Wayne never asked Jim Wright or his staff for anything at all.

On that particular evening, it was obvious that Wayne was excited about something. He fiddled nervously with the silverware and grinned a lot. Finally the stress proved too much for him. The seams burst.

"I'm going to be a father," he announced, beaming. His wife, Jane, had just received the news from her doctor, and Wayne was so exhilarated he barely nibbled at his filet. He was happy with the whole wide world and everybody in it. When the dessert and coffee came, he grew even more expansive.

"You know, Marshall, we need to do something for Jim Wright," he said. "What would you think of our organizing some kind of event—maybe a barbecue or a chili supper? It could be a fund-raiser, and I'd help you with all the arrangements."

"Where could we have it?" I asked.

"Any place you say," he said, throwing his arms open wide. "We could have it here in Washington, or in Fort Worth, or even in Austin. We could have it any place you say."

"Any place at all?" I said.

"Any place at all," he trumpeted reassuringly.

"Could you have it in Moscow?" I asked.

Wayne, uncertain he had heard correctly, sat down his coffee and leaned forward. "Moscow, like in Russia?" he asked.

"Moscow, like in Russia," I said, nodding.

"Are you kidding?" he demanded.

"No, I'm not," I said.

"You mean you're actually talking about putting on a barbecue in the Soviet Union?"

"Either that, or a chili supper."

Wayne was interested but puzzled. "Would you please tell me what the hell you are talking about?" he pleaded.

"Glad to," I said. "The Soviets have invited the Speaker to bring a delegation to Moscow. Jim Wright has talked to the State Department and the White House, and they think it might be a pretty good idea—especially right now."

"Great! Sounds really interesting. What would you guys do?"

"Well, for one thing, the Speaker would talk to this new fellow everybody's talking about—Gorbachev."

"Wow. I've been reading about him. He's got everybody stumped as to what he's really doing over there—reorganizing the government, bringing new people into the Kremlin, opening up the press and the movies."

I nodded. "Right. Nobody really can figure what he's up to."

"Do you think he's for real? Is he just craftier than the guys in the past, or is this a whole new ball game?"

"That's the main thing Jim Wright wants to try to find out."

"And the chili supper?"

"The Speaker told me he'd like to put on some kind of a reception over there, and I think he'd go for a deal like this. Even if Gorbachev ain't for real, maybe some 4-alarm Texas chili and jalapeno peppers will thaw out the Cold War."

Wayne was clearly intrigued by the idea, and accurately predicted that his boss, Buddy Langley, President of GTE, would enthusiastically approve. Wayne wryly confided to me, however, that his company rarely gave chili suppers in Moscow.

Over the next few weeks, preparations for the trip picked up momentum. The Speaker invited and got prompt acceptances from 18 colleagues, including two other members of the Democratic leadership, Majority Leader Tom Foley and Majority Whip Tony Coelho. Five Republicans also signed on, including Congressman Dick Cheney, a member of the House Select Committee on Intelligence who was destined later to become Secretary of Defense.

Jack Matlock, a seasoned diplomat who was preparing to go to Moscow as our new Ambassador to the Soviet Union, came by the office to share some insights with the Speaker. Fluent in Russian and steeped in USSR history and customs, Matlock had served three previous tours in subordinate jobs in the Moscow Embassy. He also had traveled widely in the country and knew many of the key players in the current Kremlin intrigue. I was disappointed to learn that he had serious reservations about the prospect of significant changes in Soviet policy under Gorbachev's leadership.

To work out final details of our schedule, the Speaker asked me and Spencer Oliver, a veteran staff member of the House Foreign Affairs Committee, to advance the trip by flying to Moscow a week before the delegation. Our job would be to work with our Soviet counterparts on the schedule and other arrangements. In particular, we were to make sure there were no surprises to ruffle feathers on either side. On this point I recall wondering whether Moscow might have a honkytonk named Billy Bobski's.

To me, advancing this trip was the assignment of a lifetime. For a Depression kid who used to stand on the street and sell popcorn in Bishop, this was pretty heady stuff. Here I was, flitting off to Moscow to arrange meetings for the Speaker of the United States House of Representatives—by any measure the most important legislative office on earth—with the new boss of the Soviet Union.

As Miss Myrtle Wakeland used to drum into our high school civics class, it is the President, not the Congress, whom the Constitution empowers to speak for our country in foreign affairs. Nobody in the Speaker's delegation was under any other illusion. Even so, everybody realized these Moscow sessions would offer a unique opportunity to get insights into this relatively unknown man who now had his finger on the USSR nuclear trigger.

Nobody was quite sure just where Mikhail Gorbachev was leading the Soviet Union. With his surprising new policy of "openness" at home, his "restructuring" of the Soviet bureaucracy, his aggressive new crew in the Kremlin and his flurry of fresh proposals for nuclear arms control, this looked as if it could be a whole new ball game. But after nearly half a century of the Cold War, virtually every responsible American official had grave doubts.

But what if, I fantasized, these very meetings—*my* meetings, if you please—yielded some tiny clue as to a possible detour from our existing road toward nuclear Armageddon? What if, as a lowly Congressional spear carrier, I had even a microscopic role on a world stage where we might—just might—take the first halting steps toward keeping our lush green earth from being incinerated into a lump of celestial charcoal? Wow.

Before Spencer and I left for Moscow, Jim Wright made it clear that while Gorbachev and Company were his No. 1 priority, he didn't want to spend the rest of the trip in dreary meetings with Kremlin bureaucrats. "I want a chance to meet some real, honest-to-goodness people—the everyday citizens of the Soviet Union," he said. "I want to get out in the towns and the countryside—to see where people live and work. Like on a dairy farm, for instance. Yes, that's it—make sure we get to visit a dairy farm."

If anybody questioned whether the Kremlin regarded the Speaker's upcoming visit as important, all doubt was wiped away by preparations Spencer and I found underway shortly after our arrival in Moscow. This would be the highest-ranking U.S. Congressional group ever to visit the USSR, and the Kremlin was rolling out the, uh, welcome carpet.

As a longtime staffer on the Foreign Affairs Committee, Spencer had been to the Soviet capital several times before and had good friends in our embassy. After a quick briefing there, we went to the first meeting with our Soviet counterparts. The Soviet team was headed by an impressive high-level Kremlin aide in his mid forties. His name was Nikolai Lysenko. Over the next couple of weeks, I was to come to know him pretty well. In was Nikolai, in fact, who was later to give me my most revealing personal insight into the events unfolding in his country.

Behind Kremlin walls that had been standing since an obscure Italian sailor weighed anchor from Spain in 1492, the Speaker's delegation would meet with an all-star cast of Soviet leaders-- Gorbachev, Ligachev, Gromyko and Shevardnadze. Other private meetings were laid on with Dobrynin and Shcherbitsky, our old pals from the Kremlin group we had hosted in Austin, Dallas and Fort Worth a couple of years before.

Apparently only once did the Soviet team run into any problem in arranging all these leadership talks. As Spencer and I heard the story, some Kremlin bureaucrat had not gotten the word and challenged Nikolai's authority, demanding "Who ordered this?" Nikolai cleared up matters for the poor fellow with a very brief response. "Mikhail S," he said simply—as in Mikhail Sergeyevich Gorbachev.

Even though Nikolai's people seemed to try hard to accommodate the wishes of the U.S. delegation, Spencer and I did surprise them with one request.

"A dairy farm?" asked Nikolai, blinking. "The American side would like to see a dairy farm?"

"Yes," I said. "When Mr. Khrushchev visited the United States in the 1950's, he visited a corn farm in Iowa. He wanted to see how the average farmer lived in our country. Surely you can understand how the members of our Congress would like to see how your people live, also."

Nikolai shrugged and promised to do his best.

Meanwhile, back in Washington, the Speaker had discovered that his scheduled visit to Moscow would overlap that of U.S. Secretary of State George Shultz. The Secretary would be there to negotiate with Foreign Minister Eduard Shevardnadze on some of Gorbachev's startling new arms control proposals. To avoid distracting Soviet attention from these delicate talks, Jim Wright and his colleagues stopped over two days in Madrid, where European parliamentarians were meeting, and then flew on to their first stop in the Soviet Union—Kiev, the busy, sprawling capital of the Soviet Ukraine. Here we found that my friend Nikolai, despite his reluctance, had pulled a few strings.

Along with greeting ceremonies, formal meetings and museum tours, we found that our official schedule for Kiev also provided for a visit to—you guessed it—a dairy farm. There were only two modest problems. First, the farm was no less than 30 miles south of the city. Second, we would travel by bus on roads that, well. . . just say they fell a bit short of Interstate standards. And, as any Capitol Hill staffer will tell you, there are two things you ought never, ever, to put on a bus. One is a crate of dynamite, and the other is a member of Congress. On long, bumpy trips, both are capable of generating loud and unpleasant sounds.

But on this trip, Jim Wright and his jolly crew did pretty well. We got to see parts of the city and the Ukrainian countryside that we otherwise would have missed. And besides that, Mickey Leland was aboard.

Mickey Leland was an African-American Congressman from Houston and one of the finest men I ever knew. A former Texas state legislator, he was elected to Congress in 1978 and promptly enlisted Jim Wright's help in a realizing a cherished personal dream—to help at least some the world's starving people. A Select Subcommittee on Hunger was created and Mickey was named Chairman. In this post Mickey rolled up his sleeves and launched efforts which unquestionably saved thousands of lives. In 1989, on his way to one of the countless remote, starving provinces he visited in Africa, Mickey and several members of his staff died in a plane crash.

But don't think of Mickey as some sort of stuffy do-gooder. A saint he definitely was not. He drank, gambled and, during his bachelor days, proved himself a worthy successor to Casanova. He also told raucous jokes and wonderful stories.

If Mickey enlivened the long bus trip to the dairy farm, it was probably because he was a specialist in buses. In his first race for Congress, often he crawled out of bed long before dawn and got a friend to drive him out to the furthermost point of a commuter bus line in Houston. Climbing aboard, he sat quietly until the bus filled up. Then he moved to the front of the bus, cleared his throat, and bellowed: "Good morning! My name is Mickey Leland, and I am running for Congress."

To this ultimate captive audience, Mickey spent half an hour or so making his pitch and answering questions. He said even some otherwise stoic commuters seemed impressed by his unorthodox campaign idea.

"Did the bus driver ever try to shut you up?" I asked.

"Oh, no," Mickey said. "First I made sure I had the endorsement of the bus drivers' union."

Jim Wright's idea in going to a dairy farm was, of course, to try to meet some of the ordinary working people of the Soviet Union. He wanted to see their homes, visit with their kids, and try to get some personal insights into the problems and hopes of their families. Whether deliberately or not, the Soviets took us instead to a place where we saw few workers and no families at all. While the dairy operation looked efficient and impressive, it would have been far more interesting to a group of American dairy engineers and technicians than to a gaggle of American politicians. The visit did, however, have its entertaining moments.

To comply with the dairy's sanitary standards, the Congressional visitors were asked to slip long, white sterile robes over their clothing before going through the milk production unit. Grinning wryly, Mickey Leland dutifully donned this modified bedsheet—and then went a step farther. As our bewildered Soviet escorts looked on, Mickey picked up a spare robe and fashioned for himself a pointed white hat. Still having no idea what was happening, the Soviets watched as this unusual guest extended his arms in a dramatic pose. Looking for all the world like a Grand Wizard of the Ku Klux Klan presiding at a cross-burning, Mickey laughingly called out to Jim Wright: "You see, Mr. Speaker, there's nothing I wouldn't do for you!"

In Moscow, the Soviets lodged the Jim Wright delegation in the Sovietskaya Hotel, a rambling, comfortable old place reserved for official visitors. I had barely checked in when one of our escort officers told me he was really puzzled about two other Americans who also had just arrived at the Sovietskaya.

"What's so unusual about them?" I asked.

"Well, for one thing, besides their baggage, they were carrying these large wooden spoons and soup ladles," he said. "And they had this big cardboard box they insisted on carrying themselves."

"And I guess you're going to tell me that they were wearing cowboy boots and big ten-gallon hats?"

"Yessir, they sure were," he nodded vigorously. "And one other thing. One of them kept showing people a sonogram—you know, the kind that doctors take."

"Did he say what the sonogram was?"

"He sure did. He showed it to everybody who'd look. He was the proudest guy I ever saw. He said it was a picture of his little daughter—*who won't be born for three more months!*"

I smiled a private smile. Wayne Franke had arrived.

Along with his friend, Mario Martinez, Wayne had flown in on a commercial airliner, carrying essential chili-making tools and a cardboard box containing enough Texas-style seasoning to heat Leningrad. Our Moscow chili party was a go.

Before leaving the States, Wayne was worried that Moscow butcher shops might not have the quality meat needed to make good chili. The State Department and the Air Force agreed. So from its European bases, the Air Force rounded up 90 pounds of top-grade beef, cut into half-inch cubes, and flew it to Moscow, along with 20 pounds of pinto beans and several crates of tomato sauce. To me, this supply flight had an ironic touch. I was around early in the Cold War when our Air Force pulled off the logistical miracle known as the Berlin Airlift. With around-the-clock flights in all kinds of weather, American airplanes fed a city of two million people, defying a Soviet blockade. Now, forty years later, Air Force officers of another generation were flying a shipment of food to the Soviet capital to feed perhaps at least a few of the Soviet old-timers who helped blockade Berlin. Only this time, the food was intended not to fight the Cold War, but maybe to take one tiny step toward ending it.

Ambassador Matlock made available the kitchen facilities at Spaso House, his official residence, for the chili caper. Wasting no time, Wayne and Mario donned their aprons, grabbed their big wooden spoons—and promptly were confronted by the Spaso House's veteran chef, a fiery Italian named Pietro. He apparently had never heard of a substance called chili, resented two strangers being thrust into his kitchen, and looked upon the whole enterprise with grave professional misgivings.

Since Pietro's English was limited and Wayne and Mario spoke no Italian at all, Mario began experimenting with Texas Spanish as a common channel of communication. Grudgingly at first, Pietro began responding to this overture. As he tried to make sense out of Spanish and Mario tried to fathom the intricacies of Italian, Pietro's huffiness began to evaporate. Before long he not only pitched in to help with preparations for the chili but also took Wayne and Mario out that night for a bit of Moscow bar-crawling. The next day the three of them whipped up a vat of steamy, succulent red broth that would have easily won a prize at the annual chili cookoff back in Terlingua, Texas.

On the evening of the big blast, Soviet dignitaries turned out by the score. While language differences limited standard party chitchat, our guests smiled and nodded a lot and warmly applauded a harmonica duet rendered by the Speaker and Congressman Jim Scheuer of New York. And the chili?

Wisely, Wayne and Mario had been far more sparing in their use of peppery chili seasonings here than for a crowd in Texas, and most of the American delegation bragged that the dish was zesty and wonderful. Naturally, though, everybody was anxiously watching for the reaction of our Soviet guests. Most of them, wary at first, took a few modest spoonfuls and then decided, apparently, that this was pretty tasty stuff—not nearly as fearsome as they had expected. Wayne and Mario happily dished a lot of second helpings—some even to guests whose eyes were glistening a bit. And Wayne, while cleaning up after the party, found only one bowl with the chili partly eaten. Every other bowl in the hall was spooned clean—the ultimate barometer of good chili.

It would take more than a vat of Texas chili, of course, to burn away the fog shrouding Mikhail Gorbachev's real aims. Still unanswered were the questions being asked around the world. Where was this new Kremlin leader trying to take the Soviet Union? Did his surprising actions to date portend important changes in the his country's fundamental aims? Was there really a chance of ending the Cold War? Or was all this just an attractive new coat of paint for the same old expansionist goals that the USSR had pursued for half a century?

These questions itched in the minds of the Americans as they gathered under the imposing spires and domes of the Kremlin. In the ornate Great Hall of Catherine, they assembled around an enormous conference table for a long talk with Gorbachev.

Opening on a positive note, Jim Wright told the General Secretary that recent changes in the USSR could offer the best chance in fifty years for our countries to cooperate. Gorbachev, smiling, seemingly relaxed and self-assured, said through his interpreter that the USSR wanted to work with the U.S. for several reasons—economic, political and social. To the surprise of the Americans, he added: "Thank God some movement has begun toward cooperation."

Later he complained that the U.S. had not responded adequately to generous new Soviet arms proposals, apparently feeling the USSR was cornered and "could be squeezed like a lemon." He said the Soviets would like to reduce nuclear missiles in Europe, but the Reagan Administration said this would cause difficulties with Congress. "I look you in the eyes and do not see you as being so bloodthirsty or fearful of the USSR," he declared.

Finally, after two hours, Gorbachev sheepishly apologized for talking so long, comparing himself to a garrulous preacher.

"I was about ready to take up a collection," Jim Wright joked.

In other meetings the delegation huddled with Ligachev, Gromyko, Shevardnadze, Shcherbitsky and Dobrynin, and sat in on sessions of the Supreme Soviet. When all the talking was over, the Congressmen had lots of scribbled notes and personal hunches, but nobody seemed to have any conclusions on which they were willing to bet the family jewels.

Three days before we were scheduled to leave Moscow, Nikolai showed up unexpectedly in a Kremlin hallway. "I must talk with you," he said quietly.

The two of us moved into an alcove beside a statue. From his discretion I could see he had something unusual on his mind.

"The General Secretary would like to invite the Speaker to speak on Soviet television," he said.

Assuming this was a routine courtesy, I said: "You mean on television just here in the Moscow area?"

"No," he said. "On our national television. Over the whole country. He would speak for about fifteen or twenty minutes, and we would provide an excellent translator."

This was a little bigger deal than I thought. I recalled having read somewhere that the Soviet Union had about 300 million people spread across 11 of the world's 24 time zones. This would be a somewhat bigger audience than Jim Wright reached on the 10 o'clock news over KXAS-TV in Fort Worth.

"What would he talk about?" I asked.

"Anything he wants to," Nikolai said.

"Anything at all?"

"Anything at all," he nodded.

"When would you want him to do this?"

"At the time when our audience is largest. We would like for his speech to be broadcast at the time the General Secretary always chooses for his own speeches—immediately after the 9 o'clock news on Saturday night."

I pointed out that we were scheduled to leave Moscow Saturday afternoon, and the schedule probably could not be changed.

"The speech could be recorded," Nikolai said.

"Would you edit out any of it?"

Nikolai acted hurt. "We would not do that," he said.

Frankly, the more he talked, the more flabbergasted I became. What would prompt Gorbachev to make an offer like this? The Soviet Union had been giving the world nuclear indigestion for half a century, so why would its new leader open up his own proprietary television network and tell a top-ranking American official he could say anything he pleased? Was there a joker in the deck? Was there some key question I had foolishly failed to ask?

It was an hour or so before I could get Jim Wright loose from the delegation for a private huddle back at the hotel. When I told him about the offer, he was surprised—and clearly delighted. Even so, we spent a good deal of time trying to examine its implications. On its face, the invitation to make a major speech to the entire population of the Soviet Union seemed almost too good to be true. Jim Wright and I both wanted to believe it was made in good faith, and that his remarks would not be misused or twisted in a way to compromise or embarrass the United States.

Having lived with the trickery and deceptions of the Cold War for most our adult lives, we were inclined to be wary.

Even though the speech would have to be taped and would not be broadcast until several hours after our departure, I accepted Nikolai's word that it would not be edited, and that it would be translated accurately. After all, the Soviets knew our Embassy would monitor the broadcast carefully and could spot instantly any shenanigans with the tape or the translation. For Jim Wright, it was decision time.

"Tell them we'll do it—on a couple of conditions," he said. Then he carefully spelled out the message I was to convey to Nikolai.

For Jim Wright, this was a dream come true. He was, by instinct, by experience and by choice, a political animal. And what politician in history would not have drooled down his string tie over an opportunity to deliver a personal message to a television audience spanning nearly half the earth? But for this particular politician, this would be far more than a just another ego trip.

Nearly 30 years earlier, as Christmas, 1958, approached, Jim Wright, then a young two-term Congressman, had written a visionary newsletter called *A Letter To Ivan*. Addressed to an imaginary Soviet citizen, the letter bemoaned the vast amounts of money being poured into weapons by both the Soviet Union and the United States because each feared the other. Stressing the common values shared by people in both countries, the letter proposed a peaceful contest between our two competing economic systems. Then, by a methodical, agreed-on 10 per cent a year reduction in arms spending, both countries could invest the savings in fighting disease, feeding the hungry, wiping out slums, and building schools, hospitals and libraries. "Think it over, Ivan," the letter said. "We've both been trying the other way long enough."

As he was leaving his two-hour conference with Gorbachev in the Kremlin only a day or so before, Jim Wright told him about this newsletter and gave him a copy. The General Secretary nodded agreement. "If only we had done so back then," he said.

Now, in his televised speech, Jim Wright would have a chance to echo this theme of peaceful competition and step-by-step disarmament in a fresh, updated version of his old, yellowing newsletter. The message would be the similar, but this time he wouldn't be pecking it out on a typewriter. This time, he would be talking to Ivan himself.

Nikolai was standing by at the hotel, awaiting Jim Wright's answer. "The Speaker is pleased to accept the General Secretary's generous offer—provided you can agree to two conditions," I said. "The first is very simple."

"Yes?" he said.

"I would like for you to reconfirm to me a promise you have already made—that there will be no editing, no changes, no alterations of the Speaker's remarks, and that the translation will be absolutely accurate and faithful to his meaning."

"Again, you have my absolute assurance," Nikolai said.

"Great. Now for the other condition. Jim Wright would like to offer to each listener a little emblem like this," I said, fingering the tiny replica of crossed U.S. and Soviet flags in my coat lapel.

"That is very generous. There is no problem with that."

"Yes, but I haven't finished," I said. "The Speaker would send these lapel buttons only to people who write to him in the United States. I have already checked with the Washington post office. I have been told that the letters from your country can use a simplified form of address—'Jim Wright, Washington, U.S.A.' We would like to have those words superimposed on the television screen."

"That's fine. That can be done," Nikolai said.

I frowned. "Nikolai, I want to make sure you understand. Over these past few days I have learned to like you and respect you. I don't want to cause you any trouble."

He smiled. "There will be no trouble."

I wasn't sure I believed him. "Nikolai, now please understand exactly what I am telling you. I am saying that a high official of the United States government is going to ask citizens of the Soviet Union to write personal, private letters to him in the United States. What's more, he plans to answer the persons who write and send them one of these little emblems. Do you understand what I'm saying?"

"I understand what you are saying, and it is all right," he said.

"There is no problem with your citizens engaging in private correspondence with an official of the United States? They will not get into trouble?"

"There is no problem. They will not get into trouble."

"And you can tell me this on your own responsibility? You don't need to consult with anyone?"

"I don't have to ask anybody," Nikolai declared. "I can tell you it is all right."

To me, that did it. In my own private world, I was now sure that something truly profound was unfolding in the Soviet Union. How else could Nikolai, certainly no Kremlin decision-maker, display such sublime self-confidence? How else could he personally be absolutely sure that plain, everyday Soviet citizens were perfectly free to correspond with a top-ranking official of a foreign government? Under previous regimes, wouldn't any such letter writer have been carted off by the KGB to the nearest gulag?

However ridiculous it may seem to admit it even today, I truly felt at that moment I knew the answer to the question everybody was asking. Mikhail Gorbachev was indeed for real. By design or by accident, he had pulled a couple of loose threads, and now the Communist dictatorship which had terrified its own citizens and the rest of the world for 50 years was beginning to come unraveled like an old sweater. Otherwise how could Jim Wright be granted such an astounding blank check—not only to say anything he doggoned pleased to the whole USSR, but also then to correspond privately with Soviet citizens?

In response to Jim Wright's TV speech, he received nearly 2,500 letters. About a third were in English. The rest were translated by the Library of Congress. To each was sent a reply and, as promised, a lapel pin of crossed U.S. and Soviet flags.

All the letters expressed hope for peace and cooperation. Many recalled U.S. help to the USSR during World War II. Many others appealed for nuclear disarmament. And some foresaw better days ahead.

"Great changes are going on in our country," said one Soviet citizen. "We feel it daily in our life. We have great hopes to do better."

12

The Great Washington Elephant Hunt

It began, as unusual stories sometimes do, among a handful of good friends gathered around a few convivial bottles of whisky.

The time was a few days before Christmas in 1963, and a hodgepodge group of merrymakers was partying at a home in an otherwise dignified neighborhood not far from Fort Worth's sprawling Forest Park Zoo. Among the guests was the zoo's director, Lawrence Curtis.

This fact alone should have suggested mischief, because Lawrence Curtis was not your standard bookish, pipe-smoking zoological nerd. He was a big, strapping fellow who tooled around town in an ancient Cadillac for which he was said to buy gasoline a dollar's worth at a time.

His best friend, *Star-Telegram* columnist George Dolan, described Curtis as an inveterate practical joker and, in zoo matters, an unsurpassed con man. Dolan once related how a posh Fort Worth hotel, proud of its elegant 16th Century British design, asked Curtis to help stock its picturesque fish pond. Curtis reacted, Dolan claimed, by selling the hotel a batch of ordinary Texas river carp, passing them off as incredibly rare and expensive fish which once swam in the garden pool of the Duke of Bedford.

One of Curtis's interesting companions that fateful day was Fort Worth's free-spirited young State Senator, Don Kennard. A devout populist, Kennard caused extreme nervousness among the overfed occupants of the overstuffed armchairs in the rarefied atmosphere of the Fort Worth Club. But with the people out in neighborhoods where dining room tables were covered with oilcloth rather than starched linen, Kennard was admired as the working man's champion in Austin. Most people even got vicarious enjoyment out of Kennard's personal adventures.

On one occasion he and a kindred soul, Fort Worth District Attorney Doug Crouch, decided their children knew far too little of the suffering endured by hoboes during the Depression. To remedy this educational shortcoming, Kennard took his daughter and a grade-school classmate to the Fort Worth railroad yards. Waiting there, with a fruit jar of martinis, were Crouch and a venturesome Fort Worth businessman he somehow had talked into joining the expedition. All five climbed aboard a flatcar on a departing freight train. Kennard, trying to change cars, tumbled off the train just outside Fort Worth. When the four others arrived in Weatherford, 26 bone-jarring miles away, they were arrested and jailed by railroad dicks, thus providing them with a far deeper insight than they had expected into the perils of hobo life during the Depression.

Another guest at the Christmas party was Bill Newbold, a former television newsman. Years before, while a reporter on *The Fort Worth Press*, I had worked with Bill in the squalid little basement press room of the Fort Worth Police Department. In fact it was Bill, then a reporter and cameraman for WBAP-TV, who patiently explained to me that, even apart from the matter of personal hygiene, there were other serious drawbacks in having to work in the press room. To claim our desks in the mornings, he said, it was occasionally necessary to chase away the drunks and ladies of the evening who slept on them.

But in the intervening 10 years, the fates had been kind to both Bill and me. At the time of the Christmas party in 1963, I was working for Jim Wright, and Bill, by then seasoned veteran of the State Department, was on Christmas leave, having just returned from Cambodia.

In fact, only a few months before, Bill had acquired and shipped to the Fort Worth Zoo a couple of Siberian tiger cubs. At the Christmas party, Curtis again thanked Bill for his generosity in sending the two cuddly little animals.

But Senator Kennard, also an old friend of Bill's, feigned disappointment. "You always did think small, Newbold," he said scornfully. "We don't need any mangy tiger cubs. What we need is an *elephant*."

Curtis nodded agreement. "Bill, don't get the idea we're not grateful for the lion cubs. But Don is right. We really do need an elephant, especially since Penny died."

Penny, a full-grown elephant named for the coins that Fort Worth school children contributed to purchase her many years before, had been one of the zoo's principal attractions. She had died a couple of years back, and one of Curtis's fondest hopes was that someday she could be replaced.

As whisky enlivened the conversation, Kennard zeroed in once more on what he considered Newbold's obligation to the Fort Worth zoo. "They've got a lot of elephants in Cambodia, don't they, Bill?" he persisted. "Can't you get us at least a little one?"

Listening to all this spirited discussion, but saying very little, was my boss, Jim Wright. Inside his head, however, the wheels of mischief were turning.

Back in Washington a few days later, he walked into my office and recounted the conversation between his two old friends—Newbold, who had since left for a new assignment with the State Department, and Kennard, a longtime political ally. Then, smiling devilishly, Jim Wright came to his point.

"Kennard, you know, is always as broke as I am," he said. "Wouldn't it be great if we tricked him into thinking that Bill Newbold had shipped an elephant from Cambodia—and sent it COD to him?"

"He'd croak," I laughed.

For the next few minutes we sat there in my office, giggling like schoolboys and engaging in hilarious fantasies of how Kennard would react if confronted with a gigantic bill for importing an elephant from Cambodia.

"He'd regret the day he razzed Newbold about sending an elephant," I hooted.

Jim Wright nodded enthusiastically. "Why don't you try to get a message like that delivered to Kennard. It'll have to come from a credible source. Otherwise he'll smell a rat."

"Rather than an elephant," I snickered.

"Rather than an elephant," Jim Wright agreed.

Armed with this devious commission from my boss, I started to work. Through friends in the U.S. Customs Service who shall remain forever nameless, the Great Elephant Joke was set into motion.

It was two days after Christmas, 1963. State Senator Don Kennard was headed to a pre-New Year's party staged every year in Athens, Texas, by his longtime friend in the Legislature, Bill Kugle. As Kennard was walking out the door, the telephone rang. It was an official of the U.S. Customs Service.

"I just got a message from our office in San Francisco," he said. "They're holding an elephant out there. Addressed to you. I need to find out how you want to handle it."

"An elephant?" Kennard asked, dumbfounded. "Addressed to me?"

"Yessir," said the customs man. "Shipped over by air from someplace—let's see, here it is...yeah, shipped over from Cambodia. Fourteen hundred dollars in air freight charges due on it."

"Fourteen hundred dollars?" Kennard repeated weakly.

"Yeah, not counting the fifty-dollar-a-day custodial charge during the two weeks we've got to keep it in quarantine."

"Who sent the elephant? Was it a guy named Newbold?"

"Message doesn't say," muttered the customs man.

Still stunned, Kennard said, "Look. I'm going to have to get back to you on this. I was just headed out the door for a trip to East Texas. I'll call you again in a day or so."

Jim Wright and I were in the office in Washington when we learned that our prank message had been delivered. We snickered like kids, conjuring up our own hilarious scenes of how Kennard must have reacted.

"What did he say? Did he almost faint?" I asked, pressing our secret ally in the Customs Service for lurid, juicy details.

"He sounded pretty surprised, all right," Secret Agent X agreed.

"And what did he say about the fourteen hundred dollars in air freight charges?" Jim Wright wanted to know.

"And the fifty-dollar-a-day quarantine charge?" I persisted.

"He seemed pretty surprised about all that, too."

I got the feeling that our friend in the Customs Office didn't think our joke was quite as funny as we did, but was doing his best not to spoil our private hilarity. Of course, we were certain in our own minds that the most uproarious laugh of all was yet to come.

"Just wait till Don telephones Bill Newbold in Cambodia," Jim Wright chuckled. "He'll say, 'Hey, Bill, I was just kidding about your sending an elephant to the zoo, but he's arrived and I sure want to thank you.' "

"And Bill will say, 'What in the hell are you talking about, Kennard? I didn't send you any damned elephant!' " I whooped.

"And then we can come clean and tell Kennard it was only a joke," Jim Wright said. "He'll get a big laugh out of it."

But from the very beginning, events did not follow our comic scenario. After getting the call from the Customs man, Kennard did not panic and call Bill Newbold, as we expected. Instead, to reassure himself this was not a gag, Kennard waited until the next day and then called back to check with the U.S. Customs Service. He was promptly connected to our friend who called him in the first place. He reconfirmed the original notice. Now bolstered by the solemn word of a United States Government official that the elephant message was indeed on the level, Kennard told the Customs man he needed a few more days. Our private joke was still private, all right, but it began taking some other unexpected turns.

For one thing, instead of being ridiculed for receiving a $1,400 COD elephant, Kennard had become sort of a hero. From friends and family with whom he shared the news, he received nothing but upbeat reactions. His 10-year-old daughter, Karen, was overjoyed at the prospect of having her own personal pachyderm—especially one just her size. She kept the family telephone humming for hours, telling her friends about the cute little elephant her father soon was going to get. She could visualize the cuddly little creature staked in their front yard on Potomac Street, waving his tiny trunk and enthralling the neighborhood kids.

"May I take him to school, too, Daddy?" she asked.

Lawrence Curtis was as elated as Karen—but for another reason. Even though Kennard had mentioned nothing about giving the elephant to the zoo, Curtis already was entertaining covetous thoughts.

"I'll be glad to help you with the details, Don," Curtis said. To Kennard he presented a book on the care and feeding of elephants, craftily hoping Don would see the futility of trying to maintain such an animal without proper facilities—such as, for example, the facilities at Forest Park Zoo.

Gradually Kennard began to relish the role of expectant foster father to an elephant. Moreover, he saw a promising political opportunity in the little beast. After all, politicians are always trying to cook up schemes to get good press. Here was a once-in-a-lifetime opportunity for lots of newspaper ink and television time—warm and fuzzy coverage about a generous public servant and his charming little elephant. Kennard wondered whether to take the story to the newspapers.

"Absolutely! That's a great idea!" cried Julian Reed, a prominent young public relations consultant and longtime friend of Kennard's. "Don't worry about the money. Just march down to the city desk at the *Star-Telegram* and say, 'Hey, I've got a problem I want to tell you about...' "

Which is precisely what Kennard did the following morning—and it worked. In the absence of an ax murder, most city editors are perfectly willing to settle for a for an upbeat story about an adorable little animal that somehow has been thrust into the public consciousness—even if the story marginally involves, ugh, a politician.

"Who sent this to you?" asked the guy on the *Star-Telegram* city desk.

"I think it was Bill Newbold," replied Kennard, recounting their joking conversation at Curtis's Christmas party.

The man on the city desk immediately began trying to telephone Newbold in Cambodia. What neither he nor Kennard realized was that Cambodia's King Sihanouk, charging the United States with fomenting the overthrow his government, had ousted Bill Newbold and other U.S. personnel from his country well before Christmas. Nor did either the desk man or Kennard know that Bill and his wife Elwanda were on their way to a new State Department assignment in Hong Kong.

Failing to reach Bill by telephone, the city desk man located Bill's father, Charles R. Newbold, who, as it happened, worked downstairs in the advertising department of the *Star-Telegram*. Mr. Newbold mentioned the recent political upheaval in Cambodia and said he hadn't been able to reach Bill, either.

Bill's mother was also interviewed. To her, it was perfectly obvious that her son had sent the elephant. "Bill always was something of a practical joker," she laughed. Splashed across Page One in the Sunday *Star-Telegram* was a story that began:

"State Senator Don Kennard of Fort Worth found himself the surprised and somewhat bewildered owner Saturday of 635-pound baby elephant."

The story went on to recount the customs official's call to Kennard, the unpaid $1,400 shipping charge, and reported without qualification that the elephant was a gift from Bill Newbold. Then, two days later, the news coverage took a more ominous turn.

'PACHYDERM PROMPTS ELEPHANTINE MYSTERY,' said another Page-One story, relating that nobody had been able to locate the elephant.

"The whereabouts of the baby remains a mystery," the article said. "A San Francisco newspaper Monday made a check of customs department there and could find no trace of an elephant. A telephone call from the *Star-Telegram* also proved futile."

Kennard, of course, was still worried about the $1,400 shipping charge. "How anyone could convince the people in Cambodia to send a thing like that COD is beyond me," he moaned.

He mentioned the possibility of selling the animal to the Fort Worth Zoo to pay the charges, but Curtis was quoted as saying the zoo had nothing in the budget for purchasing elephants. To Jim Wright, this raised the gravest possibility of all.

"What if Kennard gets the *Star-Telegram* to launch a campaign for public donations?" he wondered..

"And all the little school kids skimp on their lunch money so they can donate their nickels and dimes," I muttered.

"And there's no elephant," Jim Wright groaned.

It began to dawn on both of us that we may have foolishly lighted the fuse on a crate of political dynamite. The next day Jim Wright came into my office and gloomily sat down. In his hand was a newspaper story quoting zookeeper Lawrence Curtis as saying he had just talked to Jim Wright in Washington and received assurances that the animal had cleared customs and was en route to Fort Worth.

"I told him no such thing," Jim Wright protested. "Curtis may be a bigger practical joker than we are."

As the confusion deepened, the *Star-Telegram* carried another story—this one quoting the dispatcher of Local 10 of the International Longshoremen's Union in San Francisco. "None of our crews has unloaded an elephant," he said.

Neither had the Pacific Maritime Association. "We always hear about such things, and we haven't heard a thing about an elephant," said a spokesman in San Francisco.

Jim Wright put down the clippings and looked at me. "Marshall, do you think you can find an elephant?" he asked.

In the past, when the boss had asked me to do a chore, I always replied, "Sure." But never before had he asked for an elephant—small, for free, and *now.*

"I'll try," I said meekly.

In the next day or so, the pressure got worse. Thanks to the Associated Press, a large part of the world now knew about the Texas Senator who had abruptly inherited an elephant, once the little critter could be located. Kennard was besieged with calls.

From a saloon in St. Louis, a tender-hearted drunk called to say he would like to buy "thish little elephant" to take home to his kids.

A more credible offer came from the superintendent of a big amusement park which featured a petting zoo.

Kennard's patience was wearing thin. "I haven't decided what I'm going to do with it," he snorted. "I may decide to keep it myself."

"Oh, no—you surely don't want to keep an elephant," the caller protested.

"No? Why not?"

The park superintendent cleared his throat authoritatively. "Man," he said, "they get biggg."

Another call came from a Republican county chairman. He was excited over the prospect of getting a real, live mascot for his party.

"This is a Democratic elephant," Kennard proclaimed. "Do you think I'm going to turn it over to a bunch of Republicans?"
But the most worrisome calls came from newspaper and wire service reporters. They still had been unable to find the elephant. Could Kennard tell them precisely where it was located? "Call Lawrence Curtis," Kennard suggested brusquely.

As for Curtis, he gradually had come to suspect that no such creature existed. He had shared this opinion with Kennard, but having already announced the elephant's imminent arrival, neither Kennard nor Curtis had any idea what to do next.

In an effort to buy time, Curtis enlisted fellow zookeepers across the western United States in an elaborate charade. He persuaded colleagues to provide progress reports on the imaginary shipment of a non-existent elephant from San Francisco to Fort Worth.

"Yessir, the little feller came through here," a conspiratorial zookeeper in Utah might tell an inquiring reporter. "But the truck left a day or so ago, and I'm not sure which route they were taking."

In our Washington office, the pressure grew worse than that in Dr. Frankenstein's laboratory. The mad doctor had inflamed the townspeople by creating a seven-foot monster. Jim Wright and I were in grave danger of inflaming the community by failing to create an elephant—an elephant which already had been duly authenticated by an official of the U.S. Customs Service, publicly documented by the *Fort Worth Star-Telegram* and The Associated Press, and was now expectantly awaited by thousands of eager school children in Fort Worth.

And what was my responsibility in all this? Oh, not much. Just to find a baby elephant—like *now*.

Where on earth, I wondered, does one find an elephant? Barnum & Bailey? Not likely. They probably need all they have. Where, then? Animal trappers? No such listing in the Washington Yellow Pages. Well, I figured, I've got to start somewhere. I dialed the Washington Zoo.

Feeling like Bob Newhart in one of his old telephone routines, I asked the zoo superintendent if he had any idea where Congressman Wright could find an elephant—preferably a smallish one. (Already I was thinking about the potential shipping charges.)

"You're looking for an elephant?" asked the zoo superintendent. His tone suggested a degree of curiosity as to how such a creature fitted into the legislative requirements of the House of Representatives. But since he graciously refrained from voicing this question, I didn't feel it necessary to explain that the elephant was needed to keep the school children of Fort Worth from forming a mob and riding Jim Wright, Lawrence Curtis, Don Kennard and me out of town on a rail.

"Sorry—we don't happen to have any spare elephants out here," he said. "Have you checked with the State Department?"

I pondered the question for a moment. "No," I said finally. "Frankly, I thought I might have better luck with the zoo."

"I understand," he said. "But the other day some fellow from the State Department called here. He was talking about a maharajah in India trying to give an elephant to our ambassador, Chester Bowles. You might check it out."

The possibility sounded pretty far-fetched, but the zoo man gave me the telephone number and I called the fellow at State.

It seemed that the Rajah of Kollengode, in India's Kerala State, had been pestering Ambassador Bowles to accept a female baby elephant named "Shanti," meaning "Peace," as a gesture of friendship to the United States.

Bowles, a friend of Jim Wright's and a former member of the House of Representatives, was now serving for the second time as our Ambassador to India. As a busy diplomat, he was ill-suited to baby-sit an elephant, but obviously could not offend the maharajah.

Even though it was far from certain that we could get the little animal, my pulse quickened at the possibility. I suspected the diplomats wanted to find a suitable recipient as quickly as possible, because even though its imposing Washington headquarters covers four city blocks, the State Department lacks suitable accommodations for elephants.

In the next few days, a few details trickled in. When Shanti was 10 weeks old, her mother was killed in an elephant trap. The Rajah of Kollengode took the little orphan and put her under the care of his children. Reportedly the animal had the run of the house (or the palace, or whatever a Rajah lives in). Since Shanti weighed 700 pounds, this arrangement probably did not add to the longevity of the family's good china.

At this point, Bill Newbold, who had been traveling and was oblivious to the entire affair, arrived at his new post in Hong Kong, where the story had been in the newspapers. "Hi, Bill, I've heard a lot about you," said the U.S. Consul General. "How are the elephants in Cambodia?"

Bill thought that was sort of an unusual question, but didn't pursue the matter because he and Elwanda were running late for a welcoming luncheon in their honor at the Hong Kong Press Club. But no sooner had they walked into the club than Bill was confronted by an old friend he had known in Cambodia, veteran AP Correspondent Roy Essoyan. Having followed the story of the missing elephant on the international news wires, Essoyan wasted no time with pleasantries: "All right, Bill—where's the damn elephant?"

"You're the second guy in an hour to ask me about an elephant," Bill protested. "What is everybody talking about?"

Meanwhile, back in Washington, we nervously awaited official word that we could have Shanti. Jim Wright was growing edgy. He had been in touch with Ambassador Bowles, who was trying to work out the gift arrangement. But the fuse was burning perilously close to the dynamite. And then, just as we were bracing ourselves for an anticipated newspaper story exposing the elephant joke that would disappoint the children of Fort Worth, the State Department gave its final OK. Vastly relieved, Jim Wright grabbed the telephone. To Lawrence Curtis he outlined a plan.

The next day a car pulling an enclosed trailer pulled up in front of Kennard's house. Alerted by Curtis, newspaper and television reporters swarmed over the street. The celebrated day had arrived. Shanti was here. She was, wasn't she?

She was not. When the ramp from the trailer was lowered, out sauntered not an elephant but a somewhat scroungy little donkey. Affixed to his sides were signs bearing his name: "Meanwhile."

To the assembled news people, Jim Wright came clean. He admitted that the whole thing started as a joke, and that the elephant at first had been strictly imaginary. But now there was a real one, and she would be here soon. Honest she would. In the meanwhile, there was Meanwhile.

Instead of the public relations disaster we had feared, we had a bonanza of warm humor and goodwill. The papers were enthralled with the story. Not often does a private joke between politicians backfire and result in a cuddly new little beastie for the city zoo.

To handle the arrangements for bringing Shanti to the U.S., Lawrence Curtis selflessly volunteered to fly to India. So grateful was Don Kennard that he agreed to pay the zoo director's airline fare.

"And then the scoundrel kept going and flew on around the world," Kennard groused later.

When Shanti arrived in Fort Worth on April 4, 1964, she was treated like a celebrity. The little animal was featured on the television news, her picture was in the papers, and Governor John Connally bestowed honorary Texas citizenship both on Shanti and Venugopal Varma, the Rajah's 24-year-old son who came to make the formal presentation.

Even after her long trip from India, the hair on the back of Shanti's head was braided—a reminder of the loving care she got from the Rajah's daughters, who fed her at first with a baby bottle.

Despite its harrowing moments, the tale of Shanti the Elephant deserves a special niche in the annals of politics. Of the countless small dramas played out each day in Washington, there are losers as well as winners. I still am not sure who, if anybody, wound up getting stuck with the shipping charges. But apart from that, in the case of Shanti the elephant, everybody was a winner.

The Rajah of Kollengode got his wish—proudly presenting Shanti to Ambassador Chester Bowles as a gesture of friendship to the United States.

Ambassador Bowles was delighted over being allowed promptly to surrender custody of the creature to the State Department in Washington.

The State Department, relieved that Shanti would not be shipped to its own stately offices in Washington's Foggy Bottom, was more than pleased to give the little beast to a Texas Senator who seemed actually eager to get it.

Senator Kennard earned the admiration of voters for his generosity in donating Shanti to the zoo for the enjoyment of their youngsters.

Bill Newbold, who finally learned the whole story in the Hong Kong Press Club, of all places, nevertheless got credit for sending a now-you-see-it, now-you-don't elephant to the Fort Worth zoo.

Zoo boss (and globe-circling traveler) Lawrence Curtis wound up with a charming new little boarder that enthralled thousands of grateful children.

Congressman Jim Wright got to retain the services of an incredibly able Administrative Assistant. In other words, he didn't fire me.

Regrettably, though, the story had a sad ending. After several years in the Fort Worth zoo, little Shanti died. But even today, her memory can generate a lot of warm smiles among the people who knew and loved her. That's not a bad heritage for a person, or even for a little orphan elephant.

13

Chalk Up One
for the Peacemakers

If I had dreamed as a kid that someday I would go to Jerusalem to attend a family reunion between a famous son of Isaac and a famous son of Ishmael, I might have paid more attention in Sunday school.

It would have been tough, because in church I was usually squirming in my pew. My legs itched, and I was hot and bored. For one thing, as a fifth grader I couldn't understand the connection between the things we did in our little Texas farm town and the Old Testament lessons Mr. Bowers was trying to teach us. Our Sunday school lessons had drawings of strange-looking foreign people with beards. They rode donkeys and lived in desert towns with peculiar names. They dressed in long robes that looked as baggy as the cotton sacks those poor Mexican wetbacks dragged along the furrows in the sweltering farm fields outside Bishop.

Even so, their robes looked more comfortable than those miserable white linen Palm Beach pants my mother always wanted me to wear to church. I argued that I could listen to the preacher just as well and be far more comfortable in my everyday khakis. But she thought those starchy linen pants made me look nice. My mother was the kindest, gentlest person I ever knew, and I loved her very much. Rather than hurt her feelings I usually wore those linen pants, even though they were as stiff and scratchy as sandpaper. Sometimes I wore my pajama bottoms underneath and I doubt if the devil ever knew the difference.

Even worse, air conditioning had not yet made it to Bishop. Our little Southern Baptist Church had an imposing colonnaded entrance and tasteful brick trim, but for relief on sweltering Sunday mornings we had nothing but a few big overhead fans. These served only to make sure the hot air kept moving. There were, of course, the hand-held paper fans found in the pews. These were donated, I am sure, by the Kingsville funeral home whose advertising they featured.   Despite the congregation's energetic use of these fans, on some August days our church sanctuary seemed nearly as hot as another location about which the preacher frequently warned in his sermon.

Actually I'm not sure Mr. Bowers ever told our Sunday school class about Isaac and Ishmael and their father, the Jewish patriarch Abraham. In our sheltered lives as kids in the 1930's, we probably were not worldly enough to understand, even if he had. If we had been tutored in cultural values by Beavis and Butthead and Roseanne and Howard Stern, as kids are today, we probably would have snickered about Abraham's liaison with his wife's maid.

But then as now, Baptists were leery of promoting temptation. One day in the schoolyard, for example, I confided to a chum, James Edgar Whitten, that I didn't understand why Baptists thought dancing was sinful.

"It's not the dancing," he said. "It's the things that go with it."

That observation stuck with me. Years later, first in the Army and then in college, I kept visiting places where there was dancing, hoping I could run across some of the things that were supposed to go with it. Only rarely did I succeed. But I digress.

Anyhow, even if Mr. Bowers did tell us about Abraham, I doubt that he dwelt overlong on the fact that Abraham's wife Sarah, thinking she was too old to bear a child, arranged for her Egyptian maid Hagar to sleep with Abraham so he could have a son.

The son, of course, turned out to be Ishmael. And then later, when God made it possible for Sarah herself to bear Abraham another son, Isaac, things got even more complicated. Abraham ordered Hagar to take Ishmael and go away. Then Ishmael was ordained by God to father all the world's Arabic nations. His half-brother Isaac, meanwhile, received a covenant from God to become progenitor of the Jews. Today, four thousand years later, for reasons we probably are not supposed to understand, we are still seeing the results of this family upheaval.

If we kids were to have trouble in later life trying to understand the hostility which exists even today between Arab and Jew, there was a good reason. Just about everybody in Bishop had a name like Nelson or Pierce or Davis, with maybe a Spieglehauer and a Schultz here and there. This was long before the United States became hopelessly addicted to foreign oil, and even if I had heard of fellows called Arabs, I certainly had never seen any. As for Jews, I remember only two small families. Both ran dry goods stores on Bishop's one-block Main Street. One of the men was very unusual.

His name was Louis Goltzman. I used to deliver the *Corpus Christi Times* every afternoon to his store on the corner. Even though he seldom spoke to anybody except the poor farmhands buying work clothes in his store, he was always nice to me and paid his newspaper bill on time. But I never recall seeing any of the other merchants along Main Street stop by, even to pass the time of day, with Mr. Goltzman. Perhaps he appeared too shy or withdrawn. And almost certainly they were uncomfortable with his unusual appearance.

Stoop-shouldered, thin and frail, he could be seen most afternoons sitting on a stool or trash can outside his store, poring over a Yiddish newspaper he must have received by mail. It was here that passersby occasionally would steal a closer look at his face.

Even though Mr. Goltzman surely was not really old, his face was gaunt and had an unusual pallor. On his cheeks was a little fuzz but he obviously did not shave.

For a while, I believe he and his wife lived in rooms above their store, although later I think they moved to a nearby second-story apartment. Naturally they did not come to our church, and Bishop had no synagogue. I never remember any of our Christian townspeople visiting them, or even offering a perfunctory good afternoon. On the Main Street of our town of about a thousand people, Mr. Goltzman and his wife seemed doomed to live in virtual isolation.

Exactly where they came from, or how they got to Bishop, I never knew. Some said they were refugees who had been driven out of Europe or Russia or somewhere. They said they suspected Mr. Goltzman had been tortured and brutally mutilated back wherever it was he came from.

Some men in town privately joked about Mr. Goltzman's reticence and unusual appearance. Over coffee in the drug store they would privately call him by a nickname so cruel that I cannot bring myself even now, more than half a century later, to repeat it. On my paper route I used to think about how isolated and lonely Mr. and Mrs. Goltzman must have felt in our town. I was ashamed of the way people seemed to avoid and ignore them.

Only two doors from Goltzman's was another little dry goods store. This one was owned by a small, energetic fellow named Bill Sanders. He too eked out a living by selling khakis and overalls and work shoes to farm workers who didn't have a car to get to the department stores in Kingsville, six miles away. He lived in a small curtained-off area in the rear of the store with his sister, a Mrs. Friedlander, and her son—a big, good-looking kid named Harry. He was about my age, and as well as I can remember, Harry Friedlander was the only Jew I ever went to school with.

Even as a kid it struck me as unusual that both the Goltzmans and the Bill Sanders family were the only people who lived in their stores on Main Street. Not until many years later did it occur to me that people in our town might have been reluctant to have them as neighbors. But at this point I don't guess it makes any difference—to them, at least. Mr. and Mrs. Goltzman and Bill Sanders and Mrs. Friedlander are surely dead by now. And my schoolmate, young Harry Friedlander, doesn't need a place to live, either. As a GI in the infantry, he was killed fighting the Nazis in World War II.

After the war, with the whole world feeling guilty about having allowed the Holocaust to occur, I was delighted when the United Nations laid the groundwork for the nation of Israel. How great, I thought, that the Goltzmans and Friedlanders of the earth would no longer be forced to live in communities that tolerated their presence but didn't really like them. In the new nation of Israel they could, if they chose, live among their own people in a homeland secure and at peace with neighboring nations of the Middle East. This, anyhow, was my childishly naive thought.

The creation of Israel was proclaimed on May 14, 1948. The next day it was attacked by five Arab countries. The Israelis defeated the invaders, but this did not shake the Arab belief that the newborn nation had no right to exist, and they pledged to destroy it. Again in 1956, 1967 and 1973, wars raged between Israelis and Arabs.

If we Americans find such consuming hatred hard to understand, maybe it's because we, with our melting-pot heritage, do not long savor such nationalistic animosities. Indeed, we probably have the shortest collective national memory of any country on earth. A little more than fifty years ago we fought the biggest, bloodiest war in history against Germany and Japan. Today they are among our closest international allies. Yet between Arabs and Jews, hatreds intertwined with deep-rooted religious beliefs have been smoldering nearly four thousand years.

With both sides tracing their ancestry back to Abraham--the Jews through Isaac, the Arabs through Ishmael--the descendants of these two half-brothers are bloody rivals, even today, for the holy land God promised to Abraham. Abraham was told, the Bible says, that God's covenant would be with Isaac, but that Ishmael would father a great nation. In their claim to the disputed lands, the Arabs point to their conquest of this territory about 600 years after the birth of Christ and the fact that Palestinians have lived there ever since.

On the other side of the Atlantic in 1976, three years after the latest Arab-Israeli war, a significant event occurred. The people of the United States elected as their President a fellow who, unlike myself, *did* pay attention in Sunday school. His name was Jimmy Carter and he, also, was raised in small town and attended a Baptist church which undoubtedly lacked air conditioning. Yet even as a youngster, he was a devout student of the Scriptures. The only thing I can figure is, he probably didn't have to wear itchy Palm Beach pants, thus allowing him to follow the lessons more closely.

As a peanut farmer from Plains, Georgia, Jimmy Carter held somewhat shaky credentials for a man destined to become a renowned international peacemaker. Any such idea would have prompted patronizing smiles in the rarefied heights of the State Department.

Also in 1976, there was another election—this one in the U.S. House of Representatives. Jim Wright, an eleven-term Democratic Congressman from Fort Worth, was elected Majority Leader, succeeding Thomas P. (Tip) O'Neill, a big, gregarious Boston pol who was then moved up to become Speaker.

Like the toothy Georgia farmer who was preparing to move with his family to an 18-acre plot with government housing at 1600 Pennsylvania Avenue, Jim Wright as a boy had steeped himself in Bible lore and in the broad sweep of world history. Now, like Carter, he was an outlander in the eyes of Washington's elite foreign policy establishment and an untested novice in international affairs. Yet he, too, was destined to have a role in an international drama then beginning to unfold in the Middle East.

Under Tip O'Neill, it had become customary each fall for the Majority Leader to lead a group of Congressional colleagues to a spot on the globe where vital U.S. interests were in play. Even though newspapers habitually disparaged these trips as thinly-disguised pleasure junkets, they were far from that. Besides providing high-ranking colleagues with first-hand insights into international issues on which the House often was obligated to legislate, the trip helped the Majority Leader solidify his working relationship with key House movers and shakers of both political parties. The delegations were carefully selected to be bipartisan.

So it was that one afternoon in early October, 1977, I asked two close friends to join me for a meeting in Jim Wright's office. One was Eugene L. (Gene) Krizek, a former Capitol Hill staffer who was now director of Congressional liaison for the State Department. The other was General William H. (Moon) Mullins, a veteran fighter pilot who had become deputy chief of legislative liaison for the Air Force.

"Jim Wright wants to take a high-level delegation to the Middle East after adjournment," I said. "Can you guys help make the arrangements and then come along to see that things don't get screwed up?"

"Of course," said Moon.

"You bet," said Gene. "Glad he's going to the Middle East. Lot of significant things happening over there these days." In retrospect, this was a considerable understatement.

For one thing, Gene said, our State Department experts had been fretting nervously over the unexpected election in May of Menachem Begin as Israel's new Premier. A militant superhawk and ultra-Zionist, Begin had been arrested years before for "unacceptable" activity in the Lithuanian sector of the Soviet Union. Imprisoned in Siberia for a year--some of it in solitary—he arrived in Palestine in 1942 and promptly became a leader in an underground terrorist group fighting the British, who ruled Palestine then under a League of Nations mandate. After the creation of Israel, Begin had led the right-wing Likud coalition in the Knesset, or parliament.

"Our people at State don't really know what to expect of him as Premier," Gene reported.

Thanks to the help of experienced pros like Gene Krizek and Moon Mullins, travel plans were quickly put into place. But then, only two days before Jim Wright and his delegation were scheduled to depart Washington, a totally unexpected diplomatic thunderbolt came from Egypt.

In a speech that stunned the world, President Anwar Sadat abruptly announced to the Egyptian People's Assembly in Cairo on November 9 that he was willing to go to Jerusalem in a personal quest for peace with Israel.

In foreign ministries around the world, diplomats dropped their leather-covered pipes and blinked in disbelief. Could this be true? Could such a pledge really have come from the iron-willed Islamic leader who had thrown his armies into four bloody wars against the Israelis? From the fierce military commander who had vowed only months before never even to speak with Israel as long as a single one of its soldiers stood on captured Egyptian soil?

Left speechless for once, many foreign policy experts thought maybe the news dispatches from Cairo were wrong—that it was some kind of mistake, perhaps a slip of the tongue. Yet, of Sadat's exact words to his parliament, there could be no doubt:

"There is no time to lose. I am ready to go to the ends of the earth if that will save one of my soldiers, one of my officers, from being scratched. I am ready to go to their house, to the Knesset, to discuss peace with the Israeli leaders."

In these three sentences, Anwar Sadat had thrown out the rule book. There was a new day in the quest for peace between the world's most powerful Arab nation and its arch enemy, Israel.

In light of Sadat's momentous announcement, Jim Wright was even more eager to pursue the conferences he had scheduled in the Middle East, and he left Washington with his delegation as scheduled on November 11. All across the Atlantic and during our scheduled three-day stopover in Madrid, the Congressmen seized hungrily upon every scrap of news available from Cairo and Jerusalem. Between visits with President Adolfo Saurez and other Spanish leaders, the American lawmakers pored over news stories and State Department dispatches on the developing international drama in the Middle East.

Then, on November 14, our last day in Madrid, Sadat wiped away any lingering doubts about his electrifying speech to parliament. In an interview with Walter Cronkite, the Egyptian President reaffirmed that he had meant exactly what he said. If Israeli Premier Menachem Begin would extend a formal invitation, he would go to Jerusalem and speak before the Israeli parliament in a personal search for peace.

That afternoon, as our plane climbed over the Mediterranean and turned on course toward Cairo, Jim Wright and members of the delegation gathered in little clusters, speculating on where all this might lead. These men all were accomplished political pros, and they talked shop.

"It's ironic for an old Zionist warhorse like Begin to have this kind of an opportunity for peace fall right into his lap," observed one Congressman.

"Yeah, but it'll take a tough right-winger like him to make it work. It took Richard Nixon, remember, to recognize Red China. No Democrat on earth could have got away with that," remarked a colleague.

"It's not Begin who'll get into trouble about this--it's Sadat. How do you think it's going to set with the PLO and other Arabs to see Sadat go trotting off all by himself to Jerusalem?" ventured a third member.

As darkness gathered and our big jet whirred on toward Cairo, the passenger cabin crackled with a sense of excitement and expectancy unlike any I had felt in 15 years on Capitol Hill. Tomorrow we would meet President Anwar Sadat.

Accompanying the Majority Leader on this trip were 13 members of the House. Five were prominent Republicans. As Administrative Assistant to the Majority Leader, I was aboard, along with Kathy Mitchell, Jim Wright's longtime personal secretary. With us also were Gene Krizek, Moon Mullins, nine other Congressional staff members and five Air Force escort officers.

On official trips like this, protocol encouraged spouses to accompany the delegation, provided there was space available on the plane and the government incurred no expense for their food or lodging. Jim Wright's wife Betty and daughter Ginger went along, as did the wives of most other members. And I was lucky enough to find a seat for my wife Eddie.

Like most Special Air Mission transport planes based at Andrews Air Force Base near Washington, our VC-137 was a virtual flying command post. Behind the flight deck and crew quarters was a compartment jammed with high-tech electronic gear. We could talk with the White House, with the Pentagon and I suppose, if need be, with a Buddhist monk at a pay phone in Tibet.

A reconfigured version of the Boeing 707 in elegant military dress, our plane was a thing of beauty. Painted proudly on its rudder was an American flag, and on its gleaming white fuselage the words THE UNITED STATES OF AMERICA. An Air Force officer told me this particular plane was used as Air Force One by President Lyndon B. Johnson. In its forward lounge were easy chairs, a television and a comfortable sofa. Adjoining it was a coffee table that would have enthralled the editors of *Popular Mechanics*. At the punch of a button, the coffee table rose to become a desk--perfect for the times Jim Wright called Kathy up from the passenger compartment to dictate memos.

Landing about 8 o'clock that night at Cairo Airport, we were met by formal delegation headed by U.S. Ambassador Hermann Eilts. A respected, no-nonsense authority on the Middle East, Eilts also had a penchant for wanting to take charge.

As the ranking Congressional staffer on the trip, I received a message relayed to the plane from Eilts while we were taxiing up to the ramp. Eilts, whom I had never met, directed me to have the members of Congress and their wives exit the plane by the front door. Staff people, he specified, were to leave through the rear door. Instead of acquiescing to the order and then making a fool of myself by publicly bellyaching about it, as another Congressional person would do in a later year, I ignored it. I stood back, as I customarily did, until the Congressmen and their wives had finished deplaning. Then I led the staff people in marching out the same damn door.

On our way to meet President Sadat the next day, our bus drew enthusiastic welcomes from street crowds, even though it was obvious that Cairo and its citizens faced colossal problems. In a city expected to accommodate two and a half million people, it then had nine million, with another two million commuting to the city to work each day. Over the preceding 20 years, 34 per cent of Egypt's wealth had gone for war and defense.

Egypt's economy and budget, like the streets of Cairo, were a mess.

Yet the Barrages was only one of ten homes the Egyptian government maintained for President Sadat. On a tree-shaded plot beside the Nile north of Cairo, this was his favorite. Our delegation with its police escort arrived shortly after noon on Tuesday, November 15, and we were welcomed inside to a large, airy room. Because he caught cold easily, the President refused air conditioning.

Lean and handsome in a dark pin-striped suit, Sadat was exuberant as he greeted our delegation. Obviously delighted that his 50-word utterance to parliament had captured the imagination of the world, he agreed to news media requests to allow coverage of our meeting. From behind a thicket of microphones, bathed in television lights, he opened the session with a personal tribute to President Jimmy Carter as a man of peace and a man of his word. He urged continued U.S. efforts to push peace talks.

Still eager to have the word from Sadat's own lips, Jim Wright said he understood U.S. envoys soon would relay to Sadat a personal invitation from Premier Begin to visit Jerusalem. Would Sadat go?

"Whenever the invitation arrives, I will be ready to go," he declared.

Then, in an hour-long give-and-take session, Sadat gave our group what seemed to be his frank assessment of the seemingly endless list of knotty and convoluted problems that for centuries had frustrated would-be peacemakers in the Middle East.

The next day, Wednesday November 16, we left Egypt for our flight to Tel Aviv, where special buses were to take us on to Jerusalem. Aboard the airplane, the atmosphere of expectancy seemed to grow with the passing miles. But there still had been no official word on the invitation Begin was reportedly preparing.

At a table in the main passenger compartment, Jim Wright was hunched over a portable typewriter, pecking out his account of our meeting with Sadat. It was another of the daily dispatches he always tried to send to the *Fort Worth Star-Telegram*. The paper usually published them intact under his by-line. On any international trip, Jim Wright routinely did this—for two good reasons. For one, these personalized accounts let people back home know exactly what he was doing on foreign trips. Secondly, the day-by-day stories, crammed with details of official activities, virtually guaranteed that no future political opponent could ever accuse him of wasting taxpayers' money on a pleasure junket.

"What do you think of this?" he said, handing me the story.

I read it over. It was pretty good, but my 12 years as a newspaperman compelled me to pick a few nits. "Might want to take a look at a couple of little things—here and there," I said.

He did a little editing and gave the story back to me. Can you see that this gets out right away?" he asked.

"Sure," I said, immediately taking the copy forward to the VC-137's communications room. After talking with the two specialists there, I returned to our compartment. Knowing Jim Wright enjoyed feigning distrust of modern technology, I felt certain what his first question would be.

"Did you get that story sent?"

"Yes, sir,"

"What did you do—telephone somebody in Washington and dictate it to them?"

"No, sir. The communications guys up front sent it out by radio teletype."

"Radio teletype? What do you mean?"

"Well, it's a little machine like a typewriter. The communications guys punch out the story on the keyboard and it's received in the Pentagon. From there it will go to our office and the *Star-Telegram*."

"You mean it goes by radio from this airplane to the Pentagon?"

"Yes, sir, but not directly."

"What do you mean, 'not directly'?"

"Well, they bounce it off the Telstar satellite."

Jim Wright frowned. "Marshall, they can't do that," he said gravely.

"All right, you caught me," I said, laughing. "The truth is, I took your story and stuck it in an empty wine bottle I got from the steward. Then I threw it out the window. With any luck, in a day or two a passing ship will pick it up in the Mediterranean."

"At least I understand that," he said, chuckling.

As we arrived that evening in Jerusalem, there was a new development. In a nighttime briefing in the historic King David Hotel, Samuel Lewis, the American Ambassador, told us the Knesset had voted 83-3 to extend a formal invitation to Sadat. The three nay votes came from Communist members who opposed the government anyway. Begin's invitation had been sent, but no response had come from Cairo.

Still uncertain what part, in any, our delegation would play if Sadat did come to Jerusalem, we proceeded on Thursday, November 17, with our original schedule. First there was a deeply moving visit to Yad Vashem, Israel's national memorial to the six million Jews who died in Hitler's death camps. From there Jim Wright led his colleagues into meetings with Knesset leaders, including Speaker Itzhak Shamir and other top-level officials. Dominating each of these conversations was the heightening prospect of Anwar Sadat's visit.

"That will be a very great day," said Foreign Minister Moshe Dayan.

Our final visit was to the office of Premier Begin, and it was there that I shared with my wife and two treasured friends probably the most historically significant moment of my life.

While Jim Wright and the delegation waited in a nearby meeting room, Gene Krizek, Moon Mullins, Eddie and I were huddled in a small adjoining room, checking over events on our schedule.

Without warning, a door popped open and Menachem Begin himself dashed in, aflame with excitement.

"He's coming! He's coming!" he cried. "We just received word! President Sadat is coming to Jerusalem!"

Thunderstruck, we four Americans were speechless. Realizing we were probably the first persons on earth to hear this momentous news, we began trying to congratulate the ecstatic

Premier. I don't even remember what I said, but I remember exactly what he said.

"You can't tell where this will end," he bubbled. "Maybe even I will go to Cairo. I've always wanted to see the Pyramids."

I grinned.

"We built them, you know," he laughed, eyes sparkling behind his owlish, black-rimmed glasses.

Then, hurrying into the next room, the Premier made his triumphant announcement to Jim Wright and the delegation. As a wave of cheers, applause and congratulations engulfed the room, I got the idea that the visiting Americans thought maybe the diminutive Israeli statesman stood a bit taller than he had a few minutes before.

The schedule called for President Sadat to arrive in Jerusalem about 7:30 p.m. Saturday, November 19. His speech to the Knesset was set for Sunday evening. Under our present schedule, we were supposed to leave Sunday morning. While I felt sure we would be invited to stay, there was another question.

It was posed by Michael Levenson, a brainy young officer with the Israeli Foreign Ministry. Since our arrival, Michael and I had worked closely together on the schedule and arrangements. Only the night before, we had shared a few drinks in the Air Force hospitality room on the sixth floor of the King David Hotel, where our delegation's rooms were located.

Like many younger Israelis, Michael had seen fierce combat as an Israeli soldier. As we talked of his country's seemingly endless wars with Arab nations, Michael mentioned, hesitantly at first, a few personal recollections of combat. Then, with deepening emotion, he described the terror, tumult and carnage of desert battle. It was as if the implicit promise of Sadat's visit, together with our hospitality room bourbon, had enabled this upcoming young Foreign Ministry officer to share some of his innermost feelings with this balding older fellow who seemed interested and sympathetic.

Sitting in a quiet corner of the room, eyes glistening, Michael spoke in a raspy whisper that sounded almost as fervent as a prayer. "Maybe this visit will lead to a day," he said, "when my sons will not have to fight four wars just to protect their homes."

Now, on Thursday evening, Michael had returned to the King David. Pulling me aside, he said the Israeli government was preparing to impose the most stringent security measures in history to protect Anwar Sadat during his stay in Jerusalem. It would be disastrous, he emphasized, for even the slightest harm to befall the Egyptian President while here. Any such happening would enrage every Arab nation in the world and possibly trigger another war. So security teams would be on high alert every moment. Soldiers armed with Uzi submachine guns would be deployed every few feet around the King David, he said. Moreover, the hotel would be emptied of all guests except the Anwar Sadat and Jim Wright delegations. Then, apologetically, Michael came to the point.

Security experts believed the hotel's the sixth floor offered the safest location available, so the Israeli government was reluctantly requesting our delegation to move down to the fourth floor, leaving the sixth to handle Sadat and his staff. Michael apologized for the inconvenience, but said the security people considered it essential.

As Michael talked, it occurred to me that of all people, Premier Begin certainly ought to know the vulnerabilities of the King David Hotel. In his days as an anti-British terrorist in the 1940's, he tried to blow up the place. I didn't mention this, of course. However amusing it was to me, I didn't figure Michael would find it so.

Apologetic about having to ask us to move, Michael said we would given almost identical rooms on the fourth floor "for the remainder of your stay." While I was certain Jim Wright would cooperate with Israeli security, Michael's words gave me an opening to check on our own schedule.

"And what day do you think we will be leaving?" I asked.

"Your schedule calls for your departure on Sunday morning," Michael replied.

"I know. I had just thought that in view of the close relationship between Israel and the United States, the Foreign Ministry might think it would be useful for us to stay."

Michael looked me squarely in the eye. "Would the Majority Leader want to stay?"

The truth is that I had never asked Jim Wright. But to me it would have been incomprehensible to consider departing on the eve of such an historic event.

"Of course," I said.

"Let me do some checking," he said.

Even though Eddie recognized at once how essential it was to protect Sadat, she did a little good-natured grousing as she began packing our bags.

"Just think of it this way—we are giving up our bed in the cause of peace in the Middle East," I said. She threw a pillow at me.

But then, to my astonishment, a few members of the delegation said we should pick up and leave Jerusalem. It was difficult for me to believe, but they resented being asked to move down to the fourth floor.

"If they make us to change floors, let's just change countries," one member huffed.

"How do we know we are even welcome?" another demanded.

Privately surprised at these complaints on the eve of a happening of such worldwide significance, Jim Wright called his colleagues together for a hurried caucus. As the State Department's ranking official on our trip, Gene Krizek asked and received the Majority Leader's permission to address the members. By all means, he told them, they should remain.

"If we don't stay to represent the United States at this historic event, President Carter will need to send another delegation, and I'm not sure there is time for him to do that," Gene declared.

Then, in the midst of the meeting, Jim Wright was summoned to the telephone. Premier Begin was calling to invite the delegation to stay for President Sadat's speech. He said special seats were being reserved in the Knesset for the visiting American lawmakers. Jim Wright tried to demur.

"Mr. Prime Minister, we appreciate that more than you can possibly realize," he said. "This is a moment like none other in history. But it would be very selfish of us to deny your own citizens the privilege of those precious seats. I have seen the Knesset gallery, and I know its limited space. You have at least a hundred valid claims among Israelis, I am sure, for each available seat. Therefore, I really think we should decline with grateful thanks and arrange an early departure so as to relieve you of any additional security worries or—"

"You don't understand, Mr. Leader," Begin interrupted. "We very much want you and your group from the American Congress to be present with us for this event. If you look outside you will see that three flags are being raised in front of the King David Hotel—ours, Egypt's, and that of the United States. We want you as parties to this historic moment."

We stayed.

When Anwar Sadat arrived on Saturday, he was greeted at the entrance to the King David by the impressive display of flags that Begin had ordered. To those in our party, the flags stirred a glow of national pride. On another level, I suppose these three flags standing together could have been seen as two combative brothers, warily coming together under the gaze of a caring but muscular friend.

At almost precisely 8 o'clock Saturday night, Sadat's presidential Boeing 707 taxied up to a red carpet on the ramp of Ben-Gurion Airport. Security people and dignitaries stood everywhere. From an Israeli army band burst a fanfare. Hundreds of reporters, television crews and photographers scrambled for better views. President Anwar Sadat of Egypt strode down the ramp.

Greeted warmly by Premier Begin and President Ephraim Katzir, Sadat was taken in tow and introduced to other high-level Israeli leaders lined up along the red carpet. Then Sadat saw the man he was looking for.

Ariel Sharon was the Israeli army commander who, during a counter-attack in the Yom Kippur War, led his troops across the Suez Canal into Egypt.

"I wanted to catch you there," Sadat said, smiling.

"I'm glad to have you here," his old adversary replied.

As the Egyptian President stepped, confident and smiling, into the lobby of the King David Hotel amid the glare of television lights and swarming newspeople, he drew cheers and applause. Looking down from the mezzanine, I remember thinking this scene was about as close to the millennium as I was ever likely to see.

The next day, in an act of hospitality unthinkable only weeks before, Sadat was accorded and accepted an invitation to pray in

Jerusalem's Al Aksa Mosque and to visit the neighboring Dome of the Rock. This is a site revered by both Muslims and Jews. In Islamic belief, it was from here that Mohammed rose to heaven to talk with God and then, with God's blessing, returned to earth to spread Islam. To Jews, it is the holy ground where Abraham prepared to follow God's command to sacrifice his son Isaac, as well as the location of Solomon's Temple.

The home of Israel's unicameral legislature, the Knesset, is an impressive chamber whose seating is laid out in the pattern of a menorah, Judaism's symbolic seven-branch candlestick. On entering the chamber on the evening of Sunday, November 20, Sadat was greeted by more applause. He smiled, looking almost at home.

As he spoke in Arabic to the hushed chamber, Sadat's words were simultaneously translated into Hebrew and English and telecast around the world. From their special seats in the gallery, the American Congressmen listened raptly—far more attentively than a few of them were accustomed to doing in the House chamber in Washington.

In an eloquent call for peace, Sadat emphatically recognized Israel's right to exist. "If you want to live with us in this part of the world, in sincerity I tell you that we welcome you among us with all security and safety," he declared.

But he warned that Israel must abandon its dreams of conquest and its belief that force was the best method of dealing with the Arabs. He said a lasting peace in the Middle East would depend on Israel's withdrawal from occupied Arab land, including East Jerusalem, which he had visited earlier in the day.

In his response, Begin praised Sadat's courage and joined his call for peace. But referring to land occupied by Israel, he vowed that Jews "will not be put in range of fire for annihilation."

While largely symbolic, Sadat's speech and Begin's response were at least a beginning. It would be ten months later, after repeated crises and disappointments, before President Jimmy Carter was able to bring Begin and Sadat together. In the seclusion of Camp David, the presidential retreat in the mountains of Maryland, Carter shuttled tirelessly for 13 days between the cabins of his two guests, seeking to allay suspicions, build trust and fashion compromises. Finally, on September 17, 1978, Carter stood with Begin and Sadat for the signing of agreements which, six agonizing months later, established a peace which endures today between Egypt and Israel.

But ancient antagonisms do not die easily.   Hatred and bloodshed still haunt many parts of the Middle East, and perhaps they always will.   But before we write off the whole thing as hopeless, we should remember that for a few shining moments in the late 1970's, three courageous and devoutly religious men--a Christian, a Jew and a Muslim—chalked up at least one modest score for the peacemakers.   Even for this tiny, tortuous step, I believe Mr. Goltzman and Harry Friedlander would have been grateful.

14

Adventures
of an Advance Man

If a Presidential campaign reminds you of a circus, the kinship
may be closer than you think.

Both a circus and a national political campaign thrive on
crowds, color and excitement. Both feature bands, balloons,
pretty girls in glittering costumes and performers who are either
famous or soon hope to be.

Not often do these ingredients appear spontaneously. Thus
both circuses and Presidential candidates have developed methods
to create them synthetically.

America's first circus performance was presented by a Scottish
immigrant named John Bill Ricketts. His show opened in 1793 in
Philadelphia, where, of course, only six years earlier, a bunch of
wise old birds in pigtails drew up the parchment document that
made Presidential campaigns necessary in the first place. George
Washington, who had been elected to his second term in 1792,
attended the Ricketts circus opening performance.

At some point after that, perhaps when crowds began to slack
off, Mr. Ricketts or some other circus impresario may have
started looking for ways to put more paying customers in the
bleachers. History doesn't say so, but I can imagine old man
Ricketts saying:

"Hey, Sylvester—methinks I got a hot idea for stirring up
bigger crowds. How grabbest you the notion of sending out a few
guys to put up posters and handbills?"

"Everybody in Philly already knows the circus is here, boss,"
Sylvester could have replied.

"Not here, dummy. I'm talking about one-horse towns where we ain't played yet. Go out in the boonies and stir up the yokels before we get there. Get the rubes excited. You know, send in some savvy promoters—some advance men."

In the remote possibility that any conversation like this ever took place, Mr. Ricketts undoubtedly did not know he was creating a whole new breed of specialists—*genus advance circus-politicus*, the creature known today as The Advance Man..

This chapter, dear friends, is an attempt to give you an inside peek at the role of the advance man, now known as either (1) the unseen hero of political triumph or (2) the convenient fall guy for political disaster. [Check one.]

Even though political advance men today face different and more sophisticated tasks, their predecessors of the circus world also had their hands full—finding and leasing the show grounds, getting the required licenses, contracting for supplies, buying newspaper advertising, posting billboards and distributing handbills.

For modern political advance men—particularly those in Presidential campaigns—the responsibilities are considerably more imposing. These faceless technicians descend on a city several days in advance of the visit. Day and night they work feverishly to guarantee that from the moment their candidate steps out of the airplane until wheels up on departure, he wrings the maximum political benefit out of every costly and precious campaign moment.

Usually working in teams of three or four, these largely anonymous figures must find ways to stroke political friends, outwit foes, pander to the press, coordinate with the Secret Service, draw up schedules, develop routes, organize motorcades, raise crowds, build platforms, choose welcomers, arrange photo ops, hang banners, make signs, hire bands, set up sound systems, arrange dinners, rent rooms, scrounge up campaign money, jot down thank-you names, make sure there are backups for everything on this list and, most important of all, be prepared to take the blame for anything that goes wrong. And something *will* go wrong. Trust me.

While the historical record is hazy on advance men in Presidential campaigns before 1960, this highly specialized craft first began to creep into public awareness in the battle between John F. Kennedy and Richard M. Nixon. Awed by the effectiveness of these agents in the Kennedy campaign, Theodore H. White wrote in his classic book, *The Making of the President, 1960:*

" 'Advance men'—the small teams of agents who arrange the tours of major candidates—are practitioners of one of the most complicated skills in American politics; a good advance man must combine in himself the qualities of a circus tout, a carnival organizer, an accomplished diplomat and a quartermaster-general."

Considering the demands and perils of the job, what kind of people are foolish enough to take on advance assignments? Who are these political kamikazes? Where do they come from? The answer is, from just about everywhere. By and large, they are volunteers—lawyers, PR guys, lobbyists, Washington reps of large companies, political appointees or Hill staffers, local or state officeholders, you name it.

Once exclusively the domain of testosterone, the ranks of advance people today include a small number of women. Even in this enlightened age, however, males still dominate the field—especially in Presidential campaigns.

Usually they are people whose political savvy and talents have impressed the candidate they're working for. Some live in places like Dubuque or Schenectady, but most live in Washington. They generally have jobs that enable them to take off with virtually no advance notice at all. Take, for example, the experience of my friend Ken Burns.

As a young Texas lawyer, Kenneth H. Burns came to Washington in the early 1960's as a Capitol Hill staffer. When Lyndon Johnson became President, Ken was working at the Federal Maritime Commission and serving occasionally as an advance man for Johnson. A week or so before Christmas in 1967, Ken was sitting at his desk, grateful that the government bureaucracy was spooling down for the holidays. The last thing he expected was a call from Marvin Watson at the White House with an urgent question.

"Can you be at Andrews in an hour?"

"Uh, er—yes, I guess so," Ken stammered. "What is it—an advance?"

"Yes. And it's important. Are you certain you can make it to Andrews in an hour?"

"I'll make it. Where we going?"

"I'll tell you on the plane. Have you had your shots?"

"Shots? You mean like for going overseas? No, I don't think so."

"That's all right. We'll give 'em to you on the plane. Remember now—Andrews. One hour from now."

And that is how Ken Burns departed, without so much as a clean shirt or a toothbrush, for Australia. Prime Minister Harold Holt had drowned while swimming, and President Lyndon B. Johnson, as he was prone to do, made an abrupt decision. He would attend Holt's memorial service in Melbourne.

While advance men once were used mainly in high-profile political campaigns, they proved so useful that today they are dispatched to make arrangements for almost all top-level government officials on important trips. Today, whether it's a televised Presidential debate in Des Moines or an official NATO conference in Brussels, advance men are usually there to smooth out the bumps.

Of the Presidential and Congressional figures for whom I did advances, my fondest recollections center around Hubert H. Humphrey—one of the finest men I ever knew.

In the mid-1960's Humphrey, then Vice President, made a special trip to Fort Worth to speak to a big dinner staged by supporters of my boss, Jim Wright. Most arrangements for the Vice President's visit were made by one of the Congressman's staffers in Fort Worth—Joseph L. Shosid, a man of many talents.

Besides working part-time for the Congressman, Joe ran his own lucrative advertising and public relations firm. In addition, his prowess as a basketball referee kept him in demand all over the Southwest. And if all that weren't enough to keep him busy, Joe was an ambitious and tireless member of the U.S. Air Force Reserve. Eventually he worked his way up to Major General.

Like many of us, the Vice President was impressed with Joe's wide-ranging skills, his organizational ability and, perhaps most of all, his maddening thoroughness. Never in his entire life had Joe Shosid left anything to chance. Everybody occasionally makes a "things to do" list, but with Joe such a list took on almost reverential importance. Once returning to his office at midnight, his list happened to slip out of his hand and slither through a crack down an elevator shaft. Horrified, Joe rousted an elevator company workman out of bed and persuaded him to clamber down the shaft and retrieve the list.

Privately, I am sure, Humphrey thought, Aha!— a perfect advance man! So when Lyndon Johnson stunned the country by announcing on March 31, 1968, that he would not seek re-election, Humphrey launched his own campaign for President— and promptly enlisted Joe Shosid as one of his key advance men.

A week or so later, Joe gave my name to Humphrey's advance chiefs and they asked if I would like to help. Intrigued by a chance for an insider's role in a campaign for a candidate I genuinely admired, I asked Jim Wright if it would be OK. Sure, he said, as long as I did the advances on my own time, rather than when I was being paid to work for the government.

Hubert Humphrey's 1968 Presidential campaign was less than three weeks old when I found myself on an airplane, outward bound on my first advance and thoroughly intimidated—for two reasons. First, I had no idea what was in the inch-thick pile of advance instructions that was abruptly plopped into my hands just before I climbed on the plane at National Airport. Even worse, I began to consider my destination—Huntington, West Virginia.

West Virginia, I thought. Grimly I remembered that it was there, eight years before, that Hubert Humphrey had suffered probably the most humiliating defeat of his life. As a 1960 Presidential hopeful in the bellwether West Virginia primary, the Minnesota Senator was beaten 2 to 1. In some wards the defeat was a mortifying 20 to 1. The winner was a charming, bushy-haired young man with an Ivy League look, armed with apparently unlimited campaign money and the most ruthlessly efficient political organization West Virginia had ever seen. It was this thunderous primary victory that launched Senator John F. Kennedy on his course toward the White House.

Even now, as the plane cruised westward, I realized that for Hubert Humphrey, it would require a large measure of political courage even to venture back into this state where he had encountered such a devastating loss. I promised myself that at least on this advance, on my watch, I would do my doggonedest to see that everything went right and that no opportunity was missed.

For the next two days, I worked with Hal Lauth, an experienced Humphrey advance man, to make sure everything was in readiness for Humphrey's speech to students in an "Impact 68" program at Marshall University's Gullickson Hall. With the diligence of a 747 captain and first officer running through a preflight checklist, Hal and I made plans to cover every imaginable contingency. At least we thought we had.

The Vice President, as ebullient as ever, arrived at Huntington's Tri-State Airport as scheduled on April 24. He was greeted by Governor Hulett C. Smith, who had maintained a careful neutrality in the bitter Humphrey-Kennedy battles eight years earlier. After that, everything on Humphrey's latest visit went smoothly for, say, maybe 15 minutes.

Our carefully organized motorcade was speeding toward Marshall University. Suddenly the car just ahead—the one carrying the Vice President— skidded to a stop. A traffic accident? An assassination attempt? Secret Service agents began piling out of their cars. Then I saw it.

Humphrey's Drug Store, proclaimed the big sign over the building at the edge of the road. It was an advance man's dream— a one-in-a-thousand photo opportunity. A golden chance for a warm and fuzzy feature story about a small-town drug store owner in West Virginia being flabbergasted to have a drop-in visit by another Humphrey—himself once a pharmacist in the family drug store back in Huron, South Dakota. Only now the visitor was not a pharmacist. He was Vice President of the United States.

To spot an opportunity like this was one of the most important parts of an advance man's job—and I had missed it. But Hubert Humphrey hadn't—even when he was in a motorcade whistling by at 40 miles an hour. If Humphrey doesn't win the Presidency, I thought, with eyes that sharp he would have a great future as somebody's advance man.

It was in West Virginia also that I focused for the first time on what Humphrey described as his trouble with his "glands"—his own wry explanation for his inability to stop talking. He would talk anytime to anybody about any subject. In his four years as Mayor of Minneapolis, he made an estimated 4,000 speeches, or about three a day. In 15 years in the Senate, he introduced nearly 1,500 bills and resolutions. He had so much to say he simply found it difficult to shut up.

In Gullickson Hall that night, the students loved him. But then, as he droned on and on, many began to squirm. Our schedule called for him to take off for Oxford, Mississippi, at 9:10 p.m. As that time passed, I approached one of the Secret Service agents who usually traveled with Humphrey.

"Do you have any idea how much longer he's going to talk?" I whispered.

"No," he said. "But it will be 20 minutes after he says, 'Ah, my friends, we live in a great country.' "

But this verbosity, I came to believe, was nothing more than the reflection of his personal effort, however naive, to right all the wrongs in the world. When somebody once snickered that Hubert Humphrey had more solutions than there are problems, Humphrey just smiled. "What's wrong with that?" he asked.

At any political event, the one indispensable ingredient is a big crowd. It is the measure by which news reporters judge the popularity—and thus the electability—of a candidate. Thus an advance man always tries to have an event in a location that will make a crowd look biggest. In other words, if you are fairly certain to have 1,000 people, look for an auditorium that holds 750. For 100, find a room school classroom that accommodates 50.

When reporters covering the 1960 Presidential campaign became enthralled at the spectacle of crowds breaking through barriers to swarm joyously around John F. Kennedy, the lesson was not lost on Kennedy's advance man, Jerry Bruno. He began the practice of using two men, each holding one end of a rope, to restrain the crowd. Then, just at the right moment, he signaled the men to drop the rope, allowing spectators to surge forward and enthusiastically engulf Kennedy. Bruno later denied, however, that he used a handsaw to cut nearly through sawhorses to be used for crowd control, thus assuring their collapse at the most emotional moment.

With crowds occupying such a crucial role in a successful campaign appearance, advance men look for live bodies anywhere they can get them. But they must be wary of crowd-raising promises by self-promoters, screwballs and people with hare-brained ideas. This lesson I learned first-hand one pleasant June day in Florida.

With two other Humphrey advance men, I had been sent to prepare for an important campaign appearance by the Vice President. My companions were Sam Shipley, who in real life was

Secretary of Commerce for the State of Delaware, and Zel Lipsen, an up-and-coming Washington lawyer.

Outside, along the pristine white beach in the resort city of Bal Harbor, the brilliant afternoon sun glistened off the waves crashing in from the Atlantic. A bronzed young lifeguard studiously critiqued a girl in a blue bikini as she lay on a towel, rubbing lotion on her legs. Kids frolicked in the surf. All seemed right with the world.

But upstairs in Room 213 of the nearby Americana Hotel, the mood was darker.

"It's no use," Sam said, hanging up the phone. "They're still saying they can't help us."

"They've got to help us, dammit," I said. "They promised. We can't do it without them. Who did you talk to?"

"The president of the union. He said the business agent never told him anything about helping raise a crowd, and it's too late now to get his members organized."

"And this guy expects us to raise a crowd? Does he know we only got here last night? None of us knows a soul in this town."

Sam looked glum and stared at the floor.

"Well, so what are we going to do?" asked Zel, looking at me.

"Oh, it's simple," I snapped. "I'll just call Washington tell the Vice President that his advance men are glad he's coming to Florida, but sorry—we won't have anybody here to meet him."

Sam tried to look on the bright side. He pointed out that the American Federation of State, County and Municipal Employees, the group to which Humphrey was scheduled to speak the next day, would certainly have a group of its members out to meet him.

"I'm not talking about just a group," I said. "I'm talking about a *crowd*—a big crowd. People cheering and whistling. Teenagers jumping up and down. People trying to get Humphrey to kiss their babies. Come on, you guys—think."

Sam shifted in his chair. "Well, there was this one fellow..." he began.

"And?" Zel asked.

"While I was downstairs at lunch today I ran across this one fellow who acted like he might be able to help us raise a crowd," Sam continued.

"Yeah? Who is he?" I asked, frowning.

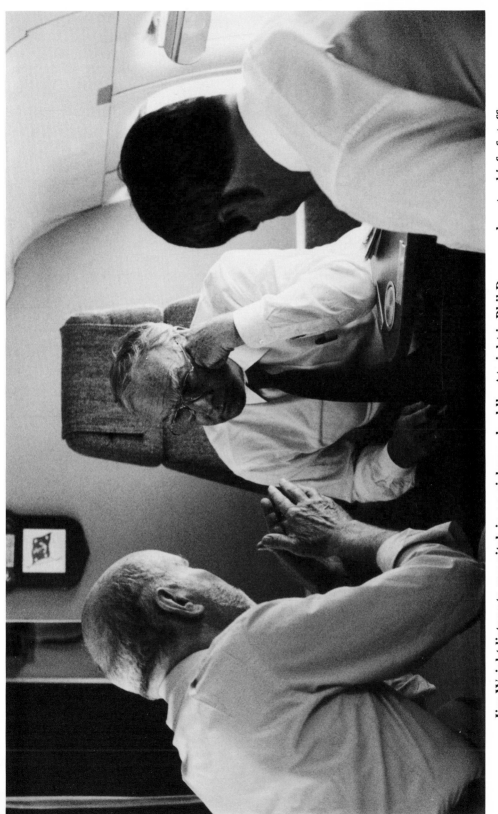

Jim Wright listens to my pitch in an airborne huddle. At right is Phil Duncan, deputy chief of staff.

My father, Lee Lynam, and his beloved flag.

Eddie returns triumphantly from a bargain-hunting expedition.

A young reporter interviews an American icon. (below)

Amid the tumult with Richard Nixon in the 1960 campaign.

On 1976 whistlestop campaign train, Jimmy Carter talks with a balding advance man (below).

**Claude D. Pepper spins one of his delightful stories
with a friend in the Speaker's office.**

**As an aviation writer in the 1950s, I volunteer
to test a new Bell Helicopter rescue device.**

Eddie and I pose proudly with our son and two daughters and their families at a Christmas gathering.

Even though experienced in the wilds of Washington, George Troutman and I are novices in the woods of East Texas on a camping trip with Hans Weichsel.

Kathy Mitchell, Eddie and I (front row) pose with Egyptian President Anwar Sadat on the eve of his historic pilgrimage to Jerusalem in 1977.

Only moments after receiving confirmation that Sadat's trip is definitely on, an elated Israeli Prime Minister Menachem Begin pauses a moment for the photographer.

The proudest achievements of Eddie and Marshall Lynam—Marsha Ann, Charles Lee and Sharon Kaye (left to right).

Twice the U.S. government has invited me to fly in a B-17 Flying Fortress. These guys—my old War War II bomber crew—were with me the first time. I'm the tall skinny guy standing second from right.

My friend Congressman Jim Oberstar of Minnesota snapped this picture
of the grizzled captain of the good ship *Emily Morgan* on the Potomac.

Three generations of Lynams—
Charles, Marshall Joseph, age one, and
Marshall Lee, somewhat older.

Eddie Lynam usually flits around
Arlington, Virginia, in her '92
Honda Accord, but in Cairo she tried
another means of conveyance.

When Eddie could not blow out all the candles on her birthday cake, a family friend graciously offered to help.

Lieutenant Colonel Lanny Lancaster, Jim Wright's first appointee to the U.S. Air Force Academy, prepares to take a hitchhiker for a ride in a Fort Worth-built F-16 fighter.

As a reporter, I found that some interview subjects were more careful than others about the notes I was taking.

Speaker Jim Wright introduces me to Mikhail Gorbachev in the Kremlin in 1987.

Leading the highest-ranking U.S. Congressional delegation ever to visit Moscow, Jim Wright arrives at Soviet war monument.

Candid shot of Mikhail Gorbachev during meeting with Speaker Wright's delegation.

With U.S.Embassy escorts, outside St. Basil's Cathedral in Red Square.

An Air Force lieutenant colonel offers congratulations on my survival
after a parachute leap into Biscayne Bay.

The logistics were far from simple, but
two Texans, Wayne Franke, right, and
Mario Martinez, left, staged a spectacu-
larly successful chili supper for our Soviet
hosts in Moscow.

Speaker Jim Wright renders a
harmonica solo at the chili supper in
Spaso House, official residence of
the U.S. ambassador.

It's been a pleasure having you aboard NORFOLK!
[signature]
CDR, USN

Spring, 1986, aboard nuclear submarine Norfolk.

I enjoyed visiting the *U.S.S. Norfolk*, but the view is considerably better from a B-17.

On a dare, I joined the native dancers at an aborigine village near Sun Moon Lake in Taiwan in 1980. Then I found out one of our group had a camera.

In an effort to surpass my performance in Taiwan, I try a Spanish dance in Madrid.

In Fort Worth, in Washington, or in Moscow, the late Seth Kantor was one of the finest friends a guy could ever have had.

My sister and brother and their spouses. From left, Richard and Gwen Tilley, Marshall and Eddie Lynam, and Marie and Jimmy Lynam.

Even in my early days as an aviation writer, I was not above hamming it up for the camera.

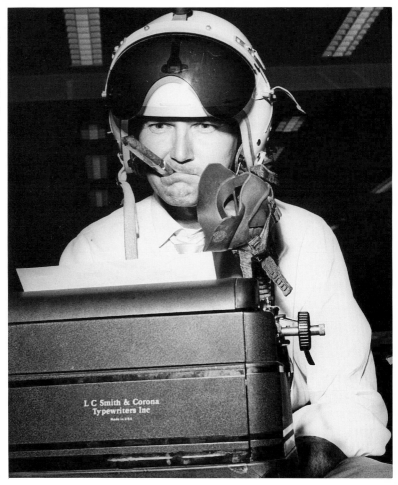

Our oldest grandson, Michael Williams, tries to straighten out President Reagan in this composite (faked, that is) photograph.

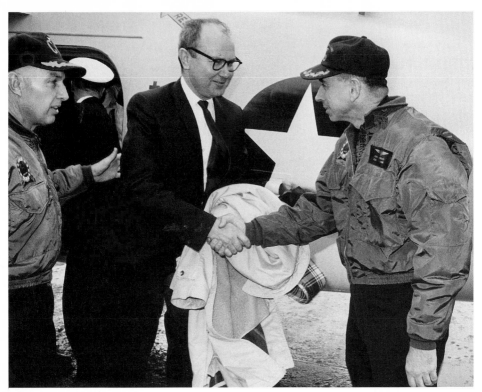

Having survived my first landing aboard an aircraft carrier, I receive warm greetings from officers of the *U.S.S. Independence.* (U.S. Navy photograph)

Two wild and wooly cow-pokes in big hats are a-fixin' to board a bus in Waco as guests of then-Con-gress-man Marvin Leath.

Sam said the man identified himself as a public relations specialist who handled all kinds of beachfront promotions. When Sam mentioned that he was one of three guys who just arrived in Bal Harbor as advance men for Hubert Humphrey, the PR guy started gushing about how much he admired the Vice President.

"How would this guy go about raising a crowd?" I asked.

"He didn't say. But he said he thought he could help us, and wouldn't charge us a cent."

"Get him on the phone. It can't hurt to ask him if he can drop by and tell us what he's got in mind."

We met later that afternoon in the hotel cocktail lounge. Having been exposed on Capitol Hill to a variety of self-promoters and con men with axes to grind, I was instinctively wary. I was not greatly reassured when this guy showed up in a sports jacket flashy enough to use as a maritime distress signal and a diamond ring that would have choked a goat. Despite my misgivings, I explained that Vice President Humphrey was arriving the next afternoon and we needed help in raising a big crowd outside the hotel.

"All right—picture this," he ordered. "First we alert the media that the Vice President is going to get a big surprise."

"Yes?"

"And then, just as the Vice President arrives, here comes the surprise! It's speeding along the ocean near the hotel! And what do we see?"

"Don't play games with us. What are you talking about?"

"The symbol of the Democratic Party!" he cried triumphantly.

Sam and Zel and I looked at each other. Clearly they were as much in the dark as I was. "OK—what is it?" I ventured.

"Don't you know what the symbol of your own party is?" our new acquaintance demanded.

"Are you talking about a donkey?" Zel asked.

"Certainly!" whooped our friend.

"You're going to bring in a donkey by boat?" demanded Sam.

"By boat? Of course not!" cried the PR man.

We three wizard advance men looked blankly at each other.

"On water skis!" he exclaimed.

I pondered this imaginary scene for a moment. "Are you trying to tell us you have a donkey that you can bring in on water skis?"

For a moment our PR friend fell silent. It was if we had ferreted out his innermost secret. "Well, actually, no. I don't have a donkey any more," he admitted.

"Did he drown?" I asked.

"No, natural causes. But I've got the next best thing."

"And what would that be?" I said.

"A Shetland pony."

"You really do have a Shetland pony that water skis?"

"You bet! How about it?"

"I'm afraid we could never pass off a Shetland pony as a Democratic donkey," I said gravely.

"Not even if I put some big ears on him?" he said hopefully.

I thanked the man for his time, gulped down a double vodka, and went back to my room to begin making some calls. I was looking for people who might like to come down and greet the Vice President the next day—preferably wearing their own ears.

Thanks to the AFSCME union members staying at the hotel, we finally rounded up a decent number to greet him on his arrival. But in addition to the crowd problem, we had another crisis. It came in an urgent telephone call only a few hours before the Vice President's plane was due to arrive.

"Say, you know those buses I was supposed to get to take those news reporters to the airport?"

"Yes, that's all set, isn't it? You've got them, haven't you?" I asked, dreading his answer.

"Well, not exactly. I wasn't able to make the arrangements," he mumbled.

Having worked 12 years in the newspaper business, I did not need to be told that political reporters expect and require exalted treatment. If disappointed in this respect, they can wreak terrible vengeance on candidates for public office. For 30 or 40 reporters and television news people to be promised a press bus which never materializes would create a scene unsuitable for small children and adults with coronary problems.

Grabbing the phone book, I looked up the bus company with the biggest advertisement in the yellow pages. By invoking the name of Vice President at 30-second intervals, I managed not only to charter a bus but also to persuade the company to send the bill to Humphrey headquarters in Washington. I guess that bill finally was paid, because I didn't receive a telephone call like the one Norman Sherman got.

As Humphrey's longtime press secretary, Norm possessed a response capability as instantaneous as one of those scary Cray supercomputers. No matter how unexpected or off-the-wall the question, Norm never failed to come up with an immediate answer which always sounded reasonable and was often accurate. In 1969, a year after the election, he was with Humphrey in Minnesota when he got a telephone call from an "action line" reporter for a Chicago newspaper.

The reporter was calling on behalf of a Peoria, Illinois, airplane pilot who complained that nobody had ever paid his $300 bill for sky-writing he performed at Humphrey campaign rallies.

"Who hired this sky-writer?" Norm asked.

Naming a key Humphrey advance man, the reporter demanded: "Why hasn't he been paid?"

"He misspelled HHH," Norm replied.

Despite this inspired response, Norm got orders from Humphrey to see that the bill was paid. Not all political campaign creditors, of course, are so fortunate. Money is always a problem. Take, for example, the Great Doughnut Crisis.

This little drama occurred in 1976, as Jimmy Carter's Presidential campaign was beginning to pick up speed. Carter's people had called me and said they needed an experienced advance man to work with some younger staffers in Newark, New Jersey. Even though I was told I would have to scare up money for whatever supplies I needed, the assignment seemed simple enough. Carter was to hold an early-morning rally in Manhattan. Then the former Georgia governor would climb aboard a special train for a whistlestop tour—similar, he hoped, to the train trips that helped Harry Truman score a spectacular upset victory over Thomas Dewey in 1948.

First stop on the Carter whistlestop would be Newark. My job would be to make sure there was a big, enthusiastic crowd there. Then, as the rally ended, I was to board the train to lend a hand at other appearances en route to a big, windup rally in Chicago.

Arriving in Newark, my first job was fairly easy. From local Carter supporters I rounded up several hundred dollars to print the handbills announcing the candidate's forthcoming visit. Arrangements already were in place for the banners, the band music and signs, but I figured we were going to need a big supply of free coffee and doughnuts to build and hold a crowd on a chilly morning at the Newark railroad station.   This was a problem, because Carter headquarters had warned us there was no money— not even for coffee and doughnuts.

So frugal was the budget that one of the campaign volunteers from Atlanta knocked on my door at midnight a couple of days before Carter's arrival. He was young enough to be my son, and he looked worried.

"Tell me, sir," he said. "Are we doing everything we possibly can to get out a big crowd for Mr. Carter?"

"Considering that we have no money, yes—we're doing everything possible. Why do you ask?"

"Campaign headquarters in Atlanta just had me on the phone," he said anxiously. "They told me if we didn't have a big crowd here, they're not even going to give me a plane ticket back to Atlanta. They're going to make me hitchhike home."

I did my best to assure the young man that somebody in Atlanta was pulling his leg, but I'm not sure be believed me—and, for that matter, I'm not sure I believed me.

The next day I was lucky enough to find a businessman to pick up the coffee bill, which would run several hundred dollars. He drew the line, though, on the doughnuts.

Then I met a labor union official who agreed to give $500 for the doughnuts—on one condition.

"Rather than giving the money directly to you, I want to handle it through the Newark Democratic organization, so they will know our union participated," he explained. "But I'm sure they will gladly pass along the money to you for the doughnuts." He was wrong.

When finally, after a half dozen calls, I got through to the local Democratic chieftain, he had a question.

"Who ordered the doughnuts?" he growled.

"I did," I said.

"Then I suppose, Mr. Lynam, it's up to you to find a way to pay for them."

He was right, and I did. The crowd which cheered Jimmy Carter at the rail station the next day enjoyed the doughnuts.

When the doughnut man asked about his money, I gave him the name and phone number of my lovable friend at Democratic headquarters. "As the local Democratic leader, he will be delighted to defray Mr. Carter's expenses here, I'm sure," I told him. Then I got on the train for Chicago.

For an advance blunder that could have been seen by millions, however, nothing stands out like an incident on opening night of the 1988 Democratic National Convention in Atlanta. It was one of the most exciting moments of my life. I was standing on the platform. At my elbow was Jim Wright, the hometown man for whom I had worked for 26 years. As a lifelong Democrat and Speaker of the House, he was chairman of the convention—the boss of the whole dazzling shebang.

In a moment he would step to the rostrum to deliver the opening speech of the convention. The hall was packed. In the heady glare of the television lights, the cameras were focused and ready. America was waiting. As Jim Wright strode to the microphone and acknowledged the welcoming applause, I was almost bursting with pride. The TelePrompTer began rolling.

"When I was a boy in West Virginia..." scrolled the first few words. With a coast-to-coast television audience awaiting my boss' opening speech, the TelePrompTer crew had put on the speech of Senate Majority Leader Robert C. Byrd of West Virginia.

I didn't know whether to commit suicide or to wait a few minutes for Jim Wright to kill me. But then, to my astonishment and gratitude, I was saved by the Speaker's polished platform skills. He simply ignored the words flowing across the screen in front of him. Without a moment's hesitation, he smoothly began intoning from memory the words of his own speech. Flawlessly and forcefully, he delivered every ringing phrase that had been so carefully and lovingly crafted—a speech whose pages I knew still rested in the breast pocket of his coat. In the hall or out across the United States, nobody could possibly have detected the difference.

"I remembered it pretty well," he told me later. To me, his words were as welcome as a last-minute reprieve from the governor. He never again mentioned the matter. I didn't either.

The richest reward of advance work is an occasional chance to get to see, close-up and for real, some of the people future generations of Americans will read about in the history books. Hubert Humphrey will never be listed among those who made it to the big prize at 1600 Pennsylvania Avenue. Even though the malignant roots of the Vietnam war stretched back through the presidencies of Eisenhower and Kennedy, it was Lyndon Johnson and Hubert Humphrey who ultimately inherited most of the political blame for America's longest and most frustrating war.

In a way, though, it may be a blessing that Humphrey never became President. His heart may simply have been too big to cope with a job where there are hardly any decisions that don't hurt somebody, somewhere. Hubert Humphrey could have been the first casualty if he ever had been confronted with a decision like the one Harry Truman was forced to make on Hiroshima and Nagasaki.

For Humphrey wanted to help everybody, as evidenced by the incredible range of interests for which he fought. Besides the broad causes of civil rights, public education, labor laws and health care, Humphrey in a typical week in the Senate might speak on migratory birds, dairy reports, disaster loans, disarmament, domestic economy, price supports, consumer problems, trade development, antitrust laws, the public debt, North African policy, passports, French politics, international civil aviation, Lithuanian independence, captive nations, wildflowers of the Northwest and the need for more office space.

Like many great men before him, Humphrey was the product of a small town and never forgot it. On one trip, during a short break between two public appearances, I escorted him to his hotel room to relax for a few minutes. He flipped on the television and happened to catch scenes of student protests which for weeks had crippled New York's Columbia University, at times through the seizure of campus buildings.

As Humphrey watched the swarms of young people storming angrily in the streets of New York, I heard him whisper, almost to himself: "Thank God for Waverly"—his tiny adopted hometown in Minnesota where, after a heroic battle with cancer, he was destined to die in January, 1978.

It was during this battle with cancer that Humphrey demonstrated once again the generous spirit that marked his life. Press secretary Norm Sherman reported later that Humphrey, knowing he would soon die, telephoned Richard Nixon, not one of his favorite persons, to convey his best wishes on Christmas Day, 1977.

And later, realizing that as a former Vice President his funeral would be held in Washington, Humphrey made an unusual deathbed request. He asked that Nixon be invited to attend his funeral—not because he had forgotten Watergate and many other Nixon acts he found appalling, but as a step toward national healing.

Knowing this would be Nixon's first trip to Washington since resigning the Presidency, Humphrey saw his impending death as a chance to bring Nixon back from political exile—a fate Humphrey believed should never befall a former President of the United States, whatever the circumstances.

"He always sought to heal, not exacerbate, differences," Norm said.

Even though the national anguish over Vietnam ultimately robbed him of the Presidency, Humphrey must have enjoyed the belated recognition and acclaim that began to blossom for him in the final weeks before the 1968 election.

One of his last major campaign swings was a triumphant six-city tour of Texas. As one of the Vice President's key political strategists, Jim Wright had not only represented him before the rules and credentials committee at the Democratic convention but also had opened a statewide Humphrey campaign headquarters in Austin.

To prepare for Humphey's eleventh-hour swing through Texas, Jim Wright set out on what most political experts thought was a hopeless task. Hoping to show a Texas Democratic Party unified solidly behind Humphrey, he began trying to negotiate at least a temporary truce between Governor John Connally and Senator Ralph Yarborough.

In Texas politics this was the equivalent of trying to mix nitric acid with glycerin. The two men had feuded for years. Connally, every inch the genteel establishment conservative, might well have come from a different planet than Yarborough, the fiery, garrulous champion of Texas liberals.

To the astonishment of virtually everybody in Texas—perhaps including himself—Jim Wright succeeded in bringing Connally and Yarborough together. Before a throng of 10,000 people in Fort Worth's Burk Burnett Park, the Governor and the

Senator radiated sweetness, light and political unity, offering rousing endorsements which allowed Humphrey to bask in the rosy glow of party harmony.

"In 24 years we've never had as united a party in Texas," Yarborough cried.

With his behind-the-scenes handiwork, Jim Wright had made Humphrey look like the world's foremost political peacemaker. This unheard-of display of Texas Democratic cohesion surprised nobody more than the savvy national political reporters traveling with Humphrey. On the plane en route to Austin that afternoon, I watched Scripps-Howard correspondent Dan Thomasson peck out the lead for his national story:

FORT WORTH—Hubert H. Humphrey may have done today what all the king's horses and all the king's men couldn't do—he put the Texas Democratic Party back together again.

At every campaign stop on the Texas swing, Humphrey was greeted by cheering, enthusiastic crowds. To me personally, the visit in San Antonio was particularly exciting. For one thing, the city stirred memories from boyhood, when I thought the old Transit Tower surely had to be the tallest building on earth. Moreover, I knew that somewhere in the welcoming crowd today was my cousin, Olive Dareos, who with her husband George ran La Louisianne, the most elegant restaurant in town.

For sheer political drama, though, I never expect to see anything to equal Humphrey's final campaign visit to Texas—a joint appearance, only two days before the election, with President Johnson in Houston's famed Astrodome. Johnson's own tenure in the White House was contaminated by the war he inherited and was able neither to win nor end. He had made this special pilgrimage to Texas to display his support for Humphrey who, ironically, was destined to lose—principally because of his unyielding support of the President.

There was no place for irony, however, that Sunday in the Astrodome. An astounding crowd of 40,000 people jammed the massive stadium. The band music, the applause, the euphoria made an unbelievable scene. I remember seeing a national television anchor man gazing upward, obviously awed by the sea of cheering humanity.

"What do you think?" I shouted over the tumult.

"I think I've never seen anything like this in my life," he said.

As the Humphrey campaign had steadily gained momentum in the few weeks just before the election, many of us dared to hope we could overcome the political damage growing out of the antiwar riots at the Democratic convention in Chicago. Even as we gathered on election night in the Lemington Hotel in Minneapolis, there were occasional moments of hope.

"Well, at least we're scaring hell out of them," Humphrey laughed at one point.

But victory was not in the cards. Out of a total popular vote of 63 million, even though Nixon got only half a million more than Humphrey, he got them in the right places. In the electoral vote count, Nixon won big, 301 to 191. Jim Wright and those of us who worked in Texas took consolation, however, in carrying the state for Humphrey. It was the only Presidential election since 1924 that a Texas majority had gone differently from the nation.

Exhausted but satisfied we had done the best we could, I climbed on an airplane, headed for Austin, where I had left a rented car. After turning it in, I boarded a bus for the 80-mile trip to San Antonio, having called my cousin, Olive Dareos, to ask her to meet me there.

Like myself, Olive was disappointed over Humphrey's loss. But as she drove toward home, it was clear that she had something else on her mind, also. I bided my time. Finally it popped out.

"You know, I think I'm beginning to understand politics," she said.

"Really? How so?"

"When you came to San Antonio a week or so ago, I watched you come down the stairs—right out of the Vice President's plane. Bands were playing. People were cheering. And there you were—right in the middle of all those important people. I was so proud. Then, two days ago, there was the election."

"Yes?"

"And today," she said, "you call and ask if I will come and pick you up at the Greyhound bus station."

15

Battle of Insiders: The Majority Leader's Race

As our Piper Apache droned deeper into the timber country of East Texas, I nervously sipped coffee from a styrofoam cup and tried to figure out what I would say after we landed. This assumed, of course, that the pilot of our little chartered plane could find Diboll, Texas, in the first place. A recent visitor had warned that the little backwoods town of 5,500 "is not so easy to find and you're out of it before you get into it."

But getting us to Diboll was the pilot's problem. My problem, once we got there, would be far more complicated. The more I tried to break it down into its component parts, the crazier it sounded. I was supposed (1) to visit a millionaire I had never met and (2) convince him to give away a lot of money (3) to a bunch of people he didn't know (4) to carry out a plan that might not work.

Moreover, this was not just your everyday millionaire. My chore would be somewhat easier if it were a kitchenware salesman who had waked up one morning and found that he had inherited a rich uncle's estate. At least I would feel less intimidated in talking with a guy like that.

As it was, in any battle of wits with the fellow I was going to meet, I would clearly be outgunned. To begin with, this particular guy had taken a little family lumber company in East Texas and built it into a multimillion dollar timber products empire. And then for an encore, in 1973, he managed to pull off the granddaddy of all corporate mergers—a deal so adroit that it flabbergasted the smart-alecks on Wall Street and put this good ol' East Texas boy on Page One of *The New York Times*. In a single master stroke, he and his family and associates acquired an astonishing 15 percent of the stock of Time Inc.

That's why it was tough to figure out what to say. Everything I came up with sounded ridiculous.

Good morning, sir. Not very original, but I've got to start somewhere.

You don't know me, but— That's stupid. Don't waste the man's time. Tell him why you're here.

I would like to talk to you about some political campaign money—Ouch. That may get me thrown out. But if he really is a no-nonsense guy like everybody says, maybe he'll admire my forthrightness.

The money? Oh, it's not for me. I want to give it to a woman in Baltimore. . . No. No. No. Entirely wrong impression. Fix it—quick.

Oh, I don't know the woman, of course. Get to the point, dammit.

But she's running for Congress, see? So what, son? So what?

And Don and Craig and I thought maybe if we can help her raise some campaign money, she may consider supporting Jim Wright. Support him for what? Tell him, you dunderhead.

Oh, yes—I should have mentioned this. Jim is running for Majority Leader of the House of Representatives.

This whole convoluted story had begun unfolding in Washington a few weeks earlier. As we were leaving the Capitol late one summer afternoon in 1976, Jim Wright asked to hitch a ride home with me. I figured he had something on his mind. Otherwise, he would not have endangered his life by accompanying me in my beat-up old Mustang into the chain of traffic careening at warp speed down the Southwest Freeway. With Jim Wright apprehensively bracing himself for a collision, I deftly executed my customary kamikaze maneuver into a stream of cars barreling hell-bent for the Virginia suburbs. A terrified fellow in a Buick yielded a slot for me. Later, after Jim Wright regained his color and composure, he started talking about the Majority Leader's race shaping up in the House.

The Speaker of the House, Carl Albert, was retiring after 30 years in Congress to return to his native Oklahoma. Certain to succeed him in the Speakership was Thomas P. (Tip) O'Neill, a tousled, friendly mountain of a man from Massachusetts. It was then only June, and the election would not be until December. But already O'Neill had nailed down enough votes among his colleagues to guarantee that he would ascend to what surely was the most powerful legislative office not just in the United States but in the world.

This would leave vacant O'Neill's present post as Majority Leader, the highly-prized No. 2 position in the House. As straw-boss to the Speaker, the Majority Leader is responsible for speaking for his party in the House, steering its legislative program, controlling the legislative schedule, resolving disputes, and, occasionally, knocking heads. Moreover, the office is the traditional stepping-stone to the Speakership, as Tip O'Neill was preparing to demonstrate anew.

With such a seat of power soon to be vacated, it's a safe bet that virtually every senior lawmaker in the House toyed at least momentarily with the idea of seeking the prize. Most realized, however, that among their House colleagues they would require a bedrock base of support similar to those claimed by the three prominent House leaders who had already announced their candidacies.

As we talked in the car that afternoon, Jim Wright mentioned that several colleagues had come to him suggesting that he ought to enter the race.

"Are you considering it?" I asked, knowing full well that he was. He had been elected to Congress in 1954. Back in those days, the old bulls who ruled the House figured that until a new member had been around for 10 years or so, he was entitled to no more attention than a doorknob. Intelligence and hard work counted a little, but not as much as the number of pages you had torn from your office calendars. For a brainy, industrious member aspiring to a larger role in the House leadership, being patronized this way was Chinese water torture.

I had watched, first as a newspaper reporter in Fort Worth and later as his Administrative Assistant, Jim Wright's growing impatience with the limited role any individual member was permitted to play in the House. Even in the 1960s, talented lawmakers moved up in the House about as fast as people renewing their tags moved up to the counter at the Division of Motor Vehicles. So frustrated did Jim Wright become at one point, I recalled, that he asked then-Vice President Lyndon B. Johnson about the possibility of either a cabinet appointment or an ambassadorship.

"You say you are frustrated?" Johnson demanded. He emphasized how frustrated he himself was, and how President Kennedy was most frustrated of all. For people with as much surplus adrenaline as Jim Wright and Lyndon Johnson, hardly anything could be as maddening as the funereal pace with which the ponderous machinery of government customarily moved.

Taking Johnson's advice, Jim Wright remained in Congress and, through the years, advanced significantly in power and prestige. Now, in 1976, with the Democrats in unchallenged control of the House, he held one of four Deputy Whip positions, an important but lower rung on the leadership ladder. Moreover, he headed an investigative subcommittee and would be in line the following year to become Chairman of the Public Works Committee, one of the most prized positions in the House. But Jim Wright was not a man for small plans.

In the car that afternoon, he pointed out that the three announced candidates had been busy for months. Not only were they collaring their House colleagues, one by one, to line up support. Also they were cozying up to Democratic Congressional candidates who, if elected in their districts in November, 1976, would be entitled to vote in the Majority Leader's election the following month.

As Jim Wright mulled the possibility of entering the race, he seemed reasonably confident of his two main bases of support— the Texas delegation and the Public Works Committee. But he realized he was far behind in another crucial area—the quiet, behind-the-scenes effort to help colleagues gather campaign money for their re-election efforts back home. From friends in the House, he knew that the three announced candidates had been busy for months, beating the bushes for money to help Democrats running for election or re-election. "It's awfully late to be getting into the race now," Jim Wright said, almost as if trying to talk himself out of it.

In those days, efforts to raise funds for colleagues seldom got much newspaper attention. Yet one of the top priorities for a Congressional leadership candidate is to have a Political Action Committee especially for that purpose. Say, for example, a popular District Attorney, campaigning hard in Cincinnati for a seat in the House, clearly has a good chance to win, but urgently needs money for a last-minute television buy. Then, out of the blue, he suddenly receives a $500 campaign contribution from a friend—a friend who just happens to be running for Majority Leader. If the newcomer wins a seat in the House, there is no guarantee, of course, that he will vote for the leadership candidate who came through with a campaign contribution when it was so urgently needed. But it never hurts anything, either.

The more we talked that afternoon, the more I realized that if Jim Wright ran for Majority Leader, it would be a race unlike any he had ever undertaken—different from his campaigns for the Texas Legislature, for Mayor of Weatherford, for Congress from the 12th District of Texas, or even his statewide race for the U.S. Senate in 1961. For this election would be essentially a private drama on a public stage. It would be acted out entirely by House insiders, quietly but vigorously seeking votes from other House insiders. And ironically, these members, who ordinarily crow about craving public input on affairs of government, actually would resent advice from a constituent or even a friend on a race like this.

To understand why, bear in mind that there is only one way to become a member of the House of Representatives, and that is to be elected by the people in your district. Under the Constitution, a person cannot be appointed to the House. Members take pride in this unique status. Senators, of course, can be appointed on an interim basis. And under the 25th Amendment, a person can even be appointed to fill a vacancy in the office of Vice President, as Gerald Ford was in 1973.

Thus, when the House elects its officers, they are "the elect of the elect"—a set of political pro's, chosen from the ranks of the 435 political pro's who make up the House. While sometimes politically bloody, these leadership contests seldom produce riveting public drama. They capture nowhere near the newspaper and television attention of a Presidential race. For one thing, the candidates are largely unknown outside their own district or state. Then, too, the maneuvering is often so subtle and complex it cannot be easily backgrounded by newspaper reporters in 500 words or by television anchors in 30 seconds.

Aboard the plane headed to Diboll with me that bright summer morning were two of Jim Wright's most valued friends and political allies. One was Craig Raupe, who had gone to Washington with the newly-elected Congressman in 1955 and had worked for him, either as a staffer or a devoted friend, ever since.

Craig squirmed uncomfortably in his seat. In the salty language he often used to conceal his essential soft-heartedness, he demanded of his seatmate: "How much further to this damn place?"

"Not much. Diboll is just south of Lufkin," replied Don Kennard, the State Senator from Fort Worth. Like Craig, Don had long been a stalwart supporter and steadfast political confederate of Jim Wright. It was Don who had arranged the appointment and chartered the plane for today's trip.

I looked down at the seemingly endless carpet of timberland. "With as much money as this fellow's got, why does he want to live out here in the sticks?"

"Maybe to keep away from guys like us," Don said, laughing. "Or maybe because these sticks, as you call 'em, made him rich in the first place."

And so they had. Arthur Temple, now one of the wealthiest men in a state full of wealthy men, was a teenager when he started work in his family's Southern Pine Lumber Company in the Depression year of 1939. When his father died in 1951, he took over the company. Hard-working and resourceful, he invented an automatic lumber sorter and steadily built what had been a little backwoods lumber firm into a forest products combine called Temple Industries, with more than 400,000 acres of East Texas timberlands.

Then, in 1973, Arthur Temple pulled off a merger with Time Inc. that gave him, his relatives and associates almost as much stock in the giant publishing empire as the 18 to 20 per cent owned by the company's executives, directors and their relatives along with the Henry R. Luce Foundation. Thus, at age 53, did a plain-spoken, sunburned good ol' boy from Diboll, Texas, become what *The New York Times* called "a major force" in the U.S. communications industry.

However impressive that description was to Craig, Don and me, we saw in this self-made East Texas timber magnate other qualities far more important. As a moderate Democrat, Arthur Temple was a rare creature indeed among Texas millionaires, some of whom were so conservative they had not yet come to terms with the French Revolution. And even though Arthur Temple had never been a close personal friend, he had supported Jim Wright in the past. Whether he would do so in the somewhat uncertain enterprise in which we were now engaged remained to be seen. But he was soon to be given that chance.

Although I had never met the man, I felt comfortable the moment I walked into his office. He wasn't wearing the green golf cap which newspapers said he often kept on at his desk, but his office was adorned with U.S. and Texas flags, along with a sign, "Do it right, but do it right now." To me, this suggested an almost spooky philosophical kinship with Jim Wright, whose own action-oriented office sign said: "Don't tell me why it can't be done. Show me how it can."

Somewhat more skillfully than I had imagined on the plane, Craig, Don and I told Arthur Temple about Jim Wright's plan to enter the race and outlined his general strategy. The election would take place in the Democratic caucus on Monday, December 6. With four candidates, there would be three separate votes, with the low man being eliminated each round.

One by one, we went over our three opponents. One was John McFall of California. Even though a likable man and presently Majority Whip, only one step down from Majority Leader, he had been politically crippled by his association with South Korean mystery man Tongsun Park. We figured he would be eliminated in the first round of voting. Thus when talking to a member who was pledged to vote for McFall, Jim Wright always asked—and often won—a pledge of support on the second round if McFall should be eliminated in the first. If enough of these second-round votes came through, the Fort Worth Congressman would have a chance to beat out the next opponent—stuffy, imperious Richard Bolling of Missouri.

Arthur Temple seemed to be listening intently, but since he asked no questions, I kept talking.

"That would leave Phil Burton. You probably have read about him. He's an ultra-liberal from San Francisco. Mean as a snake. Scares the daylights out of people. Jim believes that if he can get into a head-to-head contest with Burton, he can beat him."

Arthur Temple leaned back in his chair, rubbed his chin, chewing over what might have seemed like a highly doubtful political scenario. Like the rest of us, he was concerned about Jim Wright's late start in the race.

I realized we were on shaky ground. Here we were, asking substantial help from a shrewd, self-made millionaire who didn't know Craig and me from a loblolly pine tree. Fortunately for us, Don's presence lent our visit at least a tinge of credibility. Don had come to know Arthur Temple through a mutual friend, Congressman Charlie Wilson of Lufkin. The three of them often got together on hunting trips deep into their beloved East Texas woodlands. Today Don rode to our rescue, reminding Arthur Temple that even though Jim Wright was starting late, he had a far stronger base of support than the other candidates.

"Look at our state delegation, Arthur," he said. "Every Texas Democrat in the House is supporting Jim except for two fellows who pledged to Burton before Jim started considering the race. Now just compare that with the California delegation. It's split wide open because McFall and Burton are both from California. And besides that, those Californians are notorious for never being able to march in the same direction, anyway."

It was Craig's turn at bat. He pointed to another big source of Jim Wright's support—his colleagues on the House Public Works Committee. "He commands a lot of respect on that committee. The members would be inclined to support him because they like him and admire his work," he said. "Then too there are dozens of other House members Jim Wright has helped with highways and dams and federal buildings in their districts. A lot of them feel grateful to him."

Arthur Temple fiddled with a pencil. He looked thoughtfully at Don, Craig and me and rubbed his chin. We waited. This, we knew, was the moment of decision.

"How can I help?" he asked, smiling.

Delighted, we three Jim Wright musketeers plunged ahead. "We need you to help us round up some campaign money—not for Jim, but for his colleagues," Craig said.

"And for Democrats running for Congress who look like they have a chance to win. If they do, they'll get to vote in the Majority Lelader's race," Don explained.

"Well, first you need to organize a PAC," Arthur Temple said.

"There isn't time for that, Mr. Temple," I said. "It would take weeks to get through the legal rigmarole. We can't afford to lose any more time before we get started."

"So what do we do?"

"We need you to help gather up campaign donations from as many people as you can, with the checks made out in the names of individual members and candidates."

Arthur Temple looked skeptical. "My friends would feel a whole lot more comfortable giving to Jim than to some guy they never heard of. And besides, if Jim had a PAC, he could give the money in his own name to whoever he wanted to."

"We'd like to do it like that. But the other fellows are so far ahead of us on this, there's just not time to organize a PAC."

Arthur Temple hesitated. "Well, I don't know," he said. "I think—

His telephone rang. He picked it up. "Yeah, Charlie. No, it's all right. I can talk. What you got on your mind?"

For the next few minutes he listened, grunting an acknowledgment now and then. "Sure, Charlie, I'll do that. Sure. Say, listen, Charlie—you got any political money?"

Still on the phone, Arthur Temple looked at me and smiled mischievously. "All right," he said. "Make out a check for $500. No, don't make it out to me. Make it out to—"

As fast as a quick-draw artist at the OK Corral, I whipped out a list of names and thrust it into his outstretched hand.

"No, not to me. Make it out to Barbara Mikulski. M-I-K-U-L-S-K-I. That's right. No, Charlie, you don't need to know what it's for. Just make out the check and mail it to me. I'll take care of it."

Arthur Temple laughed. "My friends are going to find it pretty expensive to call me from now on." And so they did.

Over the next few weeks, he gathered dozens of checks made out to Democrats campaigning for the House. Jim Wright quickly dispatched each to the payee, along with a personal note explaining that the contribution came from a good friend in Texas who was eager to help in his or her race.

Emboldened by our initial success, Craig and Don and I split up and fanned out to different parts of the state. For his next pitch, Craig went for the gold. In Dallas, which then even more than now was a citadel of Republican activism, he managed to set up a meeting with a group of bankers and insurance executives.

To the conservative business leaders who gathered in a posh skyscraper office to hear Craig's story, Jim Wright's affiliation as a Democrat was accepted with noses wrinkled in spirit if not in fact. While most of the tailored suits in the room grudgingly recognized that he was not a knee-jerk liberal and was more conservative than Burton or Bolling, they would have been far happier hearing how they might help a Texas *Republican* become Majority Leader.

Because they were community leaders, most of these businessmen were aware that during his 22 years in Congress, Jim Wright had brought significant benefits to the entire Dallas-Fort Worth area, providing vital help with megabuck projects like the new Dallas/Fort Worth Airport, the Trinity Canal and General Dynamics defense contracts. Moreover, he had, after all, gone to high school in Dallas, and if the next Majority Leader simply had to be a Democrat, *sigh*, it might as well be a *Texas* Democrat.

For a while, it looked as if Craig might be successful in raising a little money in Dallas. But then, when he mentioned that the checks should be made out not to Jim Wright, but to *other Democrats*, the meeting went downhill fast.

"You're asking us to make out checks to people *we don't even know?*" demanded a man we shall call Mr. Penworthy. He was a prominent business leader Jim Wright had helped many times.

"Most of them are members of Congress," Mr. Penworthy," Craig pointed out.

"Even so, just think what you're asking. You want us to blindly give money to people in other states—people we never even heard of."

Waving his list, Craig stood his ground. "I'll tell you one thing. There's not a single soul on this list that would embarrass you."

Mr. Penworthy got out his glasses and scanned the list. Pointing to one of the names, he asked, "Isn't this the fellow in Utah I read about a few months ago?"

"What did you read about him?"

"That a Congressman by this name was arrested for propositioning an undercover policewoman," Mr. Penworthy cried triumphantly.

This, for all practical purposes, concluded the Dallas meeting. A week or so later, as Craig laughingly related to Don and me how embarrassed he had been, Don added a postscript to the story.

"That's what you get for wasting your time in Dallas," Don told Craig. "You should have been out in West Texas with me. In El Paso a lawyer friend of mine also spotted that name. He said, 'Ain't this the guy that tried to buy sex from a female police officer?' "

Don reluctantly admitted that it was. Delighted, his lawyer friend cried:

"A sonuvabitch after my own heart! Gimme my checkbook— I'm going to send the horny bastard five hundred dollars!"

From Diboll, Dallas and El Paso, we moved our strategic operations in July to New York for the Democratic National Convention. Here Jimmy Carter would win the Democratic nomination to oppose President Gerald R. Ford, the only American ever to reach the Oval Office by appointment. Picked by President Nixon and confirmed by Congress in 1973 to replace resigned Vice President Spiro T. Agnew, Ford then inherited the Presidency when Nixon resigned in 1974.

For those hoping to become Majority Leader, this national gathering in New York of the Democratic faithful was an ideal hunting ground. Sensing recapture of the White House in November, virtually every Democrat seeking election or re-election to the House was in New York, eager to help anoint our party's presidential candidate.

Philip Burton, widely regarded as the front runner, set up a hotel hospitality suite. Friends and prospective supporters were invited to drop by and pay homage to the man many thought was certain to be the next Majority Leader.

With Jim Wright's candidacy still officially unannounced, we practiced political guerrilla warfare. Craig, Don and I, along with staffers and friends like Kathy Mitchell, John Mack, Kathy Luhn and Liz Connell, quietly but methocially began tracking down House candidates, one by one, and inviting them up for private talks with Jim Wright. To outsiders campaigning for their first term, our invitation was a win-win proposition. Even if Jim Wright were not elected Majority Leader, they knew he would be the next Chairman of the House Public Works Committee. From this committee each year came authorizations for scores of new highways, bridges, dams and federal buildings—valuable hometown projects which often made the local member of Congress look like a real go-getter.

For aspiring members, who might soon be called on to deliver on a badly-needed highway project for voters back home, nothing could be more inviting than friendship with a senior lawmaker who could make it happen. For Jim Wright, those long, tedious, frustrating years as a committee back-bencher were beginning to pay rich dividends in power and prestige. Every time we managed to track down a candidate, he or she eagerly jumped at our invitation. One by one, we escorted them back to our suite in the Essex Hotel, just across from Central Park, where Jim Wright was waiting. He took it from there.

Even though we had lists showing where members of each state delegation were staying, the candidates we targeted were not always easy to find. Some we collared on the convention floor, some in hotel lobbies, and some on the street. But some we thought we weren't going to find at all. We had almost given up, for example, on Barbara Mikulski.

Ms. Mikulski was a small bundle of political dynamite from Baltimore. Short in stature but long on spirit and stamina, she had won acclaim in Maryland as a social worker, college professor and Baltimore City Councilwoman. Unsuccessful as a Democratic candidate for the U.S. Senate two years earlier, she was now a candidate for the House. But among tens of thousands at the Democratic convention, we simply couldn't find her.

After searching vainly in her hotel, among her Maryland colleagues and in the convention hall, we were beginning to think that we might never catch up with a woman of her energy.

Then Liz Connell, one of our volunteers, tired from trampling New York concrete and dispirited over her inability to find Barbara Mikulski, stopped for a bite of lunch. Stepping into a nearby sidewalk diner, she strode up to the counter and wearily took a seat. On the next stool was Barbara Mikulski.

"I've got her! I've got Barbara Mikulski here in the diner with me!" Liz shouted into the phone to Kathy Luhn, who with Kathy Mitchell was scheduling appointments back at the Essex.

At their meeting, Congresswoman-and-Senator-to-be Mikulski talked with Jim Wright about Baltimore's urgent need to fund a massive harbor project, and he talked with her about the Majority Leader's race.

Some candidates, seeing a chance to get some high-powered campaign help, urged Jim Wright to come and speak for them in their districts. Often these invitations turned out to be bigger chores than he was counting on. When he went to Pennsylvania to stump for Allen E. Ertel, for example, he learned that he had been scheduled for 23 appearances in one day. He gulped—and made them all.

On July 27, two weeks after the convention, Jim Wright formally announced his candidacy. Nobody in the press paid much attention. Among outsiders, he was a late starter and widely regarded as a long shot. But among members of the House, the announcement was received more respectfully. They knew Jim Wright.

But at this point, neither he nor any of us on his staff suspected what a desperate, hard-fought race it would turn out to be. In time to come, Congressional historians would describe it as "the closest, most volatile and least predictable" leadership election ever held.

As autumn colors came to the stately old trees on the Capitol grounds, the four-man contest began to narrow. McFall's campaign never seemed to gather steam, even though as Majority Whip he would ordinarily be considered only one stairstep away from the prize. But he had severe handicaps.

For one thing, a candidate for a leadership post traditionally counted on his own state delegation for his bedrock support. In this case, both McFall and Burton were Californians, thus dividing the 29 Democrats in their state delegation. Such a split, however, was not unusual for the Californians.

Unlike the Texas delegation, which was usually a paragon of unity, the California group included such a tangled array of personalities, preferences and prejudices that its members seldom were united on anything. Whoever said there is strength in diversity surely didn't have the California Congressional delegation in mind. As a matter of fact, four California members, bullied by Burton, quietly came to Jim Wright and promised their support in the secret balloting.

John McFall's personality was also a factor. Some members doubted that such a pleasant, easy-going guy would be forceful enough to knock heads, as the Majority Leader occasionally was required to do. He seemed to be reluctant, for example, to push a colleague for a rock-solid promise of support. Walking up to a fellow House member, McFall might say, "Hey, Joe, I sure would like to count on your support in the Majority Leader's race." The colleague, recognizing a loophole when he saw one, might grab McFall's arm, give it a fraternal squeeze and respond, "John, you would make a hell of a good Majority Leader," and McFall would naively believe he had another vote.

But McFall's biggest burden was his relationship with Tongsun Park, the wheeling-dealing South Korean businessman who materialized in Washington and began cozying up to the city's political elite. Even though McFall refused Park's offer of a campaign contribution, which would have been illegal, he admitted accepting $3,000 for an office kitty he used to entertain visiting constituents. When the newspapers reported this gift, McFall's shaky position became shakier still. While not unlawful, the gift did nothing to enhance his public image.

The Missourian in the race, Richard Bolling, had many admirers in the House, chief among whom was Richard Bolling himself. While high self-esteem is standard equipment among members of Congress, Bolling's ego loomed as monumental as that of General Douglas MacArthur, on whose staff he served during five years of Army duty. This conceit eroded the respect Bolling otherwise was due because of his intellect, his diligence and his encyclopedic knowledge of Congress. But over the years, many colleagues came to regard him as an arrogant, aloof know-it-all.

Elected to the House as a liberal Democrat in 1948, Bolling authored three books on Congress and served on the prestigious House Rules Committee. From that lofty position he seldom hesitated to publicly rebuke colleagues for wasting his time with incomplete or erroneous information about their bills. Even though he himself yearned for a leadership post in his beloved House, Bolling nevertheless resented the naked ambitiousness of Phil Burton. When the Majority Leader vacancy loomed, Bolling jumped into the race—some say as much to deny the office to Burton as to win the job himself.

The other man in the race, Phil Burton, was considered by some to be a political genius. If he was, he paid a terrible price for the distinction. While as a staff person I was spared the necessity of having personal dealings with him, he always struck me as being a continually angry, tortured man. I never remember seeing him smile. On the countless times I saw him in the Capitol, in the halls of the House Office Buildings or in watering holes like the Democratic Club, he seemed to reflect the sullen intensity of a desperately driven, unhappy man.

I am sure he must have had another side, but to a casual observer it wasn't easy to see. A San Francisco lawyer and former California State Assemblyman, Burton was elected to Congress in 1964. With political credentials liberal enough to score 90 on the Americans for Democratic Action yardstick, together with his unyielding opposition to the Vietnam War, he quickly established himself as a force to be reckoned with in the House. While impressed at Burton's skill in building coalitions, Tip O'Neill cringed at the thought of having him as the Speaker's second in command.

Undoubtedly one reason for O'Neill's feeling is cited by author John Jacobs in his biography of Burton, *A Rage for Justice.* In 1972, both Burton and O'Neill, who was then Majority Whip, attended a Democratic fund-raising dinner in California. Afterward, both men and their wives joined another couple in the Beverly Hill Hotel's cocktail lounge. Burton, angry and drinking, began using words commonly found on restroom walls.

Ever the gentleman, O'Neill pointed out that ladies were present and suggested that Burton should cease using foul language. Burton only grew more profane, and O'Neill finally snapped: "Curb your tongue."

Furious, Burton stood up and, incredibly, challenged the portly, 60-year-old O'Neill to a fight, at one point even starting to reach across the table for him. Only after another person at the table intervened did Burton relent.

"This is crazy," O'Neill muttered. "This is not the way people in the public eye behave."

Four years later, in the heat of the Majority Leader's race, Burton again displayed his darker side—this time in a Machiavellian effort to bedevil Jim Wright.

Jay Power, then a young lobbyist for the carpenters' union, recalls the incident vividly. In the Democratic Club one evening, he happened to run into Burton, whom he regarded as both a personal friend and an important ally of the carpenters' union. Burton said he was hungry, and asked Power to take him to dinner at the Monocle, a popular gathering place for people on the Hill.

Since Burton was a frequent visitor, waiters at Monocle were accustomed to his unusual behavior. At the table, he shucked off his shoes and ordered a Stolichnaya on the rocks—the first of seven or eight vodkas he would consume that evening, along with occasional sips of milk. From the waiter Burton ordered a rare steak which, Power recalls, he picked up with his hands and began eating as he would a sandwich.

Then, across the room, Power saw impending trouble. A tall man with a white hat and a western-cut business suit was looking intently at Burton. *Uh, oh*, thought Power. *This going to be bad. That guy's from Texas, and he's going to come over here and mention the Majority Leader's race.*

Sure enough, the stranger strode over, a picture of smiles and courtesy. Apologizing for the interruption, he introduced himself as a friend of Jim Wright. He had heard what a fine man Mr. Burton was, and he couldn't resist coming over to say hello.

"I'm sure it will be a good and fair race," he added.

Burton, bristling with hostility, demanded: "What are you doing here?"

The visitor explained that farm subsidies important to Texas were under attack in the pending farm bill, and he had asked Jim Wright to help save them.

Burton exploded, leaping to his feet. With bits of steak, spit and his favorite four-letter verb flying from his mouth, he vividly described what should be done to the visitor, to Jim Wright, to the farm bill, and to subsidies.

"I will single-handedly sink all this redneck Texas special interest shit," he thundered.

So violent was this outburst that even waiters accustomed to Burton's antics scurried for cover. Startled customers at nearby tables got up and moved away.

When things calmed down, Burton's companion was so angry he couldn't resist condemning his tirade. "Phil, that was completely out of line," he said.

"You still don't get it, do you?" Burton calmly asked Power. "That guy is going to be seeing Jim Wright. I don't want Jim Wright to have a single waking moment that he doesn't know I'm on his ass."

Despite such outrageous spasms of anger, calculated or not, Burton displayed rock-steady dedication to his overriding goal.

"I want to accumulate power," he told his young friend from the carpenters' union on another occasion. "I want to build benefits for the working people and benefits for the environment."

"Yeah, Phil, but you seem to enjoy power."

"Sure I enjoy power—because nobody knows how to use it as well as I do."

In 1973 Burton, then chairman of the liberal Democratic Study Group, had led a battle to make the office of Democratic Whip elective rather than appointive so he could run for the job. Defeated in that effort, the next year he methodically began building support among what later became known as the "Watergate Babies"—the enormous class of reform-minded Democrats running for the House in the wake of President Nixon's resignation.

One of Burton's allies in this enterprise was Wayne Hays of Ohio, the House Administration Committee Chairman who had not yet become known for putting hypermammiferous Elizabeth Ray on his payroll for duties she described as other than office work. At this time, Hays also happened to be Chairman of the Democratic Congressional Campaign Committee, or DCCC. From Hays, Burton would receive advance word that the DCCC was preparing to send a campaign contribution to a House candidate. Then Burton would call the candidate, schmooze with him about his race, and then say he was recommending that the DCCC send a contribution. By this and other means Burton built solid loyalties among many of the 74 new Democrats elected to the House in 1974. This base of support was crucial to Burton's election that year as Chairman of the Democratic Caucus, the overall party organization in the House.

As the Majority Leader's race heated up in the fall of 1976, the marble corridors of Capitol Hill churned with intrigue. One day the phone rang on my desk in the Rayburn Building. My good friend Nick Masters was calling. He wanted to see me. He sounded excited.

This was curious, because ordinarily Nick was about as excitable as an octogenarian Supreme Court justice. Usually the rawest emotion he displayed was a contemptuous snort, often directed at some new Republican budget "reform." Still well known in academic circles as Dr. Nicholas Masters the political scientist, he had long since been lured from his ivy cloisters by a temptress he found far more seductive—Washington politics. For many years he had been a top-ranking staffer on the House Budget Committee, as well as one of Jim Wright's closest friends.

"Shut the door," he ordered. Dragging up a chair, he drew within whispering distance. "I've just learned the three things they're going to use to try to beat Mr. Wright," he said.

"Where'd you get this?" I asked.

"I can't tell you."

"Is it good information?"

"It's as good as it gets," Nick said emphatically.

Nick's strategic intelligence had the ring of credibility. He said our opponents would try to discredit Jim Wright on three claims—that he did not have the support of the Texas delegation, that he opposed the 1964 civil rights public accommodations bill, and that he was a tool of "big oil" in Texas.

Our preemptive strikes were prompt and effective. We put out a vigorous letter of support signed by every Democrat in the Texas delegation except two, and pointed out that they had said they, too, would have endorsed Jim Wright had he announced before they pledged their support to Burton.

And while Jim Wright did, in fact, vote against the public accommodations bill—a vote he always regretted—his colleagues quickly reminded other members of his stand for civil rights nearly a decade earlier, when such views took a lot more guts. Early in his House career, Jim Wright was one of only five Congressmen from south of the Mason-Dixon line who refused to sign the so-called Southern Manifesto, condemning the 1954 Supreme Court ruling against school segregation.

Similar word-of-mouth networking by friends helped debunk the ridiculous notion that the Fort Worth Congressman was a tool of "big oil." Probably nobody found this charge more preposterous than the grand poobahs of the major oil companies themselves.

On Sunday, December 5, the day before the Majority Leader election, the Jim Wright brigade struck two telling blows. The first Jim Wright never knew about. It was carefully orchestrated by Craig Raupe and his longtime friend, Larry L. King. They both had arrived in Washington in 1955 as impecunious, fresh-faced political novices—Craig as Administrative Assistant to Jim Wright, Larry as AA to Congressman J.T. Rutherford of Odessa.

Later, Larry himself served a stint as Jim Wright's AA and then went on to become a highly successful writer. In the future he would win renown as the author of "The Best Little Whorehouse in Texas." But in December, 1976, he was far more interested in another House, even though the charms of its occupants were admittedly less obvious. And now, with the Majority Leader election only a few days away, Craig and Larry, both seasoned and resourceful in the ways of Washington, saw an opportunity to strike an unusual tactical blow in behalf of their longtime pal.

By a fortuitous coincidence, Larry had just signed up as a writer-in-residence for the old *Washington Evening Star*. Now defunct, this venerable and respected daily was required reading among the denizens of Capitol Hill.

What then could be more appropriate, Craig and Larry wondered, than for Larry to speculate, in his first article in the *Star*, which of the four Majority Leader candidates would the new President, Jimmy Carter, prefer to work with? Such a story could hardly be more timely, especially since the article would be published on the Sunday before Monday's Majority Leader election.

Of course Jimmy Carter knew full well the danger of a President's dabbling in the internal affairs of the House. In a candid moment he had admitted that yes, he had a favorite, but he wisely kept his mouth shut about which of the four it was. To any conscientious journalist, this would offer an irresistible professional challenge. After all, isn't it the solemn obligation of a sagacious newspaper writer, brimming with truths and insights hidden to lesser mortals, to shine the bright light of truth on the innermost thoughts of a President, up to and including things he would be crazy to say out loud? In the face of such a compelling journalistic responsibility, Larry wrote a long piece examining the pros and cons of each candidate and concluded that Jim Wright had more of the former and fewer of the latter than his competitors.

"Jimmy Carter has a favorite. He has said so," Larry wrote. "Mindful of the jealous prerogatives of the Congress, and respecting tradition requiring his non-intervention, he carefully has failed to name him. The suspicion here is that Jimmy Carter's favorite is Texan Jim Wright," and went on to tell why he thought so. In the meantime, from a commercial printer Craig ordered several hundred gummed labels reading: "See inside. Larry L. King on the Critical House Majority Leader Race."

At 5 a.m. Sunday, Craig climbed out of bed and met a truck bringing enough copies of the *Star* for each Democrat in the House. Above the fold on page one of each paper, Craig methodically began sticking his gummed labels. As he worked on this chore at the mail delivery entrance of the Longworth House Office Building, another early-riser unexpectedly arrived.

Congressman Phil Burton, Jim Wright's fiercest rival in the race, strode briskly past, entering the building completely oblivious to Craig and his ongoing handiwork. As Democratic members of the House received these papers, some may have mistaken Craig's gummed label as a promotional notice put on by the Sunday *Star* at its printing plant. Regrettably, such a mistake could not be helped.

Another campaign coup came Sunday afternoon. Jim Wright sponsored a luncheon to honor the latest crop of Democratic freshmen. Defying conventional logic, he not only warmly welcomed his three opponents to the luncheon but also invited each to make his campaign pitch to the newcomers. Bolling and McFall gave perfunctory talks, but Burton couldn't resist the temptation to do a little grandstanding.

Calling attention to the close working relationship he had built with the previous class of freshmen, Burton said the class of '74 had achieved significant reforms because it was so well organized. He urged these newest members to organize, just as had the previous class. Then, as Burton took his seat, Jim Wright lowered the boom.

"Phil mentioned the class of '74," he said. "We're fortunate to have with us today the president of the class of '74, Carroll Hubbard of Kentucky. Would you care to say anything, Carroll?"

"I sure would," said Hubbard, rising. "I'm for Jim Wright." Burton looked as if he had been hit in the face with a fish.

Then, in a low-key pitch of his own, the Fort Worth Congressman gave highly complimentary assessments of all the other candidates. One by one, he praised the individual qualifications of each. Then, almost as an afterthought, he said he might be the best combination of the special qualities of each. It was a vintage Jim Wright performance.

The next day, the Democratic Caucus met to choose two top leaders who, even though they were elected for terms of only two years, would ultimately serve in these same positions for 10 years. Tip O'Neill was chosen Speaker without opposition. Then, as nominations opened for Majority Leader, I leaned against a brass railing in the House chamber and watched, realizing I was witnessing one of the most important dramas of Jim Wright's life, and probably mine as well.

Nominated first was Bolling. Then came McFall, Burton and Wright. Each was lavishly praised by his nominators and seconders. As members moved restlessly about the floor, exchanging rumors, endorsements and occasional threats, one could only imagine the mixture of emotions bubbling up within their minds. No computer on earth, and certainly no human, could possibly have sorted out the individual political motives and memories, alliances and hatreds, insults and favors, loyalties and treacheries and hopes and fears running through the minds of those about to vote.

And then, in the first round of voting, McFall was eliminated. As the second round began and members scurried into small knots for hurried conferences, I was struck by the eerie feeling that I knew, even now, how all this was going to turn out. It was moving steadily in the pattern that Jim Wright had visualized as he sat in my Mustang in front of his house six months before. On the second round, Bolling was eliminated. Jim Wright now had the opportunity he craved. He was, at last, in a head-to-head contest with Phil Burton. I clutched the brass railing and waited, hardly breathing.

Charlie Wilson, the tall, dapper Congressman from Lufkin, was one of the vote counters. The vote was dead even, 147-147, as Wilson plucked the last ballot from the box. It was a vote for Jim Wright.

"You did it, Jim! You won!" cried Congressman Bill Alexander of Arkansas. The House chamber was in tumult. Many Burton supporters stood dazed and unbelieving.

Tip O'Neill, delighted over the outcome, invited his new Majority Leader over for a drink. Gary Hymel, a one-time New Orleans newspaperman who had served many years as O'Neill's top staffer, escorted the two winners through the crowd of well-wishers to his boss' impressive new office just across the hall.

A few minutes later, Jim Wright and I started back to the Rayburn Building, where another big crowd of friends had already gathered. As we loped down a deserted marble stairway in the Capitol, Jim Wright abruptly stopped in his tracks and grabbed my arm.

"Marshall," he said, laughing, "tomorrow I want you to talk to Gary Hymel and find out what the hell a Majority Leader is supposed to do."

16

Mike, Michelob, and Yankee Boy Look for Votes

Every time Mike Kestner ordered beer from the 7-Eleven, he gave specific instructions to the man he called Yankee Boy.

"Remember now. A six-pack of Michelob. Put it in a big paper sack. Then get another paper sack—a small one—and put an extra bottle of Michelob in that one. Understand?"

Delivering yard signs in a political campaign was thirsty work. Mike said he couldn't understand how Yankee Boy managed to get along with only a couple of Michelobs a day, especially with him doing all that running. Day after day, Mike would look in the rear view mirror and watch him, all smiles and bulging muscles, as he jogged along behind the pickup. He always said Yankee Boy was too damn healthy and too damn good-looking to be a real person but all sorts of unusual people lived up North, especially around Washington, D.C.

Despite his misgivings, Mike had to admit that with Yankee Boy jogging behind the pickup, the two of them could deliver twice as many yard signs as any other team of volunteers working out of Jim Wright's campaign headquarters.

Mike always drove the pickup. This was one of the laws he laid down the day they started delivering signs together. He said his 30 years as a Fort Worth postman gave him the encyclopedic knowledge necessary to navigate the city's streets.

"Besides," Mike said, "I own the damn pickup."

He always steered with his left hand, with his elbow poking out the window. In his right hand, he clutched the small paper sack and the day's list of delivery addresses—the homes of Jim Wright supporters who had asked the campaign office to send them yard signs. Chugging up one street and down another, Mike would stop the truck and point to a certain house.

At this signal, Yankee Boy sprinted up to the pickup and grabbed a red, white and blue sign, *Keep Jim Wright Working for Us*, mounted on a sharp wooden stake. Then he jogged over to the house and deftly shoved the sign into at the lawn at a location easily visible from the street. Average time for stop, signal, sign and shove: 90 seconds.

Every morning about half a dozen other yard sign crews gathered at Jim Wright headquarters to grab a cup of coffee and pick up their signs and the day's delivery addresses. They often marveled at the bristling efficiency Mike and Yankee Boy had achieved in making deliveries.

"How do you guys get 'em out so fast?" one driver asked.

"Well, first you need a silly son of a bitch that likes to jog along behind the truck," Mike growled.

"Either that or a truck that runs on Michelob," Yankee Boy shot back.

The sign operation was an outstanding success. By election day, 33,000 Tarrant County families were exhibiting Jim Wright signs in their yards.

For the amusement of their fellow campaign workers, Mike Kestner and Yankee Boy pretended to be the odd couple of Jim Wright's 1980 re-election campaign in Fort Worth. The good-natured insults and curses they exchanged served only to put a sharper focus on their camaraderie.

Their strongest common bond was loyalty to Jim Wright. As a longtime postal union officer in Fort Worth, Mike Kestner had worked closely with the Congressman for a quarter century. Now in his mid-fifties and having taken early retirement, Mike's belly muscles sagged a little but his allegiance to Jim Wright was stronger than ever.

Yankee Boy's name was Pat Holland. A fortyish bachelor who prided himself in keeping fit, he was a top-level officer in a security outfit in Washington. His friendship with Jim Wright dated back to the 1960's when they worked together on a government project, and he was familiar figure around the office. Even though he had come to Fort Worth to work for Jim Wright as an unpaid volunteer, it took him a while to establish his credentials with a fire-eating old loyalist like Mike Kestner. Almost as soon as Pat Holland walked through the door of the campaign office, Mike Kestner decided this youngish, flat-bellied interloper from Washington was nothing but a Yankee Boy. Later, after this newcomer proved his skill in fetching Michelob, Mike Kestner granted him his friendship but never an upgrade in name.

In late 1979 and the early the following year, these two friends of Jim Wright had watched—one from Fort Worth, the other from Washington—as the evidence grew that in November, 1980, the Fort Worth Congressman would face the toughest re-election battle of his career.

Having been elected House Majority Leader four years earlier, Jim Wright now was in a far better position to render service to the home folks back in Fort Worth. The flip side of this influential position, however, was that it made him a far juicier target to the Republican Congressional Campaign Committee. Few political trophies would be prized more dearly by the Republican hired guns than the scalp of the No. 2 Democrat in the House of Representatives.

Moreover, Republican strategists knew that in the 1980 elections they could count on significant behind-the-scenes help from right-wing outfits like the Moral Majority and NCPAC, the National Conservative Political Action Committee. These reactionary organizations had begun crawling out of the political woodwork some years before, but now they were stronger and better heeled than ever before. With what the law naively called "independent expenditures," these tory mossbacks were free to funnel gobs of money into campaigns to blacken the reputation of moderate candidates without having the funds count as expenditures on the part of their own frothy-mouthed right-wing candidates. Of the dozen Democratic leaders targeted by NCPAC that year, only two survived. And if the Republicans, the Moral Majority and NCPAC weren't enough, there was also Eddie Chiles.

Eddie Chiles was a Texas phenomenon. Starting as a young drilling rig roustabout, Eddie Chiles hitchhiked out of the oil fields in 1930 to earn a petroleum engineering degree from Oklahoma University. Then, in Great Depression year of 1939, he managed to buy two oil well service trucks and founded the Western Company. As a shrewd businessman in a hard hat, he built this tiny Fort Worth enterprise into a diversified oil field empire whose sales hit $275 million in 1979. But now, as a multimillionaire, Eddie began to focus on a sinister force that apparently had escaped his attention back in the days when he was just another hard-working roustabout. More and more, he zeroed in on the wild spending, runaway regulation, tyrannical bureaucracy and manifold other sins committed by that dastardly organization, the United States Government.

Other than providing $108 million in loan guarantees to help him build offshore drilling rigs, Eddie found it difficult to think of anything Washington did to benefit the nation. From time to time, upon learning his Congressman, Jim Wright, was in town, he began requesting—and later, virtually demanding—that the Congressman drop by for private chats in his office. There, armed with dispatches from squeakily conservative organizations like the United States Chamber of Commerce, Eddie would tick off one issue after another and demand to know why Jim Wright voted wrong on so many of them. When Jim Wright explained that his job was to represent all the people and not just rich oil men, Eddie decided to defeat him at the polls.

In the two years before the 1980 election, Eddie ran nearly a dozen big display ads in the *Star-Telegram* reprimanding the Fort Worth Congressman for what he considered his irresponsible liberalism. Among the grievous sins with which Eddie found fault were Jim Wright's support of President Carter and his advocacy of a loan to keep New York City from going bankrupt. And while he commended the Congressman's vote to free domestic oil from price controls, he was infuriated by his gall in supporting a windfall profits tax on oil. In one spectacular full-page ad, Eddie crowed that Jim Wright no longer represented his district. "Come home, Jim," he thundered. This ad, like all the rest, were signed, "Your friend, Eddie."

So enthralled was Eddie with his profound political insights that he decided to share them with a large part of the nation. Twice a day on 465 radio stations in 14 Western and Midwestern states, an announcer would ask: "Are you mad today, Eddie Chiles?"

"Yes, I'm mad," Eddie would proclaim. "I'm sad for the Americans who are trying to raise a family and trying to buy a home when the liberals in Washington are spending more and more to destroy the American dream. You get mad, too."

Aside from whatever personal gratification Eddie got from these anti-government radio spots, they had another advantage. Since they mentioned the Western Company, they were aired as "commercials" and thus tax deductible as a "business expense."

Not a man for half-way measures, Eddie began searching for a candidate to oppose Jim Wright in the 1980 election, reportedly promising to raise $500,000 for any challenger he deemed acceptable. In his opinion, the Congressman who had served Fort Worth for 26 years and the House as Majority Leader for four years simply had to go.

"Jim Wright is a socialist," Eddie told *Time* magazine.

In his quest for a challenger he came up with a surprising choice. It was Jim Bradshaw, a personable sort of a guy who owned a chain of auto parts stores. He had rendered creditable service as Mayor Pro Tem of Fort Worth but had never publicly expressed interest in running for Congress. Nor had he ever been known to utter any criticism about Jim Wright's service in Washington. Yet now, in December, 1979, he announced he, as a Republican, would devote the next 11 months to a full-time campaign to beat Jim Wright.

Nobody was taken more aback than his intended victim. At a country club dinner less than a year before, Jim Bradshaw had virtually gushed with gratitude to Jim Wright for his role in getting a federal grant to improve downtown Fort Worth. More surprising still, only two months before announcing his candidacy, Jim Bradshaw had basked in the glow of the head table at a tremendous Fort Worth dinner in which the business community honored Jim Wright for his 25 years of service in Congress.

While all this political intrigue bubbled in Fort Worth in late 1979 and most of 1980, my duties as Administrative Assistant kept me busy in Washington. Our staff in Fort Worth kept me updated by phone and fax, but I seldom got a chance to acquire any first-hand information. And then, one evening another staffer and I dropped into a Capitol Hill bar for a couple of vodkas.

Back in my Army Air Force days I remember big posters warning us to keep our mouth shut about future operations. This was easy for me, because nobody ever told me about future operations. I was lucky to find out late the night before that we would be flying a bombing mission the next morning. That never left me time to locate a seductive blonde Nazi spy who would ply me with expensive liquor and employ all her feminine charms to get me to talk. But as I eavesdropped in a Washington bar that night 35 years later, I finally realized that, as silly as they seemed at the time, those old posters had a point about keeping your mouth shut.

The people at the next table were not exactly seductive blondes. They were more like two hairy-legged older guys who, exhausted after a day's work, had stopped by for a belt on their way home. Unexpectedly, I heard one of them mention Jim Wright. After that, I couldn't help hearing what they said because I was listening very intently. The longer I listened, the more obvious it became that they were worker bees in the Republican Congressional Campaign Committee.

I didn't know them, nor they me. But they were talking shop, and it was quickly apparent that the subject under discussion at their office that day had been the Republican effort against Jim Wright in Fort Worth. As a diversion I occasionally made small talk with the fellow staffer at my table, but I did get a few unvarnished insights into the priorities that our pals in the Grand Old Party were assigning to their forthcoming attack against my boss.

"We need to put some money in that race, sure," one was saying. "It'll be an uphill fight, but that guy is going to be awful hard to beat."

"That's not entirely the point. We need to keep him so damn busy at home he can't go around the country campaigning for other Democrats," the other guy said.

True, this and a few other shreds of intelligence I picked up that night were not exactly the political equivalent of a smoking gun. Even so, it was interesting to know that while the

Republican pros wanted to prevent Jim Wright from campaigning for his House colleagues, privately they held scant hope of defeating him on his own home turf.

Recognizing that the Republicans and their right-wing cohorts were out for blood, Jim Wright and our staff began to mobilize for the most comprehensive political campaign we had ever waged. Craig Raupe, who in 1954 had accompanied the newly-elected Congressman to Washington to become his first Administrative Assistant, returned to Fort Worth and opened a campaign headquarters in Ridglea.

Just down the street, our longtime friend Carlos Moore set up a telephone boiler room and meticulously selected a crew of politically knowledgeable and articulate people to begin calling the household of every voter in the 12th Congressional District. From a computerized voter list, we began the immense job of identifying our friends and asking their help in specific ways—to display yard signs and bumper stickers, to work at campaign headquarters, to serve as block captains, and on and on.

We found a level of support that surprised even Jim Wright. An astonishing number of people remembered specific instances in which the Congressman or his staff had gone to bat for them to straighten out a problem they personally had encountered with a government agency. In our office, we called this "case work," and the boss never let us forget how important it was to people back home. Even today, in 1997, you can run across countless men and women in Fort Worth who fondly remember how Jim Wright stepped in and helped Aunt Mary get her Social Security or how the Congressman got the Army to send Willie home from Okinawa when his father was desperately ill.

In previous campaigns I had gone around with a tape recorder and talked with scores of these people. In some cases they would become emotional, even years later, when they recounted in vivid detail how their home-town Congressman had fought and won a battle for them against a faceless government bureaucracy.

So dramatic were some of these little stories that in previous campaigns we had used them as one-minute radio spots. In their own words, constituents described how Jim Wright had given them personal help when nobody else seemed to care. Never in any of these spots was there a request to vote for Jim Wright nor, for that matter, even any mention that an election was coming up.

Rather, these spots were simple little stories told by real people, using their real names, about the personal help they got from their home-town Congressman, period.

Once again in the 1980 campaign we decided to use these spots. Looking through our files, I found a dozen or so fresh instances in which Jim Wright or his staff had resolved a genuine crisis for a Fort Worth citizen or family. One of these persons was a prominent African-American minister. Together with Kathy Mitchell, the Congressman's personal secretary, I called his home and made an appointment.

When we arrived with our tape recorder, we went through our customary explanation. To the minister we emphasized that if he had even the slightest reservation about describing the help he got from Jim Wright, we would certainly understand. There was no obligation at all.

The minister, a scholarly-looking fellow with close-cropped gray hair, listened patiently. I didn't realize it, but he was thinking far, far ahead of me.

"Mr. Lynam," he said, "if your purpose is to make a recording of my voice that you can broadcast on the radio, I will certainly be delighted to do that for you."

"Fine," I said.

"If, on the other hand," he said, "your purpose is to encourage people to vote for Mr. Wright, I can accomplish that in a far more efficient manner. Next Sunday, I will merely instruct members of my congregation to vote for Mr. Wright, and they will do so. My congregation always heeds my advice on such matters."

Kathy, the minister and I all burst into laughter. "Wonderful! We would like to take you up on both offers," I said.

As it turned out, this minister had lots of company, thanks in large measure to one of Jim Wright's good friends in the House, Congressman Bill Gray of Pennsylvania. Tall, soft-spoken and articulate, Gray was himself a Baptist minister who headed a large African-American church in Philadelphia. Elected to the House in 1978, he promptly was named secretary of the Congressional Black Caucus. In 1980 he came to Fort Worth specifically to organize his ministerial colleagues to rally support for the Majority Leader. Two dozen African-American ministers promised him they would help turn out the vote for Jim Wright.

Meanwhile, in campaign speeches all across the district, Bradshaw pounded tirelessly on his claim that Jim Wright was a hopeless liberal who squandered hard-earned tax money. Whether voters were buying this story or not, Republican campaign poobahs in Washington probably were happy that Bradshaw at least was having some success in keeping Jim Wright tied up at home. Although he managed to make three out-of-state trips to campaign for Democratic colleagues in other parts of the country, this was far fewer than in previous election years.

At the urging of fellow House members, Jim Wright gave top priority to his own campaign, accepting even more invitations than usual to speak to local groups. While most of these appearances have faded into the mists of passing years, one speaking engagement stands out vividly, even today, in the memory of our friend and campaign staffer Carlos Moore.

The audience that day was a group of real estate dealers. They had gathered at a Mid-Cities hotel for an early breakfast meeting. Let it be noted here that to Jim Wright, the desirability of such early-morning gatherings ranks only slightly ahead of root canals. He is one of the millions of Americans who prefer to saunter, rather than leap, into the day's activities—preferably after a good night's sleep followed by copious quantities of black coffee. Having been denied the sleep by a late night strategy meeting and the coffee by a traffic tie-up, his eyelids hung limply at half-mast when he and Carlos Moore walked into the hotel that morning. Even so, he gave a lively greeting to the first fellow he met walking toward the meeting room.

"Good morning, Red!" he cried. "Great to see you."

I don't think that guy's name is Red, Carlos thought to himself.

At the door of the meeting room, Jim Wright met another man.

"Good morning, Red!" he bubbled. "How've you been?"

I know damn well that fellow's name is not Red, Carlos thought.

Only after entering the room and being seated did Carlos and Jim Wright discover the truth. Each of the fifty or so real estate dealers gathered at the tables wore a name tag, imprinted with big, box letters: "RED CARPET." Below that, in much smaller type, was the word, "Breakfast." And below that, in still smaller letters, was the name of the wearer.

"I didn't really get into trouble until I called that first woman Mrs. Carpet," Jim Wright joked.

Even so, a few days later, he issued a strict order that our staff, in preparing name tags, should always to put the name of the person at the very top, in block letters at least half an inch high.

With election day now only weeks away, Bradshaw steadily increased the drumbeat of anti-Jim Wright television spots he had begun many months before. Using half-truths and dark innuendoes, these spots accused Jim Wright of voting to give away the Panama Canal to the Communists, of frittering away tax dollars to keep a wasteful New York City afloat, and of supporting a devastating windfall profits tax on oil and a 10-cent-a-gallon tax on gasoline. These attack ads even claimed the Fort Worth Congressman was soft of defense—an accusation which must have sounded ridiculous to his friends at the Fort Worth General Dynamics plant. Thousands of GD executives, engineers and production workers personally remembered his efforts in behalf of the B-58, the F-111 and the F-16.

While many Jim Wright supporters brushed aside Bradshaw's charges as ludicrous campaign rhetoric, not everybody found them amusing. Yankee Boy, for one, itched for an opportunity to strike back. Late one night, tired after a long day of delivering yard signs, he and Mike Kestner were relaxing at our campaign headquarters. Mike was taking nourishment from his customary small paper sack, and even Yankee Boy was sipping a Michelob, albeit a naked one. Leaning back with their feet on a desk, the two demon delivery men were watching television. When one of Bradshaw's attack ads came on, Yankee Boy watched in silence. Then, sitting his beer on the desk, he got up and said he wanted to talk to me privately.

"I wonder what you would think," he said, "if I took a few ___ s off to work in the Bradshaw campaign."

"Do you know something I don't?" I asked, laughing.

"No, I'm serious," he said. "I'm sick of the crap they've ___ tting out on Jim Wright. I would like to do a little work ___ r communications."

Their communications? What are you talking about?"

"I thought it would be nice to get into their headquarters and glue all their phones together."

"You're kidding, aren't you?"

"Not at all. All it takes is a couple of drops of crazy glue in the cradles of their telephones. The next morning they couldn't pick up the receivers. They couldn't make any calls or answer any calls."

From his expression I could see he wasn't joking. "Are you nuts?" I demanded. "That's the looniest idea I ever heard of."

"I've seen it done. It really works. I think it would be pretty funny."

"No, absolutely not. Do you have any idea what Jim Wright would say about a harebrained idea like that? He's always run clean campaigns. A dirty trick like that would make Bradshaw"'s people furious—with good reason. What's more, the newspapers would have a field day. Everybody would know we did it. Can you imagine Jim Wright having to explain that? No—hell, no. Forget it. We're not going to do anything like that."

Even though I was astonished that Yankee Boy had even toyed with such an idea, I was kind of proud that I had rejected the idea so forcefully. I had made it abundantly clear that nobody in our campaign was ever to engage in this kind of campaign shenanigans. At least I thought I had.

Three weeks before the election, things were looking good. Our block-captain organization was in place, our spot telephone polling looked good, and Jim Wright was drawing warm, enthusiastic crowds wherever he spoke. The only bad news was that hundreds of our yard signs were being stolen or vandalized. Our sign crews, headed by Mike Kestner and Yankee Boy, had long since finished distributing signs to the thousands of Jim Wright supporters who had requested them. But in the dead of night many of these were being uprooted, defaced or stolen. In the River Oaks section alone, 200 signs had to be replaced in one week. It seemed obvious that this was an organized effort.

While I suspected that such vandalism might once again stir thoughts of revenge in Yankee Boy's mind, I took comfort in the fact that he never again brought up the subject to me. I was smugly confident that my stern lecture against gluing phones together had cured him once and for all of even thinking about such stunts. From now on, he surely would not dream of undertaking any campaign mischief, even in retribution for the methodical theft and destruction of our yard signs. After all, hadn't I made it clear that Jim Wright simply would not tolerate any dirty tricks by his campaign staff? Surely neither Yankee Boy nor Mike Kestner would ever ignore my clear warning. Ha.

Not until several months after the election did Yankee Boy break down and tell me about two escapades that, even up to now, I have not dared to disclose to Jim Wright.

Still gloating with satisfaction, Yankee Boy finally admitted what he and Mike did to a fund-raising barbecue that Bradshaw supporters were planning at an elegant ranch home west of Fort Worth. The day before the event, the two of them decided to climb in their infamous red pickup and drive out to check the location. Upon reaching the area, they saw that in order to enter the driveway to the ranch home, Bradshaw's campaign contributors would have to pass through an impressive arched gate just off the main highway. They also noticed one other thing.

Beside the gate stood a steel tower perhaps 60 feet in height. As a stranger to Texas, Yankee Boy had no idea what purpose the tower served, but of one thing he was sure.

"What a great place for a Jim Wright sign!" he cried.

"You bet! A real big one--right at the top!" whooped Mike.

That night, as an occasional car whizzed by on the highway, Yankee Boy made a sign delivery unlike any he had ever made before. This one wasn't simply a matter of jogging up in the bright sunshine and thrusting a sign into a lush green lawn. Instead it was a matter of climbing nervously up a cold steel ladder in the darkness with a few tools and a rope. In the gloom below he could barely make out the figure of Mike.

"It didn't look this high from the ground," Yankee Boy said weakly.

"What's the matter—no guts?" Mike snickered.

"Shut up, you bastard! Have you got the sign tied onto the rope?"

"It's all set on my end. Just pull your end of the rope and haul it up."

Clinging onto the tower ladder with one hand while struggling in the darkness with the other hand to work the sign into position, Yankee Boy finally got it securely fixed in place. Then began the most delicate, dangerous part. Carefully, slowly, he began working his way down, stopping to unbolt the ladder, section by section, and remove it from the tower. After going to this much trouble to get the sign up there, he damn sure didn't want anybody climbing up to take it down.

It was, Yankee Boy admitted, a foolish, perilous stunt. But the next day, when he and Mike drove back out to the scene, he decided it was almost worth the risk.

"A big bunch of fat cats had come out to the fund raiser, and they were standing around, looking at the Jim Wright sign and talking and laughing," Yankee Boy recounted. "Somebody had brought up a big steam shovel, and one poor guy was standing in the bucket, way up in the air, trying to reach that big Jim Wright sign on the tower."

And if that little episode wasn't bad enough to give Jim Wright nervous indigestion, Yankee Boy's next story certainly was.

The way he remembered it, one day about two weeks before the election, he and Mike were on their way to lunch and decided to drive past Bradshaw headquarters. "They look pretty busy," Yankee Boy observed. "I think I'll ask if they need any help."

From a pay phone, he called and identified himself as a dedicated Republican who wanted to help Jim Bradshaw beat that worthless scalawag Jim Wright. He asked if he could do anything to help.

Yes, by all means, he was told. The Bradshaw people were running late in getting out their yard signs, and a large number of volunteers were being mobilized. At 8 o'clock Saturday morning, they were to report to a warehouse where the signs were stored. There would be coffee and doughnuts, and volunteers would be given a number of signs to distribute. Yankee Boy jotted down the address of the warehouse and promised that he and a friend would be delighted to help.

On Friday night the notorious red pickup, occupied by these two unlikely Jim Bradshaw volunteers, pulled up to the warehouse. Located in an isolated industrial area, it was a corrugated metal building with only one entrance. The two swinging doors were fastened by a chain and a small lock.

"That looks like a mighty puny little lock," observed Mike Kestner.

"Just what I was thinking," said Yankee Boy. "Suppose a thief wanted to break in. No way that little bitty lock would stop him."

"And if he got inside, he might steal all those yard signs."

"And we wouldn't have anything to deliver tomorrow morning."

"That'd be awful. We can't let that happen."

"Hell, no. It's our duty to put a stronger lock on this chain."

"Right. And I know exactly where I can find one."

Within an hour or so, the additional lock was in place. Where it came from is uncertain, but from its size it would have been suitable for the Fort Knox Gold Vault.

"There—that ought to keep all those yard signs safe from thieves," said Yankee Boy.

"Not so fast," Mike cautioned. "If it's a professional thief, he might pick the lock."

"You're right. How can we keep that from happening, I wonder."

"Maybe if we broke the key off in the lock, a thief couldn't pick it."

"Great idea. You got any pliers in the pickup?"

True to their word, Mike and Yankee Boy showed up as scheduled at the warehouse Saturday morning. The Bradshaw people were serving coffee and doughnuts to the volunteers.

"How long before we can get our signs?" Yankee boy asked.

"Not long. We're trying to find out who has the key to the warehouse," replied a Bradshaw aide. "Go ahead and have another cup of coffee while you're waiting."

Almost an hour passed.

Walking up to the Bradshaw aide, Yankee Boy made a show of looking at his watch. "We can't wait any longer. We've got some other chores this morning."

"Sorry about this," said the Bradshaw aide, "but we're going to have to reschedule the sign deliveries for another day. There's been some kind of a mix-up about getting into the warehouse."

"Some kind of a mix-up?" Yankee Boy demanded. "Well, if you people aren't any better organized than that, we're leaving—and we won't be back!"

On election day, Jim Wright scored a spectacular victory, receiving 61 per cent of the votes in an overwhelming endorsement of his work as Congressman for the 12th District of Texas.

Despite the assistance of Eddie Chiles, NCPAC, the Republican Congressional Campaign Committee and his own vigorous efforts, Bradshaw wound up the race with 38 per cent of the votes and a campaign debt of $126,500.

But it could have been worse. At least I kept Yankee Boy from gluing his phones together.

17

Craig Raupe—Pigs, Politics and Presidents

Craig Raupe had a dream. He wanted to go back to the little Texas town of Granbury, buy a farm and raise hundreds and hundreds of pigs. "I'm not talking about just a few pigs," he used to say. "I'm talking about pork production."

Despite a fascinating and useful life, Craig never quite managed to realize his dream. He got sidetracked into politics which, next to pigs, he loved better than anything. After working thirty years in a multitude of jobs in Washington, he wound up with thousands of friends but only two pigs. They were given to him as a spoof by several members of Congress, and he kept them for a time under his desk in the House of Representatives.

One day a grizzled old tourist, shuffling along the ornate marble hallway outside the Majority Leader's office, suddenly froze in his tracks, looking puzzled. "I hear a pig," he said.

"Shush, papa!" ordered his wife. "Don't be silly. We're in the Capitol of the United States."

Before the health department could discover his secret, Craig crated up the pigs, intending to send them to Texas by air freight. But the airline refused to accept them, saying the Agriculture Department prohibited interstate shipment of livestock by air. Undaunted, Craig appealed to a friend in the airline business.

Listing the rancid little creatures on the shipping invoice as "rare dogs," the friend smuggled them aboard a plane bound for Dallas/Fort Worth Airport. That was close as Craig ever came to becoming a big-time pork producer in Texas.

Even in the face of this professional disappointment, the life of this amiable country boy with stooped shoulders and level head could never have been called dull. Once he sat at the right hand of the Majority Leader, helping orchestrate the schedule and legislation of the U.S. House of Representatives. Another time he managed a large chunk of Eastern Airlines. He helped fight the Cold War in Indochina and Indonesia, achieved two bizarre meetings with Harry S. Truman, saved Lyndon B. Johnson from a major embarrassment, and set his subcommittee chairman's hair on fire. Through all these incarnations there remained only one unchanging component—the abiding respect and loyalty that he and Jim Wright felt toward each other. No two brothers were ever closer.

Like the man he would serve for 35 years, Craig was a child of the Depression. He grew up in the tiny farming community of Granbury, a village which slid off Norman Rockwell's easel and wound up 40 miles southwest of Fort Worth. Even today the town retains much of the charm and neighborliness of a bygone era. Nestled alongside a magnificent lake spawned by the Brazos River, the town has a square dominated by its historic courthouse. Around the square are buildings dating back to days when we prefer to believe life was simpler.

"After the second World War other Texas towns started modernizing their buildings," Craig told me. "But Granbury had no industry and was too damn poor to fix up anything. So things look today pretty much the way they did about a hundred years ago."

In the 1960's Granbury's quiet seductiveness began to attract wealthy retirees from Fort Worth and Dallas, along with an assortment of musicians, actors, writers and poets—"the artsy-fartsy set," Craig snorted. Even with these newcomers threatening to infiltrate, if not to overwhelm, the local citizenry, and even with the town getting a new Wal-Mart big enough to hold an airport, Craig would never have forsaken the little community. Hardly would a day go by that he did not mention his plan eventually to return to his childhood home on the shady banks of the Brazos, only a few blocks from the courthouse square. "If I have a paramour," he said, "it's Granbury."

Uprooted by World War II from this idyllic little community, Craig wound up as a teenage sailor aboard a battleship in the Pacific. Whenever the ship went to general quarters, he once recalled, he would scurry to his battle station in the powder magazine deep in the bowels of the ship. There he worked feverishly amid tons of explosives, knowing that even the tiniest spark could spell disaster for the ship and everybody in it. It would have taken nothing more than a couple of matches rubbing together in the pocket of a careless shipmate, or maybe even a spark from a carelessly-dropped wrench striking the steel deck. The ship would have gone up like an 800-foot-long firecracker.

Thus, while he was busily sending up powder bags so the gun crews could shoot at the bad guys, it was also crucial for Craig to keep the good guys from blowing themselves up by acting without thinking. Curiously enough, this was pretty close to the jobs he was later destined to do in Washington.

Craig Raupe and Jim Wright met in Weatherford in 1953. Craig had come to town to accept a job teaching history at Weatherford Junior College, and Jim Wright was the town's youthful Mayor. When Craig received one of the letters the Mayor routinely sent out to welcome new citizens, Craig responded by asking him for a job to tide him over the summer, until he began his teaching job.

From the very beginning the Mayor liked this gangly young newcomer who somehow radiated an impossible but delightful combination of earthiness and intellectuality. He cursed like a longshoreman, as if a swearword were as essential as a period to a properly structured sentence. Regardless of whether he picked up his purple prose as a boy, as a teenager in the Navy, or as a conscious safeguard against pomposity, his language always hit the mark.

For he was, in fact, an intellectual. Interspersed with his profanity were occasional observations on subjects as obscure as the political theories of Thomas Hobbes. It didn't take Jim Wright long to perceive that here was a man who loved the kindred arts of politics and government as much as he himself did. Better still, this new citizen of Weatherford had an abiding sense of right and wrong—a quality Jim Wright would see demonstrated shortly after hiring him to supervise the city swimming pool.

In 1953 Weatherford's pool, like those of virtually every other city in Texas which even had a pool, was closed to African-Americans. It was simply the way things were. True, Ku Kluxers and diehard segregationists could be found in almost every town in our state, but most white people were not mean-spirited or cruel. My mother would almost cry whenever anybody recalled the lynching of a black man in our little town a quarter century before.

Our main sin, I suppose, was in accepting the world the way we found it. In grammar school, I knew that white kids went to one school, Negro kids to another, and Mexican kids to a third. Today I can see now how wrong that was, but I didn't then. In those Depression days, the desperate poverty of Negro and Mexican families used to sadden me far more than the fact that their world was isolated from ours. Even when our family was evicted from our home and had little more than pinto beans and cornbread for supper, I knew we were far better off than the families living in shacks with dirt floors and eating flour tortillas on the other side of the Missouri-Pacific tracks. On the scale of human priorities, having food and shelter outweighs social equality every time. And in those days, the connection between the two had not yet dawned on many of us.

It was only later, after my generation came home from World War II, that the fundamental unfairness of segregation began to gnaw at our consciences. It happened to a lot of us, including Craig Raupe and Jim Wright.

After the Mayor hired him to run Weatherford's swimming pool, Craig used to stand at the gate day after day, fretting at the sight of little black kids sweltering outside the chain link fence as white youngsters frolicked and shrieked with joy in the pool. Finally Craig could stand it no longer.

"Dammit to hell, Jim—this just ain't fair," Craig said. "But what am I going to do? I don't know how long I can live with this. Before long some of those litttle colored kids are going to come up and ask me to get in the pool."

Today it seems unthinkable that any such subject would even need to be discussed. Yet in small town Texas, a full year before the U.S. Supreme Court outlawed school segregation, only a local city official of extreme naivity would have summarily wiped out a social norm, however misguided, that had been observed in his community for more than a century. As Mayor, Jim Wright knew that in the past, incidents less consequential than this had triggered racial upheavals in other Texas towns. There could be no doubt that opening the pool was the right thing to do. Yet it could trigger grave political consequences, perhaps even violence. Of course, he realized, a decision of this magnitude did not necessarily have to be announced to the blare of trumpets. As a matter of fact, it did not have to be announced at all.

"If it happens," he said quietly to Craig, "let it happen."

Eventually it did happen. When the first few little black kids showed up, apparently nobody in Weatherford even blinked. So quietly and gradually was the pool opened that only a handful of people were even aware of it. Except, of course, for a small number of black kids who found the searing Texas summers much more enjoyable than before. In retrospect, the subdued opening of the pool may have been Craig's first hint that in politics, as in the Navy, a fellow could help the good guys without blowing up the ship.

This, incidentally, was not the only racially-charged controversy defused by Craig's new friend the Mayor. In the days before the historic verdict in Brown vs. the Board of Education, black students in Weatherford had no high school of their own, yet they were barred from the high school white kids attended. Thus, for African-American students, public education ended with grade school. Appalled by this unfairness, Jim Wright quietly persuaded the City Council to provide bus service to take black youngsters to high school in Fort Worth.

In achieving these two subdued victories without triggering a major upheaval in a small, tightly-segregated Texas town in 1953, Jim Wright and Craig Raupe had displayed masterful political skills. Jim Wright did not know it at the time, but his ingenuity soon would be tested again. As unlikely it might seem, Craig was about to be engulfed in a controversy involving, of all things, a municipal water shortage.

In 1954 Weatherford was in the grip of a devastating seven-year drouth. So severe did the water shortage eventually become that the City Council was forced to put a complete ban on lawn and shrub watering. A few conscientious homeowners observed the ordinance, but many ignored the no-watering edict and continued to irrigate the grass and plants around their homes.

By then Craig had left his job at the swimming pool and was working at the city-owned water and electric plant. His boss there was Conrad Russell. A former Mayor and widely-known civic leader, Conrad at this time was superintendent of the city's utility plant, and he was deeply worried about Weatherford's dwindling water supply.

"People don't realize just how serious this is," Conrad told Craig. "Nobody's paying any attention to this new city ordinance. If people keep watering their lawns, one day they may try to get a glass of water and find their kitchen faucet as dry as the Sahara Desert."

"What can we do?" Craig asked.

"We've got to find somebody watering their lawn in violation of the law and make an example of them. Prove to the public that we mean business."

"Have you talked to the police about trying to catch somebody?"

"Humph!" snorted Conrad. "We can't depend on the police to do this. We have got to do it."

"We?" asked Craig.

"You," said Conrad.

Craig Raupe, hardly a zealous enforcer, dutifully accepted the summons book that was thrust into his hands the next morning. He reluctantly set out on patrol, hoping against hope he found no lawn waterers. This was not to be. On Oyster Hill, a curious name for a bone-dry residential area 300 miles from the Gulf of Mexico, he happened to walk up on an unlikely suspect—a pretty housewife, blissfully watering the plants around her expensive home.

Hating himself, Craig said, "Ma'm, I'm awfully sorry, but I'm going to have to give you a ticket for watering your shrubs."

"A ticket for watering my shrubs?" she asked, obviously mystified.

"Yes, ma'm. Because of the water shortage. There's a city ordinance against watering lawns and shrubs."

"Oh, I'm sorry. I didn't know. We've been out of town on vacation."

Guiltily, Craig handed her the summons filled out in the name she gave him, Mrs. Dotti Doss.

"This is going to be very embarrassing to my husband," she said.

"Why is that, ma'm?" said Craig, sounding to himself like Joe Friday.

"He is President of the Water Board," she said.

Petrified, Craig wondered what to do. Obviously he couldn't backtrack now. Yet what were Conrad and Jim Wright going to say? *Thank you, Craig, for ticketing the wife of one of Weatherford's leading citizens who just happens to be in charge of the city water works.* Craig entertained grave doubts that this was exactly the kind of person Conrad wanted to hold up as an example of selfish, irresponsible citizenship. Then, to make matters worse, Craig learned something else.

The husband, James Doss, was also President of the Farmers & Merchants State Bank as well as one of Mayor Jim Wright's best friends.

James Doss was not pleased when his wife told him about the ticket. Furious that she would be singled out when she hadn't even heard there was a ban on watering, Doss summoned City Councilman Byron Patrick for a talk. Patrick invited a colleague, Councilman Burette Hobson, to join them. The three met at Weatherford's traditional hotbed of political intrigue, the Texas Cafe. As the two Councilmen tried to placate the angry Water Board President, Mayor Jim Wright walked in.

"Please don't come over here, Jim. There's no need for you to get mixed up in this," said Patrick.

Ignoring the advice, Jim Wright joined the crisis group over coffee as they hunted for a way out of the dilemma. On the one hand, nobody wanted to embarrass Mrs. Doss or her husband, the prominent banker. Yet, if she were let off scot free, citizens of lesser prominence surely would continue to ignore the city's urgent water-saving law. Meanwhile, the shortage would grow steadily worse until one day there might be no water at all. Then, in a moment of inspired political insight, Jim Wright demonstrated the type of innovative thinking that was later to serve him well for 35 years in Congress.

"Look, James," he told the banker. "Why don't you make this a matter of pride? Go public with an announcement. Say, 'I *insist* on paying this fine. True, my wife wasn't aware of the watering ban. But I insist on paying the penalty as a good citizen because our city is facing a desperate water shortage. Every one of us must stand together in this crisis. As Water Board President, I want to set an example of responsible citizenship.' "

However bizarre episodes like this may seem today, these were the shared experiences which welded together the lifelong friendship between Jim Wright and Craig Raupe. Their fateful meeting in Weatherford in 1953 would be a high point in both their lives. And while neither realized it, this was just the beginning.

Politically savvy and intensely loyal, Craig was destined to help Jim Wright either as a staffer or as a tireless friend for the rest of his life. Early in their acquaintance, Craig bestowed on his new friend a tribute he reserved for selected people.

"Jim Wright," he would say, "you're a great man."

One sweltering afternoon later that summer, Craig was sitting at home in his undershirt, trying to keep cool, when there was a knock on the door. It was Jim Wright, and he had come to tell Craig he was thinking about running for Congress. Under no illusion, he knew it would be an uphill fight against the basic power structure of the Fort Worth area. He would be challenging Wingate Lucas, an entrenched incumbent, as well as his powerful patron, Amon G. Carter, publisher of the *Star-Telegram*.

Excited by the prospect of a race even against such staggering odds, Craig's political juices began flow. Damn right you ought to run, he told Jim Wright. Together they began a series of meetings with potential supporters and political leaders.

"Jim Wright said he wanted to ask their advice, but that was just bull," Craig told *Star-Telegram* reporter Larry Neal years afterward. "He already had his mind made up. I was the only one there who told him unreservedly to go."

In defiance of all political logic, Jim Wright won the election. The new Congressman packed up and headed for Washington, along with his one-time swimming pool superintendent. Craig was now Administrative Assistant, or chief of staff, to the new Congressman for the 12th District of Texas, which at that time covered all of Tarrant and four neighboring counties.

Having driven to Washington in his elderly green Chrysler, Craig began setting up Jim Wright's office in the Longworth Building, just across busy Independence Avenue from the gleaming white dome of the Capitol. It was in this office, during those first few weeks, that he met two people destined to play significant roles in his life.

The first was Larry L. King, a brash, talented former newspaper reporter from the far reaches of West Texas. Like Craig, Larry privately considered himself an unabashed, free-thinking liberal, if not a closet socialist. Larry, too, had just arrived in Washington. He was Administrative Assistant to another new Texas Congressman, J.T. Rutherford of Odessa. In later years Larry would achieve fame as an author and playwright, but in those first heady but bewildering days at the Capitol, he and Craig were content to share advice, political gossip and an occasional beer or two at a now-defunct Congressional watering hole called Mike Palm's.

One day, while Larry was huddled with Craig on either pressing matters of state or some ribald new joke, another person walked through the office door—a person who, even as much as Craig himself, would affect Jim Wright's life for decades to come. Kathy Mitchell had heard that the new Congressman was looking for a secretary to work temporarily in his district office in Fort Worth, and she had decided to apply. She had never been to Texas and, up to now, had never entertained any idea of going. But she was young, single, attractive and adventuresome, and she was here to check on the job possibility.

In an interview, Craig was impressed with her quiet charm, her credentials and her alert brown eyes that appeared to sweep in far more information than she felt it necessary to share. It took Craig only a few minutes to decide to hire her, and it was one of the finest things he ever did for Jim Wright. For a few weeks she worked in the new Washington office with Craig and two other staff members, Helen Lee Fletcher and Opal Beland. Then, with sublime self-confidence, Kathy climbed into her convertible and struck out alone for Texas. It was the beginning of a career in which she would serve Jim Wright with keen intelligence, sound judgment and unswerving loyalty for the rest of her working life.

Getting a Congressional office set up and running smoothly is like wrestling an octopus. Every time you think you've got one tentacle of responsibility under control, two more reach out and grab you. Craig and the other staffers worked with Jim Wright on endless details of hiring, payrolls, supplies, schedules, appointments, legislation, committees, reports, hearings, visits, trips, telephones and, of course, constituent cases—cases, cases, cases.

A "case" is a letter or phone call from a constituent asking his Congressman for help with a problem involving a government agency. It may be a foulup over Aunt Martha's Social Security check. Or maybe a businessman making an urgent trip to Europe needs help in getting a passport processed in time. It can be any one of a thousand things, and Craig soon found himself neck deep in helping resolve such problems.

By habit an early riser, he would arrive in the office about 6 a.m. If the morning mail contained a favorable case decision, Craig would pick up the phone and call the constituent back home to pass along the good news. In those days, Texas was not on daylight savings time and Washington was two hours ahead of Fort Worth.

Often, after asking Craig to thank Congressman Wright for his help, the sleepy constituent would ask, "By the way, what time do you fellows start to work up there?" Years later, Craig told me he was so busy in those days that he once met himself coming back.

Today newly-elected members of Congress can easily make themselves heard on major issues. But in 1955, freshmen legislators were expected to be seen but not heard, especially on major issues. It would have been unthinkable for a new Congressman to be given a role in shaping crucial House decisions such as those on taxes and defense. These were the exclusive domain of the old bulls--mostly elderly Southerners who, with decades of seniority, chaired the key committees. The crucial House Rules Committee, for example, was headed by crusty old Howard Smith of Virginia, who had been in Congress since 1931.

Carl Vinson of Georgia, chairman of the Armed Services Committee, was elected in 1914.

Bowing to reality, the freshman Congressman from Fort Worth decided to zero in on a relatively less prominent issue and try to make it his own. Looking around, he found a perfect niche—soil conservation. The need to preserve this precious resource had been one of his genuine interests for many years, and it was a subject in which the old curmudgeons of the House had shown little interest. Moreover, an ideal opportunity had just popped up.

Because of the work he had done in this field before coming to Congress, Jim Wright had been invited to deliver the keynote speech at a major national soil conservation meeting in New Orleans. It would be the first important national forum for the new Congressman from Fort Worth, and he was determined to make his speech a real bell-ringer. For several days he worked diligently, crafting and honing a dramatic call for America to wake up to the dangers of soil erosion. Finally he finished the speech—except for one important point. On his way out of the office one day, he handed the text to Craig, using his customary nickname.

"Judge, in this speech I point out that we're losing our top soil at the rate of one inch every sixteen years," he said. "But I also want to say how long it takes nature to make an inch of top soil. I'd like for you to get the Library of Congress to research this, please. Then just insert the correct figure in the speech, OK?"

Craig nodded, intending to do so right away. But he was fighting a whole battalion of octopuses that day, and he forgot about the speech.

Several days later, as Jim Wright was preparing to leave for New Orleans, he stuck his head out the door of his private office and asked Craig if the speech was ready.

Caught entirely off guard, Craig thought fast. "Yes, sir," he lied. "I'll bring it right in." Then, rummaging through the piles of papers on his desk, he found the forgotten speech. With only minutes to act, he seized the first figure that popped into his head and frantically typed 'one million years' in the blank space Jim Wright had thoughtfully provided.

At the New Orleans meeting the speech was a resounding success. Elated by the applause and favorable comments he received, Jim Wright returned to Washington and promptly arranged for time on the House floor to repeat his urgent call for an all-out war against soil erosion.

"It took nature a million years to build a single inch of topsoil," he declared in words preserved today in yellowing copies of the *Congressional Record*. "We are depleting it at the rate of one-sixteenth inch each year. Thus in a meager sixteen years, we are denuding the earth of a million years of nature's labor."

While Craig didn't tell Jim Wright that he had made up the figure, he began having pangs of conscience. As a professional educator, he felt guilty for having put an inaccurate figure out into the public domain. Worse still, he knew he had done so for no reason except to protect himself. For many months, he wondered what the figure should have been. Finally, for his own peace of mind, he telephoned the Library of Congress. In a few days, he got a call back.

"I found the figure you wanted," the researcher said, "It takes approximately a million years for nature to make an inch of topsoil."

"A million years!" Craig whooped. "That's wonderful—just wonderful."

Puzzled at this reaction, the researcher said, "I'm glad you are pleased."

"Can you give me the documentation on this? Did it come from an authoritative source?"

"Oh, yes," replied the researcher. "This figure came from the keynote speech at last year's national soil conservation meeting in New Orleans."

Unlike many Americans, Craig did not consider politics a dirty word. On the contrary, he regarded politics as the essential ingredient to self-government. Nobody did he admire more than politicians who had the guts to make decisions which, however unpopular at the time, they believed to be in the best interests of the nation. One of his special heroes was Harry S. Truman.

Once disparaged as nothing more than a stooge for the Pendergast political machine, this once obscure county judge from Kansas City came to exemplify Craig's vision of all that is right and noble in American politics. He marveled at the courage of this plain-spoken, everyday American who stood alone and

Alan's last wor
"A vision without a plan
allucination." Ambassad
on Kirk at Friday night
n the Margaret Hunt Hi
ridge.

in the face of some of the most torturous judgments a
s ever had to make—the decision to drop the atomic
nd American troops to defend South Korea, to fight
gic and remorseless Senator Joseph McCarthy, and to
e to the vainglorious Douglas MacArthur that the
n put elected civilian officials, not five-star generals,
f making U.S. foreign policy.

Craig, even such acts of Presidential heroism paled in
with the courage Truman displayed in the Presidential
1948. The Republican candidate was Thomas E.
Dewey of New York, a dapper, mustachioed former district
attorney whom some people said reminded them of the little man
on top of a wedding cake. Political pollsters and pundits had led
the nation to believe Dewey's election was a foregone conclusion.
Poor little Harry Truman, the Kansas City haberdasher who
somehow got himself elected Vice President and then inherited
the White House when President Franklin D. Roosevelt died in
1945, was given virtually no chance at all of winning his own
term in the White House.

One of the few persons who refused to believe the pundits and
the polls was Truman himself. Even though he had to scrounge
even for enough money to pay for his campaign train, he set off
on a rousing whistlestop tour that stirred the nation and soon had
thunderous crowds shouting, "Give 'em hell, Harry!" Ignoring
this upsurge in support for the scrappy little fellow speaking from
the rear of the train, the know-it-all columnists and pollsters
persisted in their smug predictions of a decisive Dewey victory.
On election night, Truman, beaming and confident, didn't even
bother to stay up to watch the returns. He went to bed, slept
soundly and woke up having achieved probably the most
astonishing come-from-behind election victory in American
history, beating Dewey by more than 2 million popular votes and
an electoral vote of 303 to 189.

Everyday people from coast to coast were thrilled by this
spectacular victory, but none more than Craig, who at the time
was a student under the GI Bill at North Texas State College in
Denton, Texas. Here he was engaged in twin pursuits. One was
courting Joyce Adkins, the brilliant and beautiful campus queen he
was destined to marry. Craig's other pursuit was steeping himself

in the subjects he loved—American history and government. Recognizing that Truman's election would stand as a significant watermark in U.S. political lore, Craig undertook an exhaustive research project that led him to write his master's thesis on how he believed his Democratic hero had managed to pull it off. He worked hard on this paper and was inordinately proud of it. His fondest hope was that somewhere, someday, he might be able to present it personally to Harry Truman. Now, in 1956, in Washington as a faceless young Congressional staffer for a freshman Congressman from Texas, he saw his chance.

Bursting with the news, Craig called his pal Larry L. King to say he had learned Harry Truman was coming to Washington for the first time since leaving the White House. He was to speak to the Jefferson-Jackson Day dinner, and would be staying at the Mayflower Hotel. If Craig could somehow wangle his way in to give Truman his study on the 1948 election, would Larry come along and take their picture? Perhaps realizing Craig would never accept no for an answer, Larry agreed to go along with the scheme.

"Larry King," Craig said, "you're a great man."

Borrowing the office camera he used to take pictures of constituents who visited his boss, Larry set out with Craig early in the morning for the Mayflower. With sublime confidence, Craig strode up to a house phone and rang upstairs. "Let me speak to Harry Truman," he said.

"This is Harry Truman," bounced back a flat Missouri twang.

Only in the innocent America of yesteryear could such a thing have happened, but the former President invited Craig and Larry up for coffee. With Midwestern graciousness, Truman made the two young Texans feel welcome. He smiled and accepted the thesis and shook hands and smiled some more as Larry energetically manipulated the camera for what he thought was about a dozen pictures. But shortly afterward, at a quick-service photo shop, all the film turned out to be blank.

"Raupe cursed and abused me at great length," Larry said in recounting the incident in *The Washington Post* many years later. But Craig was nothing if not resourceful.

Knowing that Truman, in a habit dating from his days as a World War I artillery captain, still enjoyed starting each day with a vigorous early-morning walk, Craig called Larry at home that night. Get your expletive-deleted camera and meet me in the morning so we can try to catch him on the street outside the hotel, Craig ordered. Today, dear friends, any two strangers attempting to intercept a President on the street would be set upon by large numbers of muscular young men in trench coats and tiny trademark earphones. But believe it or not, in that tranquil and far more civilized year of 1956, they caught the energetic Mr. Truman. Larry demonstrated his mastery over the cantankerous camera, and Craig got the picture he wanted. He got it for the same reason Harry Truman got his own term in the White House. He was too damn stubborn to give up.

After his first six years with Jim Wright in Washington, Craig began to get restless. The United States was being drawn ever more deeply into the war in Indochina, and Craig yearned for a piece of the action. Signing up as a State Department foreign service officer, he took his wife Joyce on assignments to Vietnam and Indonesia. On their return to Washington the following year, Craig signed up with Agency for International Development for duty far more hazardous—the job of convincing Congress what a grand idea it was to keep appropriating tax money year after year for foreign aid. This was one of the toughest, most thankless jobs in town.

On the Hill, foreign aid is unsurpassed as an arena for shameless political demagoguery. The idea of sending American dollars overseas enrages millions of hard-working American taxpayers, especially when they have been led to believe the money goes into projects that look ridiculous. Nearly any Congressional office can count on a steady drumbeat of angry mail demanding to know why we are pouring our money down a rathole in Afghanistan or Cambodia. Regrettably those wretched little African kids with matchstick arms and legs and swollen bellies have foolishly neglected to hire fat-cat Washington lobbyists to fight for the cups of gruel they occasionally get with U.S. foreign aid money.

Then too, foreign aid, however beneficial it may be to U.S. foreign policy, has seldom failed to get a bad rap in the press. Newspapers down through the years have specialized in exposing harebrained projects in which our foreign aid money has been foolishly frittered away. While lawmakers could have dug into these abuses and corrected a large number of them, it was far easier just to go along with a large segment of the American people in condemning the whole shebang as a senseless waste of our money. Yet in the 1960s it was Craig's job to convince Congress that U.S. foreign aid served worthwhile diplomatic as well as moral purposes. This was not easy.

One day, for example, Craig found himself in a high-level policy meeting where AID officials were discussing plans to use U.S. foreign aid money to build a brewery in Turkey. *A brewery in Turkey?* At first he could not believe what he was hearing.

AID officials, brimming with enthusiasm for the project, were convinced that the brewery would bring significant benefits to the sluggish Turkish economy.

"That's just dumb!" Craig protested. "When we take our appropriations bill to the Senate next week, can't you imagine them asking why we are using tax dollars to build breweries?"

Despite his arguments, the policy-makers gave formal approval to the brewery project. As a creature of the Hill, Craig realized the decision represented sheer idiocy in the agency's relations with Congress. Already he could visualize the scene:

"A brewery? Did you say a. . . a brewery, suh?" the chairman demanded, almost choking on the word.

A hush fell over the crowded Congressional hearing room. From his seat high on the rostrum the chairman peered down at the witness in thunderstruck disbelief.

"Ah cannot bring mahself to believe what you are tellin' me, suh," he cried. "You are sayin' that those striped-pants do-gooders down at the State Department have... are pouring mill-yones of ouh hard-earned Amurrican tax dollars into building a... a (choke) brewery, suh, in Turkey?"

The AID official in the witness chair squirmed and wished he were dead. "Yes, sir," he croaked.

Reporters at the press table overturned several chairs as they scrambled out to their telephones. "If you want to hear about a screwup, listen to this!" one newsman whooped to his bureau in the National Press Building. "Guess what those oddballs at State have done now!" shouted a radio reporter. "Boyoboy—the White House is going to love explaining this one!" laughed a wire service man.

Within an hour the story was in the hands of every right-wing radio talk show host in the nation. Their lines were jammed as thousands of Americans called to protest to this latest example of Washington stupidity. For three days the story and its fallout were splashed across page one of every newspaper in America.

But none of this happened. It didn't happen because a one-time sailor who learned his trade in the powder magazine of battleship still recognized how easily the good guys could do something stupid and blow themselves up.

Back in his office, Craig did a lot of soul-searching. To whom did he owe his loyalty—the Agency for International Development or the best interests of the United States Government? It didn't take long for the answer to become clear. He picked up the phone and called his friend Walter Jenkins, right-hand man to President Lyndon B. Johnson.

On Jenkins's orders, he reported to the White House and was immediately whisked into the Oval Office. He told his story to the President.

Johnson listened quietly, without comment. Then he picked up the phone and called Secretary of State Dean Rusk.

"Dean, I don't know what's going on over there," he said. "I've heard some tales. But I want you to know one thing—I don't want any breweries built anywhere with federal money."

Having left unquenched the thirst of uncounted Turkish citizens, Craig left his post at AID for an entirely new and unfamiliar professional challenge—a job as chief lobbyist for Eastern Airlines. Now defunct, Eastern in those days was one of the premier trunk airlines, especially dominant on East Coast routes. So pleased was Eastern's management with Craig's performance in Washington that he soon was promoted to Vice President in charge of the airline's Southeast region, based in Miami.

Although few people were as wise as Craig in the ways of Washington, it took him a while to get acclimated to the rarefied heights of airline management. He discovered, for example, that straight-line logic was not always practicable. Once at a high-level Eastern management meeting in New York, he listened to an exhaustive report from the Vice President in charge of baggage.

"It's a privilege to report that this year we have managed to reduce our baggage losses by nearly three percentage points," the executive said proudly. "Moreover, we plan in the coming year to reduce our baggage losses even more."

At this point, Craig characteristically went to the heart of the matter. "Why don't we try not to lose any baggage?"he asked.

While other Eastern executives laughed uproariously at the idea of trying to run an airline without losing any bags, Craig told me later they were far less amused at the airline's occasional loss of a coffin being flown as cargo. Many well-to-do New Yorkers who moved to Florida in retirement would leave instructions with their families to return them home for burial. After making arrangements, the grieving widow often would ask for assurance, "Now my husband will be going back on the same plane I am on, won't he?" In those cases where the coffin somehow was placed on the wrong flight and taken to another destination, the airline would be turned upside down until it was located and returned.

Despite small dramas like this, Craig turned out to be an exceptional airline man. He won repeated raises, citations and awards from Eastern, but the airline at that time was being wracked by a desperate fight for corporate control. As Craig related the story to me, one day he got an abrupt call: "You're a hell of a good man, Craig, and we're sure sorry to have to let you go. But we've been running two airlines here, and you've been working for the wrong one."

This was the most devastating professional insult of Craig's life. It shook him to the marrow of his bones. Never before had he failed at anything. Even though he was blameless and was fired as part of the corporate upheaval, he was haunted by the illusion that he somehow had fallen short. To him, being fired even under these circumstances represented a humiliating personal defeat. He began drinking heavily. Finally, jobless, despondent and leaning ever more heavily on the bottle, he turned to his best friend for help.

At that time, Jim Wright had just become chairman of the House Public Works Subcommittee on Investigations, a panel that had earned enormous prestige by rooting out corruption in the Interstate Highway Program. Without hesitation he hired Craig as one of his staff investigators. Here, after a desperate personal battle against booze, he regained control of his life. Never a person for half-way measures, Craig underwent an astounding change. At the height of his addiction, he seemed to guzzle enough whiskey to put a Kentucky distillery on overtime. And then, virtually overnight, he threw himself with the same zeal into the battle against alcoholism. He would attend three Alcoholics Anonymous meetings a day—one at noon, two in the evening. In between he went to hospitals or homes to help others in their battle against booze. In later years, after Jim Wright became Majority Leader, Craig quietly extended his AA work even to the floor of the House.

"If he saw a Congressman chronically nipping, he would write him a private note or get together with him for a talk," recalled his friend Gary Hymel, chief staffer to Speaker Tip O'Neill.

Never once after Craig's astonishing transformation did he fall off the wagon. Especially do I want to assure you he was cold sober the day he set Jim Wright's hair on fire.

It happened while the Investigations Subcommittee was examining various means of improving airline passenger safety. One company had come up with an intriguing idea—a simple transparent hood, made of fireproof material. In the event of a crash, the company believed such a hood would give a passenger a few more precious seconds to escape from a fiery, smoke-filled cabin.

Parade magazine heard about this, and expressed interest in getting a cover picture of the subcommittee chairman, Jim Wright, demonstrating this new safety hood in the face of an honest-to-goodness burst of flame inside an honest-to-goodness airplane. There was, fortunately, no suggestion of first arranging for the airplane to crash.

Suspecting that hardly any airline would enthusiastically welcome a blazing torch inside one of its aeronautical machines even to make a picture for *Parade*, Craig came up with an alternative. He figured that a railroad passenger car interior might bear some resemblance to an aircraft cabin, at least to a camera. Moreover, railroad people were known to be far less finicky than airline people about igniting fires inside their public conveyances.

After arranging to use an idle railroad car at Washington's Union Station, Craig stopped by a neighborhood hardware store and picked up a butane blowtorch. While he had never used one of these, he knew that sometimes plumbers did, although he wasn't sure exactly for what, or how.

As the intrepid crew gathered for the camera shoot, Jim Wright fiddled with the mask and Craig fiddled with the blowtorch. Even though neither had ever used a particular device of this kind, Jim Wright seemed to know more about the hood than Craig did about the blowtorch. Eventually, however, this dutiful friend and employee of the Congressman managed to evoke large billows of flame from the torch with at least some measure of control.

With confidence born of having survived both World War II air combat in Pacific and one term in the Texas Legislature, Jim Wright gamely pulled the hood over his head. From inside came muffled words that sounded as if he were saying he was ready. Or maybe, in retrospect, he was saying, please pull down the hood a little further in the back. Anyhow, with gradually diminishing enthusiasm for this entire enterprise, Craig orchestrated a fearsome tongue of flame into what he hoped was Jim Wright's securely protected head. It was hard to tell exactly what went wrong.

Maybe Craig's aim was faulty. Or maybe Jim Wright didn't have the hood pulled down far enough in the back. Or perhaps the company never anticipated its product would be tested by a Congressional aide making his solo flight with a butane blowtorch. Anyhow, Jim Wright's hair caught fire. For a minute there was so much excitement it was hard to tell who was trying to do what. The Congressman removed the hood with somewhat greater dexterity than he had put it on. The cameraman and Craig frantically started beating the flames, an operation which, of course, marginally involved pounding the top of Jim Wright's head.

Fortunately, however, he wasn't hurt, and suffered only a negligible loss hair. Courageously he volunteered for a second picture, and this one wound up on the cover of *Parade*. Somehow, though, the idea of fireproof protective hoods never seemed to catch on, either with the airlines or with the blowtorch companies.

While I had known Craig for many years, it was not until Jim Wright decided to run for Majority Leader in 1976 that I got a chance to work closely with him. First we were thrown together during the campaign and then, after Jim Wright succeeded in winning this No. 2 position in the House, Craig became his Executive Assistant to work the House floor. I soon learned what I had suspected from Craig's work in AA—namely that he was utterly incapable of half-way measures. His credo could be summed up in only six words—go wide open, never give up. Once his brother Hugh bought a bicycle shop, and Craig kept telling me how healthy it was to ride a bicycle. Then I found that this skinny, almost gaunt fellow would go out and ride a bicycle *for a hundred miles.* On one jaunt he fell and cut a big gash in his head. He climbed back on and kept riding, waving aside motorists offering a ride to this crazy fellow pedaling down the highway with blood streaming down his face and soaking his shirt.

He never flaunted his values, but they were as solid as the Hood County Courthouse. He devoutly believed in the sanctity of democratic government, and that there was no greater honor or responsibility than to have been elected by the people to serve in public office. He was infuriated by staff members who became intoxicated with personal power.

"There are two kinds of people around here—members of Congress and clerks. You just need to remember which one you are," he used to say.

His day-to-day work reflected his deep concern for poor, the sick, the elderly and the homeless, but he would have cursed anybody who called him soft-hearted. Probably his closest approach to sentimentality was once when he gave an autographed picture to Jim Wright. Its handwritten inscription: "To the best sonuvabitch there ever was."

While Craig never gave me that much gooey affection, once he came pretty close. He and I had been trying to reason with an cantankerous committee chairman, purple with anger, who was about to fire a staffer he mistakenly believed had changed the language in a bill. It would have been a foolish action and I came right out and told him why. Furious at me, the chairman stalked off—but he didn't fire the guy. Afterward Craig looked at me and smiled.

"Marshall Lynam," he said, "you're a great man."

For three years Craig worked the floor and helped orchestrate the flow of legislation to the House floor. While he handled it with unsurpassed skill and diligence, the pressure began to tell on him. In 1979, at the age of 54, he decided to hang it up and perhaps realize his lifelong dream of raising pigs—er, that is, producing pork—in Granbury. With Joyce he went back and they built a beautiful home a stone's throw from the spot where he grew up. But then, in 1983, Joyce developed cancer and died in a matter of months. After that, Craig was never quite the same.

For a time he taught some college courses in Texas and then, perhaps drawn by Washington, a geographic paramour second only to Granbury, he returned to the capital and founded a lobbying firm with Jeanne Campbell, herself a longtime Congressional staffer.

In January of 1987, at the convening of the 100th Congress of the United States, Craig realized one of his most cherished dreams. He sat and watched as his best friend, Jim Wright, was sworn in as Speaker of the House of Representatives—the most powerful legislative office on earth. Then, almost as if he realized his life was complete because his best friend had achieved the ultimate success for an American lawmaker, Craig died suddenly of an aneurysm on October 14, 1988. He was buried beside his beloved wife Joyce in the soil of his beloved paramour, Granbury, Texas.

We human beings are not supposed to sit in judgment of such matters. But I like to think that when Craig reached the Pearly Gates, Saint Peter may have looked in his ledger, smiled and said:

"Craig Raupe, you're a great man."

18

A Nearsighted B-17 Gunner Flies Again

On two separate occasions in my life the United States Government has accorded me the honor of flying in a B-17 bomber. The first invitation came when I was a spindly, nearsighted teenager with an abdominal hernia. And then, 44 years later, as a Capitol Hill aide, still nearsighted but by then sporting a modest little tummy, I was invited to fly in another B-17. The second invitation was far more desirable for a number of reasons.

This time, for example, nobody forced me, time after time, to march naked, except for an overcoat, past dozens of giggling young women. But before delving further into those anguishing episodes, let us consider a bit of aeronautical history.

For those of you who arrived on this planet too recently to know what a B-17 is, much less why anybody would want to fly in one, I respectfully refer you to the late, late show almost anywhere in America. There, before long, you are bound to see such old-time stars as Gregory Peck, Clark Gable or Steve McQueen heroically flying one of these beautiful old airplanes which belong, alas, to another, nobler era in American history.

By any measure the most famous warplane in World War II, the B-17 was a magnificent metal monster with four engines and a hundred-foot wing. Bristling with thirteen fifty-caliber machine guns, it was known as the Flying Fortress. It carried ten young men who, usually only a year or so before, were movie ushers, farm boys, college students and soda jerks who had received what some of us regarded as a crash course, so to speak, in flight training. Then, to their astonishment, they found themselves five miles high over Germany, being kept alive by oxygen hoses in sort of an airborne deep freeze, battling Messerschmitts and plowing through malignant black clouds of flak while dropping bombs on railroad yards, oil refineries, tank factories and occasionally, through error, potato farms.

High in this surreal, sub-zero world where few men before had dared even to venture, must less wage war, droned thousands of these old airplanes. To focus the fire from their machine guns, the planes flew clustered together like puppies seeking warmth. So tight were these bomber formations that pilots dared not relax for an instant. So tense and demanding was their task that they soaked their underclothes with sweat even as ice crystallized on their oxygen masks. They knew that even a moment's inattention at the controls might mean a collision with that other B-17—the one flying just fifty feet ahead and fifty feet off their wing. At the target, the bombardier took over and each formation was forced to fly straight and level at a constant speed for several terrifying minutes that seemed to take hours. Nazi flak gunners knew that once the Fortresses began their bomb run, they were committed not to vary their course, altitude or speed. This allowed the flak batteries to calculate with mathematical precision exactly where to fire the next barrage of 88- or 105-millimeter shells.

Thus these B-17s, along with B-24 Liberators and many other types of bombers and fighters, fought a war that is unique today and will remain so forever. Never before in history had such vast armadas of airplanes waged such monumental battles in the sky. Nor ever again, now that a single thermonuclear missile can set fire to an area the size of Delaware, will man meet man in such titanic aerial conflict.

For their role in helping achieve victory in Europe, American B-17s and their crews paid a terrible price. A total of 12,731 Flying Fortresses were built. Of these, about 4,750 were lost in combat. Each carried a pilot, co-pilot, engineer, bombardier, navigator, radio operator and four gunners.

In its day, the B-17 was a technological marvel. Today it is largely a museum piece. To the kids weaned on Star Wars, these antique airplanes must seem as dated as the awkward machine Wilbur and Orville coaxed into the air in 1903 at Kitty Hawk. Luke Skywalker fans probably would smile patronizingly at a plane which had four old-timey gasoline engines, driving quaint, fan-like devices called propellers, which engineers in those days believed was necessary to make an airplane fly. Amusing to today's youngsters, too, would be the contrast between a Flying Fortress, plodding along at 165 m.p.h. with a dozen five-hundred pound bombs, and one of our modern jet fighters. Today an F-18 or F-16, flown by a lone pilot, can carry twice the bomb load, twice as high and three times as fast. But to me, performance figures don't tell the whole story. To the guys who entrusted their lives to her and survived, the B-17 will always be the most magnificent airplane ever built.

In 1987, when Jim Wright became Speaker and I was given a small office in the Capitol, my friend Colonel Frank (Mick) McKeown, an Air Force liaison officer, came in with a magnificent gift—a color print of *Fortresses Under Fire*, personally inscribed to me by the artist, Keith Ferris. The print was taken from the great B-17 mural that occupies an entire wall at the Smithsonian's Air and Space Museum. But even as a dedicated B-17 groupie with this picture dominating my office wall, I never expected the phone call I got one day in the autumn of 1988.

On the line was Major General Roger P. Scheer, a fighter pilot with 160 combat missions in Vietnam and more decorations than the National Christmas Tree, including three Silver Stars and four Distinguished Flying Crosses. Before being summoned to duty in the Pentagon, Roger Scheer had commanded the 301st Fighter Wing, a Reserve unit based at Carswell Air Force Base in Fort Worth. There he had become friends with my brother, Chief Master Sergeant Jimmy Lynam, who had diligently supervised maintenance of the F-105 Thunderchiefs in the 301st. In a casual conversation one day, Jimmy mentioned that his brother Marshall had flown as a B-17 waist gunner back in the big war.

Later, after Roger Scheer was promoted to Major General and assigned to the Pentagon as Chief of the Air Force Reserve, I occasionally worked with him on legislative matters on the Hill. He appreciated this, I'm sure. But I am convinced that if it had

not been for his friendship and respect for Jimmy Lynam, I would
never have received such an astonishing invitation.

"Would you like to take a flight in a B-17?" he asked.

"In a what?"

"In a B-17. Completely reconditioned. Just like it was in
combat. Its a long story. If you're interested, I'll tell you about
it."

Dumbfounded, it took me a few seconds to react. I couldn't
have been more surprised if he had invited me to take a quick hop
in The Spirit of St. Louis. As far as I knew, there were only four
or five B-17s, in various states of airworthiness, left in the world.
But a completely reconditioned B-17? Stunned at the offer, I
nevertheless accepted quickly—so quickly, in fact, that General
Scheer failed to mention, er, uh, a few small facts.

For example, I don't remember his telling me that the
particular B-17 on which I was being invited to ride had been
purchased by the U.S. Air Force for 20 cents.

Twenty cents? That's right. In 1971, after negotiations with
the French government, the U.S. Air Force was given title to the
skeletonized hulk of this airplane. Long since stripped of its
engines and salvageable parts, the plane had been sitting for ten
years, cannibalized and forgotten, on a remote airfield north of
Paris. For what the French undoubtedly regarded as a pile of
useless aeronautical junk, they agreed to sell for a token price of
one franc—about 20 cents.

But even more astonishing than the price was the history of
this fabulous airplane. Little by little, from General Scheer and
from an absorbing feature article entitled *Song of a Valiant Lady*
by Nathan M. Adams in the March, 1986, issue of The Reader's
Digest, I learned the whole story.

This airplane, rolled out of the Boeing plant in Seattle in
January, 1944, turned out to be *Shoo Shoo Baby*, second perhaps
only to *The Memphis Belle* as the most famous Flying Fortress of
World War II.

Flown across the Atlantic to join the growing American air
armada in England, *Shoo Shoo Baby* performed with such grace
and stability in flight she captured the heart of the first Eighth Air
Force pilot to fly her, 2nd Lt. Paul G. McDuffee. After taking
her on 16 missions, half of them deep into Germany, he was

convinced that this was a very special airplane indeed. But then McDuffee, having completed his tour of 30 missions, returned to the States. *Shoo Shoo Baby* was assigned to another crew, with 1st Lt. Robert J. Guenther as pilot. Despite her reputation as a lucky airplane, Guenther had an ominous feeling. Was she *too* lucky? Could she be overdue for a change in her unbroken streak of good fortune? His foreboding turned out to be justified.

On May 29, Guenther flew *Shoo Shoo Baby* on a raid against a Focke-Wulf fighter assembly plant in Posen, Poland. First an engine overheated and had to be feathered. Then, over the target, a burst of flak shook the plane and another engine started gushing oil, splattering the cockpit windows. This engine, too, had to be shut down.

With the two remaining engines pushed to the limit, *Shoo Shoo Baby* managed to drop her bombs on the target. But then, turning off the bomb run, she began to lose altitude. A third engine began to fail.

Realizing he could never get the plane back to England, Lieutenant Guenther turned on a course toward neutral Sweden. Fighting to stay barely 1,000 feet above the waves of the Baltic, he skillfully brought the crippled craft to a harrowing but safe landing near Malmo. Five months later, Lieutenant Guenther and his crew were flown to Scotland and freed. But in the meantime, the Swedish government had negotiated with U.S. authorities to purchase the severely-damaged bomber for $1. They repaired the plane and converted it to an airliner. Seven months after the war in Europe ended in May, 1945, *Shoo Shoo Baby*, in her new identity as Danish Airlines Flight 1750, developed landing gear trouble and made a wheels-up crash landing at Blackbushe airfield in England.

This time, too, all her occupants escaped injury, and once again the former warplane was hauled in for repairs. Restored to Danish Airline service the spring of 1946, she pioneered passenger routes to Greenland and Africa and made occasional flights to Moscow. Then, by the end of 1947, this durable old aircraft underwent yet another metamorphosis.

At that time the Royal Danish Army and Navy, together with Denmark's Geodetic Institute, were searching for a long-range aircraft to carry out an extensive photo-mapping project of Greenland's polar icecap. Because of her stability, reliability and high-altitude performance, they chose *Shoo Shoo Baby*. For this unique mission she was equipped with special cameras, larger fuel tanks and metal shields to protect the fuselage from chunks of ice thrown by the propellers. In some of the worst flying weather on earth, the tireless four-engined workhorse crosscrossed vast, forbidding areas of the Arctic month after month for the next four years, helping compile the most detailed air survey to date of the storm-swept reaches of northern Greenland. Her mission done, on October 1, 1953, she was put up for sale.

After sitting idle and unprotected on a Danish airfield for 16 months, she was purchased by France's Institut Geographique National for even more high-altitude   photo-mapping duty. Between 1956 and 1961, *Shoo Shoo Baby* mapped Lebanon, Madagascar, Algeria, Niger, Chad, Cameroon, Martinique, Guyana, Gabon and the French Congo. By this time she had logged an astounding total of 5,500 hours—more than seven months—in the air. Her reward, at last, was the boneyard.

By 1968, *Shoo Shoo Baby*, stripped of her engines, her salvageable parts and her dignity, stood as a forgotten hulk, a weathered aluminum skeleton—wings, fuselage and tail—at the lonely French airfield. But in another part of the world, an incredible aviation detective story was nearing a climax.

From Sydney, Australia, came a telephone call from Steve Birdsall, whose hobby was tracing B-17s that had survived the war and evaded the scrap heap. Through painstaking research he had tracked down both *Shoo Shoo Baby* and her very first pilot, Paul G. McDuffee. Now a retired insurance broker living in Tampa, McDuffee often had thought about the remarkable airplane he had flown on her first 16 missions. After his initial astonishment at Birdcall's call, McDuffee got excited about the discovery and launched an all-out campaign to try to retrieve this aerial ghost from the past.

Mobilizing the support of former Air Force comrades and veterans groups, McDuffee finally succeeded in persuading the Air Force to negotiate a homecoming for *Shoo Shoo Baby*. For the token fee which today would not even buy a U.S. postage stamp, the French government sold the weather-beaten hulk to the U.S. Air Force. Disassembled and packed in 27 crates, the plane was loaded on a giant C-5A and delivered to Dover Air Force Base in Delaware.

There, in 1978, a dedicated group of Air Force Reserve mechanics undertook the painstaking job of restoring the aircraft to her 1944 identity. Devoting 50,000 hours of their time, using public and private funds and scrounging parts from other junked B-17s, the Reservists completed their task in 1988. By any measure, theirs was a spectacular achievement.

With elaborate ceremonies and rousing band music, the reincarnated *Shoo Shoo Baby* was rolled out of the hangar at Dover Air Force Base on September 10, 1988. Except for her wartime-style olive drab paint job and the string of bombs stenciled on her nose to represent her combat missions, she probably looked pretty much the way she did when she rolled out of the Boeing plant as a glistening aluminum beauty in 1944. Even her old serial number, 232076, once again graced her rudder.

My wife Eddie and I were guests of General Scheer and wife Sandy for the rollout program. While I feel sheepish about admitting it, the ceremony evoked a bit more nostalgia than I had counted on. Only a fool would be sentimental about a war, but I suppose it's understandable to be sentimental about, well, a friend. True, I had never seen this particular B-17 before. But having known a number of her sisters, I felt sort of like a friend of the family. Only thing was, during the ceremony Eddie thought I might be coming down with a cold. I had to keep blowing my nose.

Later that afternoon, with General Scheer and me aboard, *Shoo Shoo Baby*'s newest flight crew cranked up the first of her four 1,200-horsepower Wright Cyclone engines. To me, there is no sound in the world as distinctive as a B-17 starting its engines—a whine, a tentative sputter, a couple of coughs and then a thunder that seems to shake the earth. Like a long-forgotten song, the roar of the engines magically rolled back the years and stirred deep-rooted memories—a few sad, a few funny...

The time was December, 1943. The place was the Army Reception Center at Fort Sam Houston, San Antonio, Texas.

"What you want to do in the Army, soldier?" asked the sergeant.

"I don't know. I've never given it much thought."

"Well, you got any particular skills? Automobile mechanic, maybe?"

"No, but I've studied a little radio. I took a correspondence course and built some radios, and things like that."

"Aha!" cried the sergeant. "Now we're getting somewhere!"

"Could you put me in the Signal Corps?"

"Nope, the Signal Corps is all full up. They're not taking any more men right now. You know how to do anything else?"

I shrugged. "Well, I don't know, then. What do you think?"

"How about the Air Force? The Air Force uses a lot of radio operators."

"Sounds OK to me. I could do radio repairs or something like that."

The sergeant's face clouded and he shook his head. "Well, we got a little problem here. The Air Force is not taking any more enlisted men. The only way you can get in the Air Force these days is to sign up as a flying cadet."

"That lets me out, I guess. I'm pretty nearsighted. I work as a movie projectionist, and I've always had to wear glasses to keep the screen in focus."

"Where are your glasses now?"

"I threw them away when they drafted me. I didn't figure I'd have to focus very many movie projectors in the Army."

The sergeant leaned over and lowered his voice. "Look," he whispered. "There's a way we can do this."

"What do you mean?"

"Simple. I sign you up for flying cadet training, right? That puts you in the Air Force. I send you to Sheppard Field for basic training. Half way through basic training, you go to your CO and say, 'Sir, I've decided I don't want to be a flying cadet.' Then the CO will say, 'OK, Lynam. We'll give you another assignment.' And then, presto!—they'll send you to radio school."

"Do you really think that will work?"

"Trust me," said the sergeant.

Strangely enough, over the next few weeks things worked out just like the sergeant predicted—up to a point. The CO did, in fact, tell me that I would be taken off the cadet roster and given another assignment. Only thing was, he didn't say what assignment it would be, or when. In the meantime, I stayed in basic training, which included military discipline, rifle practice, close order drill and, of course, marching around Sheppard Field naked.

Well, actually not quite naked. We were permitted to wear our overcoats and GI shoes. Every week or so, my squadron would be ordered to report to the base hospital for another physical exam. Since the hospital didn't have enough room for a hundred men to undress there, we were ordered first to strip naked in our barracks and then to march, like a military unit of parkbench flashers, to the hospital.

Often our marches took us past base headquarters, where offices were staffed by large numbers of civilian employees— mostly young women. As icy winds whipped up under my overcoat to chill parts of my anatomy never before exposed to a Texas blue norther, I always devoutly hoped that the pretty typists and stenographers were too busy at their desks to be looking out the window. Usually they were not. As we strode resolutely past headquarters on bony, milk-white legs, we stared stonily ahead as legions of young women pressed their noses to the windows and snickered. Sherman was right.

At the hospital, while doctors thumped on us with little rubber hammers and peered into various bodily orifices, a few enlisted medical corpsmen amused themselves by scaring the daylights out of the guys waiting in line. From the base veterinarian one medic had borrowed a gigantic hypodermic syringe used to give injections to horses. Its needle was about a foot long and the diameter of lead pencil. Often as GI's stood in line awaiting their physical exams, the medic would pick up this horrendous instrument and turn to a fellow medic with a question: "Did Dr. Schwartz want me to give this next guy his injection in his left testicle, or in his right?" On occasion a GI would faint.

In an old trunk at home I still have my copy, believe it or not, of a yellowing War Department Form 64, Physical Examination for Flying, in which a Medical Corps doctor at Sheppard Field examined me and concluded that I shouldn't be allowed to fly, at least not on our side.

In his report the doctor, one Captain M. L. Goldhamer, didn't comment on my nearsightedness. Nor did he mention the hernia I knew I had received in tumbling off a desk when I was a baby. But he said I was 12 pounds underweight and furthermore, my aptitude was so low he didn't even see any need to waste time examining me again later on. I'm not sure what made him decide

I was too inept to fly, but it didn't really matter to me. I was bound for radio school, anyhow. Sure I was.

Anyhow, when our troop train arrived at an air base just outside Las Vegas a few weeks later, nobody was more surprised than I to find out that this was a field where the Army Air Force trained gunners to fly on bombers. The only thing I could figure is that Dr. Goldhamer got so busy asking naked cadets to turn their heads and cough that he accidentally put my report in the wrong file basket. I felt sure somebody would find it, sooner or later. All this having happened 54 years ago, however, my confidence is beginning to wane.

In gunnery school I began to wonder whether, in the interest of the fellows I might be flying with, I ought to tell somebody about my nearsightedness. But I figured that my buddies would think I was just scared. I was, but I knew they were, too. Besides, chances are that if an enemy fighter got close enough to shoot at our plane, it probably would be close enough for me to see. I kept quiet.

After gunnery school the Army Air Force sent me to for air crew training to a field in Alexandria, Louisiana, where a flight surgeon promptly discovered my hernia.

"We can't let you fly with this," he said. "If you ever had to bail out, all your intestines would fall down into another part of your body."

"You mean into my—"

"Yes," he said.

"So what happens now?"

"We can operate on you and fix the tear in your abdominal wall. But we will need your permission to operate."

"And if I don't give you permission?"

"You'll be taken off flying status and assigned to other duties."

"Can I have a day or so to think about it?"

"Sure," said the flight surgeon. "I'll just notify your squadron."

Back at the barracks I stretched on my bunk, enjoyed a luxurious nap and read magazines for several hours. About mid-afternoon a sergeant came in. "Is your name Lynam?" he asked. I nodded.

"Come on," he said. "Let's go to the mess hall."

"It's not time for chow, is it?"

"You're not going for chow. You're going to do KP."

"KP? What are you talking about?" I demanded. "Flight crews don't have to do KP."

The sergeant waved a piece of paper. "You're not on a flight crew any more. I just got this notice. You're being assigned to permanent KP."

"Permanent KP? You mean like, every day?"

"That's right," he said smugly.

The choice before me was clear. Some things in this world are worse than flying in an airplane that people are shooting at. I turned to the sergeant. "Before I report to the mess hall," I said, "do you mind if I run down to the base hospital? I want to see the flight surgeon for a minute."

"Better hurry," the sergeant said, grinning triumphantly. I wondered how many times he had performed this routine. My surgery went well.

A few weeks later I had pretty much recovered and was assigned to a new combat crew. The pilot was a tall, gangly young man named Samuel E. Holt, Jr. A Mormon from Salt Lake City, he kept to himself and didn't talk much. I remember hoping that he knew more about piloting than I did about gunnery. Several weeks later, I discovered he did. He saved our lives.

It happened on a practice bombing mission. Along with about a dozen other B-17's flown by amateur air crews like ours, we had been ordered out to a remote target range in southern Louisiana to drop ten practice bombs. These bombs, filled mostly with sand, carried only enough explosive to make a puff of smoke where they hit. All the planes, including ours, were to fly at 10,000 feet over an oval course, a safe distance apart, and take turns dropping bombs, one at a time, on the clearly defined ground target. All the planes were under strict orders to fly in a clockwise direction, and all of them did. Except one.

On a B-17, the bombardier had a magnificent view of whatever he happened to be trying to destroy. He sat in a clear Plexiglas bubble in the very nose of the plane. Just a few feet behind him was a tiny desk where the navigator worked. This forward compartment was below and completely isolated from the flight deck. To reach the pilot, co-pilot and engineer, you had to crawl back through a little tunnel under the flight deck and pop up out of the floor. Everybody was connected to everybody else by interphone, but the forward compartment and the flight deck were two separate little worlds.

As always on a bomb run, the bombardier that day had complete control of the plane. Peering down through the bombsight at the target, he was making minor corrections in our course by turning little knobs of the bombsight. Completely absorbed in his work, he didn't see the other airplane. Neither did the navigator. Nor, until the very last second, did anybody on the flight deck.

Back at my waist gun position toward the rear of the plane, I was gazing out the window, bored stiff. It was a warm, sunshiny day, but at 10,000 feet with the wind whistling in around the ball turret, it was getting a little chilly. I sat down on small raised walkway to put on my fleece-lined flying boots. Then I felt the plane shudder.

I grabbed the walkway and braced myself. Instinct told me something very unusual was about to happen, and I was right. With the bombardier using the bombsight to control the airplane through the autopilot, the pilot had glanced away from the windscreen for just a moment. When he looked up, twenty men were only seconds from death. Another B-17 was dead ahead, meeting us head-on at a closing speed of nearly 350 miles an hour. In one movement, Sam Holt flipped off the autopilot and shoved the control yoke forward. There was no time to chop the throttles. We plunged toward the earth like a comet.

Back in the waist section, all hell broke loose. Everything not tied down flew into the air and hung there. As I clung to the walkway, I watched a the Gibson Girl emergency radio float gently through the cabin, followed by a coffee bottle and several interphone headsets. Then, to my horror, I saw a fifty-caliber machine gum rise eerily from its swivel mount and hang motionless in mid-air, still linked to an ammunition belt. Months of dirt and grime, having collected in tiny cracks ever since the plane rolled out of the factory, suddenly were no longer held in place by gravity and leaped into the drafty cabin air in weird little swirls. Virtually paralyzed with fear as the plane plunged downward, I kept hanging to the raised structure where I had taken a seat to put on my boots. And then I saw the boots.

From where I had placed them, side by side, on the cabin floor, they now floated gracefully in my direction. Still sitting upright and side by side, as if beside a bed, they then hung motionless, bathed in a cathedral-like shaft of light from the waist window. A few feet forward in his radio room, operator Clyde Jontz clung to his small desk and watched his parachute pack float lazily upward through the cabin. Then, instantly, the parachute, boots, machine guns and everything else slammed into the floor. I heard the engine power ease off and I felt myself getting so heavy I could barely lift my arms. As we screamed downward, Sam was trying to pull out.

Somehow he managed to do it without ripping off the wings. To me, it was a superb feat of airmanship. It surely saved everybody on our plane, not to mention the guys flying with that idiot in the other one. The entire episode cannot have lasted over 10 or 15 seconds, but even today, when I see television pictures of our astronauts frolicking weightlessly in space, I get a spooky feeling.

The rest of our crew training went very smoothly, unless you count the time a P-63 fighter slammed into a B-17 just off our right wing during a practice mission over Memphis. Or perhaps I might mention our taking off from Lincoln, Nebraska, without remembering to remove the canvas cover from out pitot tube, thus leaving to sheer guesswork how close we were to stalling speed on our nighttime landing approach. Then too, there was the occasion when our pilot, Sam Holt, and our navigator, Donald Urry, were given separate briefings for our nighttime flight across the Atlantic. Only trouble was, one was told that the highest mountain on our course over Greenland was 10,000 feet. The other was told it was 9,000. That was the night we successfully demonstrated that a B-17, while big and cumbersome, could be made to climb very swiftly given full military power and quick, fervent prayer.

Over the late summer and early fall of 1944, the nine other fellows and I were fused into what the Army Air Force considered an adequately trained combat crew. Looking back, it's obvious that we were virtual novices at our jobs. Even our pilot, Sam Holt, could hardly be called an old pro, even though he had saved our bacon that day over Louisiana and probably other times I didn't know about. The average bomber pilot going into combat in those days probably had no more than 450 hours of flying time. Today a captain for a major airline would be likely to have 20,000 hours, or more than 40 times the experience. But ready or not, we went to war.

In November, 1944, we were given a brand-new B-17G and, over the next few days, flew from Grenier Field in Manchester, New Hampshire, to Goose Bay, Labrador; Keflavik, Iceland; Valley, Wales, England; Marrakech, Morocco; Tunis, Tunisia; landing finally in Gioia, Italy. As a welcoming gesture, 15th Air Force functionaries immediately seized our shiny new airplane and loaded us in the back of a truck. Over blacked-out roads which seemed to date from the Julius Caesar administration, we rumbled about a hundred miles to the sad, war-torn little town of Foggia, Italy.

Dog-tired, cold and hungry, we were given a midnight supper of scrambled eggs. Then Pete Olivo, our armorer and left waist gunner, asked where we six enlisted men were going to sleep.

"In that tent," said a sleepy sergeant, pointing to an enormous pile of canvas in a corner of the room. "I'll show you where you can put it up."

In basic training we learned about pup tents, but this tent seemed to be the size of an auditorium. Cursing, stumbling over big rocks, untangling ropes and trying to figure out which poles went into which holes in chill black hours before dawn, it's a miracle we ever got the damn thing up. When daylight came, by looking at other tents, we discovered an ingenious method for heating our new home.

From a wrecked airplane we got a section of aluminum tubing and connected it to a nifty power source—a barrel of 100-octane aviation gasoline. The barrel was placed on a wooden stand just outside the tent. Then we ran the tubing into the tent and crimped the end so the gasoline dripped slowly into a metal pan. It only took one match to activate the heating system we used all that winter. When you're about to be shot at in an airplane, you don't worry too much about your heating system being dangerous.

Our airfield was one of a group built around Foggia by the Luftwaffe before the Allies captured southern Italy in 1943. The outfit we joined, the 97th Bomb Group, shared the field with units of the Royal Air Force. In good weather, our Fortresses took off early in the morning, usually hit their targets in massive formations around noon, and returned—the lucky ones, that is— about mid-afternoon. Then, as sunset neared, the RAF bombers began thundering into the sky. Since our tent was located near the end of the matted steel runway, our eardrums usually took a beating during the late afternoon and early evening.

Instead of sending bombers over the target in massive formations during daylight hours as we Americans did, the British always flew singly and at night. They took their planes over the target, one at a time, every few minutes for long periods. One day I asked an RAF sergeant how they expected to put their bombs on the target in the dark.

"We may not hit anything," he admitted. "But we damn well keep the bastards awake all night."

Based at Cerignola, another airfield near Foggia, were several groups of American B-24 Liberators. Like our B-17's, these were four-engined heavy bombers. They flew the same missions we did, and their planes, like ours, were manned largely by boy warriors sent into battle shortly after learning how to use a safety razor.

While I didn't know him in those days, one young hot-shot B-24 pilot at Cerignola was destined to play a large role in my life. When we met twenty years later in Washington, George G.Troutman, by then a retired Air Force lieutenant colonel, was working on Capitol Hill for General Dynamics, then the largest employer in Jim Wright's district. George and I developed a solid friendship that will surely endure—at least until I tell this story about what happened to him at Cerignola.

At 19, George was a second lieutenant who had proved so skillful at the controls of a ponderous B-24 that he was designated, after flying only a handful of combat missions, as one of the group's lead pilots.

In this capacity he was required, between regular combat missions, to log far more training hours than other pilots. One day he was assigned to go aloft and put several hours of "slow time" on a new engine just installed in one of the group's lead aircraft. For easy identification in the air, all lead planes had the same distinctive paint jobs.

With seven members of his regular crew, George tooled around the sky for several hours, relaxing and making small talk, as he broke in the new engine. Then, on the way back to the base, six of his crewmen asked if they could watch the landing from the flight deck, right behind the pilot.

"Sure—why not?" George answered off-handedly.

As he prepared to land, there were several things George didn't know. He was unaware, first of all, that in a command car, waiting anxiously beside the landing strip, was the group commander, a full colonel. He was worried because his very good friend, the deputy commander, had led the combat mission that day, and radioed back that his plane had sustained severe battle damage to its left landing gear. His plane, a lead aircraft like the one George was flying, had been given first priority to land.

There was one other thing George didn't know. When he good-naturedly allowed his six crewmen to gather on the fight deck, he drastically changed the center of gravity in his plane, making it perilously nose-heavy.

As the landing field loomed ahead, George made a textbook final approach. Then, as he neared the runway, he tried to pull up the nose and level out. The nose wouldn't come up.

The big bomber hit the runway like a falling anvil. The left tire exploded. George fought for control as the plane careened off the runway. Sirens whined. Crash trucks and ambulances roared up. Photographers appeared. The group commander lurched up in his command car. Seeing the plane damaged but largely intact, he waved happily in George's direction.

"Great landing, Colonel!" he shouted from his command car.

Great landing? Colonel? Bewildered, George hissed an order to his crew: "You guys say nothing—understand?"

As the commander strode closer to the plane, he stopped abruptly. "You're not Charlie," he said. "Where's Charlie?"

Puzzled, George said, "I don't know, sir."

"Wasn't Charlie Thompson, my deputy commander, supposed to be flying this plane?"

"I don't think so, sir."

"Well, who the hell are you?"

"I'm Lieutenant Troutman, sir."

"Are you the ones with the battle damage to the landing gear?"

"No, sir," George replied. "I didn't fly the mission."

"But this one of our lead planes," cried the colonel.

"I've had it up slow-timing it, sir. It just got a new engine."

"But Charlie was supposed to have damage to his left gear. Isn't that what happened to you?"

"No, sir. I just blew a tire on landing."

"On landing? Well, where's Charlie, then?"

"I don't know, sir. Maybe he hasn't returned yet."

The colonel looked around, nonplussed. This young man, heaven knows how, had almost wrecked one of his lead airplanes. Yet the commander painfully remembered that he had enthusiastically congratulated him on a great landing. And everybody knows group commanders don't make mistakes.

Climbing back into his command car, the commander shook his head. "Well son," he said, "you really...er, uh—you really know how to handle a blowout," he said.

For his first taste of combat, each new air crewmen arriving in Foggia was singled out to fly a mission with an experienced crew. The target on my first trip was the railroad marshaling yard in Verona in northern Italy. This was a critical point on the Brenner Pass through the Alps, over which German supplies came in from Austria. We caught a little flak, but no fighters. Or at least none that I saw, if you know what I mean.

For flight crews, it was a nightly ritual to grab a flashlight and walk down to check the squadron bulletin board. Posted there, usually by 9 o'clock, was the next day's Battle Order. For the first few times, it was a sobering experience to find yourself and your crew listed, matter of factly, on something labeled, Battle Order, 342nd Bomb Squadron, 97th Bomb Group. While you always knew, deep down, that this time would come, it still took a moment to realize they were really talking about *you*. Then, in sort of a forced bravado, you might turn to a buddy and try to make a joke about it: "Willie, please inform the Colonel that I'm sorry, but I don't do battles."

Back in the States I guess a few of us tried to delude ourselves into thinking that something—we had no idea what—would suddenly pop up to keep us from being exposed to honest-to-goodness bullets. Yet, on a black, cold and lonely night in a strange land, there it was. These guys were *serious*. You go back to the tent, worry for a few minutes, then crawl onto your canvas cot and, surprisingly, sleep pretty well.   Until that SOB from squadron headquarters barges into our tent before dawn, blowing a police whistle.

It was a chore just to get suited up for a six- or seven-hour high altitude mission, considering all the clothes and gadgets you needed to put on.   You started out, of course, with your highly-fashionable olive drab long underwear, followed by wool shirt and pants.   Over these you pulled on an electrically-heated flying suit whose shoes, trousers, coat and gloves all plugged into each other.   Then, over your electric suit, you climbed into insulated trousers and jacket.   The extension cord for your electric suit hung out, embarrassingly enough, from your fly.   I had some misgivings about plugging it in for the first time.

Next came your heavy flying boots, followed by your inflatable Mae West life preserver, parachute harness and throat microphone.   Then, after takeoff, you slipped on thin nylon gloves to keep your hands from sticking to any freezing metal you had to touch without your heated gloves.   Later, when you reached 10,000 feet, you put on your leather flying helmet with built-in earphones which had a cord to plug into the intercom terminal near your machine gun.   After that you donned your oxygen mask and connected its hose to the ship's supply system. Then you made sure the electric wire was hooked up to keep your oxygen mask from freezing. At this point you were strung with enough wires to look like a utility pole.

Later, on the bomb run, it was advisable to put on your steel helmet and a flak vest weighing maybe 30 pounds.   Also, of course, you needed to keep handy your chest-pack parachute designed to be snapped on to your harness.   You then needed to make sure your regular GI shoes were tied securely to your parachute harness.   This was necessary because your boots usually popped off when your parachute opened and it would be difficult to walk out of Germany barefooted.   At this point you usually checked to make sure you remembered your shoulder holster and 45-caliber pistol, as well as your waterproof escape kit.   This contained maps and a bundle of American currency which, believe it or not, escaping flyers said Germans preferred to their own money.

When our crew began flying together, I secretly wished I had not thrown away the eyeglasses that helped me see the screen back at the Rio Theatre in Kingsville, Texas. Sure enough, before long the interphone in our plane was crackling with urgent advisories from other gunners. As we tooled at 25,000 feet over Germany, our tail gunner, Willie Pigg, would say, "Hey, Tex—watch that fighter out there at 3 o'clock."

If the fighter was reasonably close, I could usually see it. But even if I couldn't, I decided this would be an inappropriate time to say so. "Roger, Willie—I've got my eye on him," I would respond.

This was not quite as stupid as it may sound. For one thing, any fighter we saw was almost always ours. On virtually every mission we were protected by our "little friends." Often these were long-range P-51's with distinctive checkered tails, flown by African-American pilots now famous as the Tuskegee Airmen. Once our plane lost an engine half an hour before we reached Linz, Austria. The formation left us behind and we went over the target all by ourselves. I hadn't realized it before, but when yours is the only plane in the sky, it's hard to pretend the flak gunners are shooting at somebody else. Departing from the target, we were exactly the type of lone, crippled straggler that would delight any Luftwaffe fighters in the neighborhood. By radio we asked for help, and two checkered-tail P-51's came back to keep an eye on us. Crisscrossing each other in the sky 5,000 feet above us like protective angels, they etched beautiful and comforting con trails as they escorted us home.

To the courageous bomber crews and fighter pilots who flew the really tough missions before we arrived overseas in late 1944, we owe our gratitude—and quite possibly, our lives. Thanks to their sacrifices in knocking out key industrial and petroleum targets like Schweinfurt and Ploesti, the Luftwaffe was practically out of business during our watch. Nearly all the Me-109's and FW-190's we saw were five miles below us, grounded for lack of fuel, parts or pilots—or maybe all three. What the German still did have, however, was a limited number of Me-262's.

These were the first operational jet fighters in the world, capable of sweeping through our bomber formations at nearly 600 miles an hour while we plodded along in our B-17's at 165. The Luftwaffe sent up a force of Me-262's to meet us over Berlin on

March 24, 1945, and shot down two B-17s in another formation. While on my eighteen missions our plane never came under direct fighter attack, but the Germans proved to us they still had plenty of flak.

Vienna alone was reported to have five hundred anti-aircraft guns, and to me personally that estimate seemed a bit low. It was because of these ferocious German flak barrages that gunners like myself were given an additional responsibility. It was our job to throw out, of all things, tiny strips of tinfoil. Folded into packages about eighteen inches long, these strips were designed to confuse German gunners by registering on their radar scopes as dozens of other B-17's. Thus their radar operator could not be sure which blips on his screen were real planes and which were the tinfoil strips, or chaff, that we were happily scattering over the sky.

On the bomb run, where flak was usually heaviest, I threw out this stuff through a small opening on the floor near my gun position. My orders were to dump two bundles every thirty seconds, but the thicker the flak, the faster I worked. Probably it really did confuse German radar, but even if not I felt better having something to do when those big, nasty explosions were blackening the sky. And besides, once on a mission to Vienna, some unpleasant fellow on the ground shot out my waist window the moment after I had ducked down to throw out chaff. My gun position got a little drafty on the way home.

Today *Shoo Shoo Baby* is on permanent display at Wright-Patterson Air Force Base in Ohio. On that day in 1988 when she made her ceremonial flight around Dover, a small chase plane eased alongside to let an Air Force photographer shoot new pictures of the old but distinguished lady. It was as if a movie queen of yesteryear were being allowed to preen herself before an audience of new admirers.

Once again on that flight I stood peering out the right waist window—a spot where, nearsighted or not, I had been privileged to see man at his worst, and at his best. For this same privilege, thousands of other fellows had paid a far higher price.

Uprooted at 18 or 19 and sent to war and killed, many of them never had a chance to make love to a woman or to build a career or to buy a house or to wipe a grandkid's nose or to grow old and die in bed. I think about my schoolmate Ishmael Valverde, who died at Ploesti long before I first saw my name on a Battle Order, and my cousin, Weldon Lacy, a B-29 gunner killed on one of the first raids on Japan. I think about the crew in the next tent, whose co-pilot was decapitated by a shell fragment over Vienna. I think about my barracks buddies Ted Gilson and Mort Carlis and Clyde Plants who were killed with their whole crew at Blechhammer on their very first mission. It's strange for a guy 72 years old to feel a close kinship, even now, with kids who died as kids, yet somehow I do.

Today we've got an entirely different world, and I hope we've got a little more sense, but I wouldn't bet on it. We've already had so many wars that children have trouble remembering which is which. When our first grandson, Michael Williams, was about six years old, one day he happened to discover the old trunk in my room.

"What's in the trunk, Papa?" he asked.

"Just a bunch of old stuff from the war."

"Were you in the war?"

"Yes, I was."

"Who did you fight for—the Blue or the Gray?"

19

Such Interesting People

Sherwood L. Boehlert

Today my old friend Sherwood Boehlert is an influential member of Congress. What's more, he has become widely recognized as one of the nation's foremost guardians of the environment. If he gets any more important I may forgive him for making me parachute into Biscayne Bay.

What's more I might even consider forgiving him for nearly causing my wife to throw me out of the house. But I'll tell you about that later.

Already chairman of a key House subcommittee, Congressman Boehlert seems destined in the future for even more significant roles on the Hill. Yet he is still the personable, easy-going guy I knew during his 15 years as a House staffer. A real down-to-earth fellow, he considers the name Sherwood to be a bit stuffy, and he still encourages his friends to call him Sherry.

He was elected to Congress in 1982 from the district around Utica, New York. He's so busy these days I don't see him much any more, but back in the early 70s, when he was chief of staff to Congressman Alexander Pirnie, he and I used to do a lot of traveling together.

In those Cold War days, Sherry's boss, like my own, was vitally interested in defense issues. As their staff representatives, Sherry and I occasionally were invited, along with a dozen or so other fellows in similar jobs, to tour various military bases as guests of the Pentagon. On behalf of our bosses, we looked at weapons, watched maneuvers and sat through endless flip-chart briefings. These, as I remember, usually consisted of 4,832 incomprehensible charts with lines drawn between dozens of boxes to show the command structures of various military units. These charts were tightly-guarded secrets because of their awesome power. Ten of them in succession could have incapacitated the entire Soviet army. By putting it to sleep, I mean. Now and then, however, the military people showed us some real interesting stuff.

One day in 1972, for example, we found ourselves at the U.S. Air Force's Water Survival School at Homestead Air Force Base, Florida. Here, in a four-day course, fighter and bomber pilots were taught the latest techniques for surviving at sea in case they had to bail out or ditch their planes. Far from getting lessons only from textbooks, these Air Force fliers were given actual, honest-to-goodness water survival training in Biscayne Bay, at a restricted site thirteen miles from the main base.

In our group on that trip were a dozen or so flabby and bookish guys from Capitol Hill who seldom exercised any more vigorously than to get up from their desks to fetch another cup of coffee. To us, watching these pilots in their training exercises was a new and fascinating experience. After a few preliminaries, each flier in turn was taken and fitted into a Mae West and a parachute harness. Once equipped, he was placed near the edge of a large, open deck which stood about twelve feet above the water, some distance out in Biscayne Bay. At that point, an open parachute was attached to his harness. To keep the flier from being dragged backward off the deck, the billowing chute was held in place by the wind against a big wire screen resembling the backstop on a baseball field.

Then a steel cable with a quick-release mechanism was hooked directly to the front of the flier's parachute harness. The cable stretched out maybe eight hundred feet to a powerful vessel about the size of a PT boat. When the instructor gave the signal, the pilot began walking forward as the boat gunned its engines. If everything went right, the boat made the parachute act like a big kite and the trainee was lifted into the air. Not so different from recreational parasailing, right? Right. So far.

But then, when the trainee reached about five hundred feet, a guy on the boat waved a flag. That was the signal for the trainee to cut himself loose from the cable and to parachute to a big, spectacular splashdown in Biscayne Bay. There, if he didn't get tangled up in the canopy or the shroud lines and drown, the trainee was fished out of the water by the boat. Watching from the platform, we were enthralled.

"Great!" whooped Sherry. "That's really great!"

If he had shut up at that point, everything would have been fine. But to my astonishment, he turned eagerly to one of our Air Force escort officers.

"Will you let us do that?" he asked.

The officer frowned. He probably suspected there was a regulation somewhere against Air Force officers drowning Congressional staffers, even at their request. Anyhow, after mulling over the question for a minute, the officer went into a worried, whispered huddle with another officer. Then the other officer went off somewhere to talk, I presume, to yet another officer. In the military this is known as coordinating, or spreading the blame.

Frankly I didn't think there was even a remote chance of Sherry's request being granted. After all, killing from one to twelve visiting Congressional aides might be a detriment to an Air Force officer's prospects for future promotions. Unless, of course, the victim happened to represent a Congressman who opposed an increase in the defense budget.

A few minutes later the first officer came back. To my surprise, he was wearing a big smile. "Sure," he said enthusiastically. "We'll be glad to let you fellows try the exercise."

I winced. "Sherry," I said, "you got a big mouth."

A few minutes later an Air Force instructor started giving us preliminary directions. "Be sure you listen to this," he said. "We've only got an hour or so."

"Let me ask a question," I said. "When Air Force pilots come here for this training, how long does the training last?"

"The course lasts four days," he said.

"Experienced Air Force pilots get four days of training in this and you're giving us only an hour before we parachute into Biscayne Bay?"

The instructor smiled. "Don't worry," he said. "It'll be all right."

The first part of our training was simple. All we did was line up and jump, one at a time, into the water directly below the platform. The instructor explained that our velocity on this twelve-foot jump would give us an idea of the force with which we would hit the water when our parachute came down.

As I awaited my turn, the guy in line just ahead walked gingerly up to the platform edge. Looking wide-eyed down at the water, which appeared to be about a mile and a half below, he nervously crossed himself.

To the instructor, this seemed ridiculous. "C'mon, now," he chided. "It's only twelve feet. Why are you crossing yourself?"

"Want to hear something even funnier than that?" asked my apprehensive companion. "I'm not even a Catholic."

He made it OK, of course, as we all did. But I had an important question for our instructor.

"What happens if I get up there in my parachute and I get too scared to cut loose from the cable?" I asked.

The instructor pondered the question. "Well, if you want to land in the water with about eight hundred feet of steel cable tied to you, I suppose that's up to you," he replied.

Despite my reservations, the experience wasn't all that bad. As I might have expected, the future Congressman from Utica, New York, insisted on being the first to soar off into the brilliant Florida sky. When he managed to parachute successfully into the bay and then get fished out alive, drenched but elated, the rest of us felt better about our prospects for survival. Most of us made it with everything but our dignity intact. What's more, it was kind of fun. I especially liked the part where I came back up to the surface.

As our little group of Congressional aides swaggered into the Officers Club bar that night to celebrate our having ventured into the wet blue as well as the wild blue, nobody would have suspected that, at heart, many of us were really whimpering cowards. But before the evening was over, we were feeling so smug and acting like we had been so contemptuous of danger that we could easily have been mistaken for the Mercury Astronauts.

Years later Sherry met and married a pretty girl named Marianne Willey. Herself a former Congressional staffer, she went on to become an outstanding commercial photographer.   As Marianne and Sherry got to know my wife Eddie, we all became close friends and traveled a lot together.   Eddie liked the Boehlerts so much she finally was able to laugh about what happened the night many years before when Sherry and I came back from Florida.

It had been dark for hours when our plane arrived at Andrews Air Force Base.   Our escort officer dropped us off at the Rayburn House Office Building.   But when I got to the basement garage, I found my pride and joy, a beat-up old Ford Mustang, was missing from my parking spot.   I rushed to a telephone and called home.

"Hi, darling," I said to Eddie.   "We just got in from Florida. I'm in the Rayburn building but my Mustang isn't here.   Do you know where it is?"

"Charles is using it.   I'll drive down to pick you up."

"No, wait a minute—I don't want you driving alone down here at night.   Sherry and I just came in from Andrews and stopped here to pick up our cars.   I believe I can hitch a ride out to Virginia."

"If that's what you want to do, all right," said Eddie.

Two years passed.   I tried several times to tell Eddie about my exciting trip to Florida, but she didn't seem to be interested.

Then one night I worked in the office until nearly midnight. Even though I didn't like the idea of Eddie driving alone to the Hill at night, I was so exhausted I called and asked her to come after me.   Her answer was brusque.

"Why don't you get your girl friend to bring you home?" she asked.

I almost dropped the phone.   "My girl friend?   What do you mean by that?"

"I just thought you maybe you could get Sherry to bring you home again, like she did the last time."

"Can you please tell me what the hell you're talking about?"

"I'm talking about Sherry—that bitch you took to Florida a couple of years ago," she said.

Claude D. Pepper

When I finally got a chance to meet Claude Pepper, he was nearing the end of an incredibly eventful life. He wore a pacemaker, had a hearing aid in each ear, and took a nap every afternoon. Long before he died at 89, he had become a genuine national institution.

Millions of Americans loved him, for a lot of different reasons.

To senior citizens, Mr. Pepper was the savior of Social Security and the father of Medicare. To his colleagues on the Hill, he was a paragon of integrity as towering and unshakable as the Washington Monument.

To old-time liberals, he was one of the last surviving stalwarts of the boldest economic revival program in American history— President Franklin D. Roosevelt's New Deal. To me, he was a truly admirable gentleman, a fascinating storyteller and, most importantly, a living link to a cherished memory of my father.

My dad died in 1969. Having lived most of his life in the tiny South Texas farm town of Bishop, he never got a chance to meet Mr. Pepper. That's a shame, because he would have admired him as one of the national leaders who offered hope back in the days when hope was a very scarce commodity indeed.

Somehow I never got around to telling Mr. Pepper about a tiny incident, on a day ever so long ago, that gave me my first glimpse into how a person's spirit sometimes can be buoyed and infused with hope by a seemingly insignificant symbol or act. It was years before I really understood, but one bleak day during the Depression, I saw how a spark of hope can be generated by nothing more than piece of printed cardboard. It happened in the cramped little office of the Lynam Auto Company in Bishop.

To most people today, this long-ago incident will sound inconsequential, maybe even silly. But I'll bet Mr. Pepper would have loved hearing about it. At least he would have understood.

I was privileged to meet this remarkable man because he and my boss the Speaker were good friends. In fact, Jim Wright was still in his Army Air Force uniform the first time he saw Mr. Pepper. Returning from combat duty in the Pacific, the young red-headed flyer had been assigned to a base in Florida. Deeply interested even then in the art of politics, he went to a Claude

Pepper campaign rally to hear for himself the Senator everybody described as a spellbinding orator. He was not disappointed.

Mr. Pepper had been elected to the Senate nearly a decade before, in 1936. Despite his extraordinary record as a stalwart champion of President Roosevelt's leadership in the New Deal and World War II, he was defeated fourteen years later by George A. Smathers, a onetime friend and political ally. Even today, many people still consider that race as one of the dirtiest political campaigns in U.S. history. In a speech spiked with cruel innuendo, Smathers reportedly accused Senator Pepper of being "a shameless extrovert" who committed "nepotism with his sister-in-law," whose sister was "once a thespian in wicked New York" and who "practiced celibacy" before he was married. Senator Pepper also was denounced as a "Nigger-lover," a tool of union bosses and a Communist sympathizer.

After this devastating defeat, Mr. Pepper practiced law for twelve years while he got his life and his finances back in order. Then, in a 1962 comeback, he was elected to the House of Representatives. During this campaign Vice President Lyndon B. Johnson came down to Florida to speak at one of his fund-raisers. Afterward he asked Johnson to suggest another good speaker in case he needed to hold an additional fund-raiser. In his autobiography Mr. Pepper quoted the Vice President's reply: "I'd suggest Congressman Jim Wright from Texas. He's an eloquent, forceful speaker who always makes a great speech."

Even though Jim Wright was never called on for a campaign speech, the two men became good friends after Mr. Pepper's election to the House. In 1977, with Jim Wright in his new role as Majority Leader, Mr. Pepper was named Chairman of the newly-created House Select Committee on Aging. It was in this role that he achieved national recognition as the indefatigable champion of America's senior citizens.

In those days and later, as Chairman of the Rules Committee, Mr. Pepper dropped by occasionally to talk with Jim Wright. At times when my boss happened to be out of the office, Mr. Pepper would rap on the door of my adjoining office and ask, "May I come in, Mr. Lynam?"

It isn't every day you get to talk with a five-foot, eight-inch chunk of history in a three-piece suit. I was delighted by these visits, and as we waited for the Speaker, I always tried to lead Mr.

Pepper into a story. This wasn't difficult, because he enjoyed telling them as much as I enjoyed hearing them.

And what stories he could tell. Born in 1900, he was the embodiment of 20th Century America. He had met Orville Wright and greeted the Apollo Astronauts. He saw Halley's comet in 1910 and again in 1986.

He foresaw war after hearing Adolf Hitler speak in Nuremberg in 1938 and introduced the first lend-lease legislation in 1940. In 1945, as the Cold War loomed, he talked with Josef Stalin.

But the role for which history may remember him best was as a close friend and confidant of Franklin D. Roosevelt. Even though Mr. Pepper's election to the Senate came in 1936, four years after Roosevelt's first election, the two had been friends and political allies since 1928. In that year Mr. Pepper wrote a personal letting urging him to seek the White House. "I was a New Dealer before there was a New Deal," he liked to say.

Once Mr. Pepper was elected to the Senate, President Roosevelt had no more vigorous supporter. Even though forced by his conscience to oppose the President's "court packing" plan, he remained Roosevelt's ideological soulmate. So consistently and forcefully did he speak in behalf of New Deal programs that the *New York Herald-Tribune* observed: "When the White House has an important balloon to send up, it invites Senator Pepper to supply the necessary oratorical helium for the ascension." In his memoirs Roosevelt praised him as "a fighting liberal" and "a model for a new kind of Southern political leader."

While Washington struggled to find policies and programs to end the Depression, out in everyday America the matter was far less academic. In Bishop, it robbed people not only of food and housing but, more importantly, of hope as well. To kids like me, it was all very confusing. We understood that jobs and money were scarce, but we could not understand why. Nor did anybody seem to know what to do about it. Our family was lucky enough never to go hungry. But it seemed strange that something called a Depression could make us give up our house, and even cause my granddad to lose his beloved blackland farm with its beautiful picnic grounds out on Caesar Creek. I wondered, too, what his thing could be that forced some people to line up every day on Main Street in our town to get a bowl of stew. And why did the

Depression cause the bank down by Hart's hardware store to close one day and never reopen?

Still open at that time was the Lynam Auto Company, located only a block from Main Street. It was a Ford dealership owned by my dad, Lee Lynam, and his brother Roy. Once the company had displayed gleaming new Model A's in the showroom and did a thriving business selling cars to the farm families.

But now the showrooms were empty. When farmers would come in, they often would shuffle glumly up to my dad and talk in a low voice, like they were ashamed. "Lee, I'm already two payments behind and I can't make this one, either. The car's out at the house. I'll bring it in and give it back to you."

"What am I going to do with it, Charlie?" my dad would ask. "Go ahead and keep your car. Pay me when you can."

The finance company, however, was not as generous as Lee and Roy Lynam. Before long the business went bankrupt and, like the bank around the corner, was closed forever.

But one day before the padlock was put on the front door, my dad took me to the office with him. It must have been on a Sunday, because there was nobody else around.

As I toyed with the office typewriter, my dad sat down at his desk and started opening a pile of mail. One of the large envelopes contained a cardboard poster. He looked at it, smiled, and got up to show it to me. It was a strange sign.

Printed in red, white and blue, it carried a drawing of an eagle. In one of its claws it held lightning bolts. In the other it held what looked like a gear wheel. On it were the words, *We Do Our Part. National Recovery Administration.*

Then my dad walked to the office window, raised the blind and placed the sign in a prominent spot. In a simple expression of hope that would have been gratifying to the elderly New Dealer who would be sitting in my office half a century later, my dad looked at me and grinned.

"Happy days are here again," he said.

George H. Mahon

If your job was to decide how to spend $325 billion a year, what would you eat for lunch?

George Mahon usually had a baloney sandwich and a glass of milk.

After patiently waiting in line with the clerks and secretaries, he would pick up his modest lunch in the cafeteria line in the Rayburn Building. Then, using both hands to balance his tray, he walked carefully out to the seating area. On occasion he stopped at my table.

"May I sit with you, Marshall?" he would always ask.

"By all means, Mr. Chairman," I answered, arising to help him get settled and to dispose of his empty tray. I try to be friendly to everybody. It would have been rude to brush him off merely because he exercised more control over more money than probably anybody else on earth. Besides, I admired the old gentleman.

Like Claude Pepper, George Mahon was born in 1900. His father, a cotton farmer in Louisiana, moved the family to the remote West Texas town of Loraine when George was eight. After high school he won a teacher's certificate and rode a bicycle fourteen miles a day to hold classes in a grammar school. He won a law degree from the University of Texas in 1925, began practicing law in Colorado City, Texas, and was elected county attorney in 1926 and district attorney in 1927.

In 1934, with West Texas in the grip of both the Depression and disastrous dust storms, Mr. Mahon was elected to Congress. Five years later he won an appointment to the House Appropriations Committee and became Chairman in 1963. When he used to visit with me in the 1970s, his was clearly one of the most influential voices in the nation on how the government spent its money.

Even today I'm not sure why he used to single me out as a luncheon companion. One reason, I suppose, was that I never asked him for anything. As the Congressman mainly in charge of divvying up federal dollars, he was forever being importuned by colleagues wanting funds favorite projects, as well as by business people with special interests.

Mr. Mahon knew, of course, that I worked for his friend Jim Wright, and that in a previous incarnation I was a reporter for the *Fort Worth Star-Telegram*, which in the old days used to specialize in covering West Texas. Several times he asked me to explain the inner workings of the newspaper business—the motives of the publishers, for example. I used to chat with him about that, but I finally had to tell him the truth. I didn't have a clue.

To a disciple of rectitude like Mr. Mahon, who paid for his own baloney sandwich in the House cafeteria when any lobbyist in town would have been delighted to fly him to Paris for lunch, newspaper coverage of the Hill was disheartening. He couldn't understand why so many stories promoted political fights, nor why they took such zest in intrigues and scandals. Imbued with a sense of responsibility and thrift that would have gratified his Scottish forebears, Mr. Mahon didn't generate much hot copy. His 44 years in Congress must have surely left cobwebs on the typewriters of sensation-hungry journalists. Himself frugal, he expected frugality in others. Take his Metro visit, for example.

While Washington's subway system was being constructed back in the early 1970s, one of Mr. Mahon's good friends, Congressman Bob Poage of Waco, wanted to take a first-hand look at the tunnel-building work. Mr. Poage's bristlingly efficient Administrative Assistant, Dayle Henington, promptly called Metro officials and set up a tour. Then, at Mr. Poage's invitation, Chairman Mahon decided to come along, also.

When Dayle Henington called about this additional guest, the Metro official gasped.

"What? The Chairman himself is coming?" he asked in almost reverential tones.

To Metro, this was a very big deal indeed. Building the subway system was an enormously expensive undertaking, and its officials were acutely conscious of Mr. Mahon's grip on the federal money faucet. A top-ranking Metro official, in New York at the time, hurried back to Washington. To the two Texas Congressmen, he gave positive, upbeat briefings on the massive project, as well as an on-the-spot look at the tunneling work going on under the streets.

Where the tunnel was being dug beneath the National Portrait Gallery, construction crews were working with an enormous hydraulic lift. Enthralled by this operation, Mr. Poage turned excitedly to his friend and asked, "George, did you ever see such a fascinating piece of machinery?"

Mr. Mahon grunted. "I wonder how much it cost," he said.

When the tour was over, the two lawmakers from Texas expressed their thanks, and Dayle Henington still remembers the Chairman's final word to the Metro bosses.

"Just be sure that you don't have any scandals on this project," Mr. Mahon ordered. "We don't need any scandals."

For a man in his seventies, Mr. Mahon seemed extremely fit. He stood six two, weighed about 175 pounds and still had a full head of hair. But one day Keith Mainland noticed him limping.

Keith was one of his most trusted aides on the House Appropriations Committee. Many mornings he came by the apartment where Mr. Mahon lived with his wife, Helen, to pick up the boss and drive him to the Capitol.

"You're limping, Mr. Chairman," Keith said. "Are you all right?"

"Oh, yes, I'm fine."

Obviously he did not care to elaborate, so Keith let the matter drop—until the next day. The Chairman's limp was more pronounced than ever.

"Mr. Chairman, I'm worried about you. Why are you limping?" Keith demanded.

"Oh, I'll be all right, Keith. It's nothing."

"No, you're obviously in pain. Now I insist that you tell me what's wrong."

"Well, I guess I sprained my ankle a little."

"What happened? Did you twist it stepping off a curb?"

"No, not really."

"Then how did you hurt it?"

It was a moment before an answer came from this dignified-looking gentleman in his mid-seventies who approved the tax dollars used for everything from subway systems to moon rockets. Finally, with a sheepish look on his face, he came clean.

"Well," he said, "when you brought me home a couple of days ago, there were some children playing out on the sidewalk. They had a piece of chalk. On the sidewalk they drew this game of hop-scotch...."

Billy Graham

In Washington the National Prayer Breakfast is a very big deal indeed. Started in 1953 when Dwight D. Eisenhower was President, it has become a renowned Washington tradition. Held in one of the big hotels every February, the event today attracts about 4,000 people, including heads of state and all manner of famous poobahs.

After Jim Wright became Majority Leader, he was one of the invited speakers. He invited me to accompany him to the breakfast, but reminded me that we needed to get back to the office early. We were scheduled to fly to Texas together that evening.

Among notable guests at the Prayer Breakfast was the Reverend Billy Graham, a man I had always admired. He didn't know me, of course, but I had seen him several times during his appearances in Fort Worth.

From time to time he spoke at the Southwestern Baptist Theological Seminary on the far south side of Fort Worth. Eddie and I happened to live in that neighborhood. In fact I used to trade at a little filling station only a stone's throw from the campus. It was owned by a portly, gregarious fellow I knew only as Mr. Ward.

Many of his customers were seminary students, and Mr. Ward always kept a Bible in plain sight beside the cash register. Its presence never deterred him from being a shrewd trader, however. He once sold me an ancient Buick whose shock absorbers soon afterward stopped absorbing shocks. I still remember kids on the street laughing uproariously as my Buick hiccupped in short, spectacular bounces along Jones Street, whose maintenance, in another day, could well have been under the direction of Marion Barry. Even so, Mr. Ward tried to take good care of people living near the seminary. Only thing was, when the station got real busy, sometimes he became momentarily distracted.

In the 1950s filling stations had attendants who routinely checked the water level in a car's radiator. One day Mr. Ward got so busy servicing cars he absent-mindedly started running a water hose into a customer's gas tank.

"Hey, Ward! What are you doing?" shrieked a helper.

Embarrassed, Mr. Ward jerked back the water hose only a moment before the owner returned and drove off in the car. Knowing what was sure to happen, he went inside and waited by his telephone. In a few minutes it rang.

"Mr. Ward, I'm over here on Hemphill and my car has stalled. Can you come and help me?"

"Be right there," said Mr. Ward, jumping behind the wheel of his wrecker.

Once he had towed the car back to the station, he wasted no time. He ordered his mechanic to drain the tank and refill it, using nothing but gasoline this time. The car was running beautifully when he owner returned.

"Good job," he said. "What do you think was wrong with it?"

"You had a little water in your gasoline," Mr. Ward said.

"Hmm—that's curious. I wonder how on earth water got in there."

Mr. Ward chose his words carefully. "I'm not saying this is what happened, mind you. But I know of cases where condensation has caused water in a gas tank."

"Well, thanks for fixing it, anyway. How much do I owe you?"

"Not a thing," Mr. Ward said. "This is on me."

The owner looked puzzled. "What do you mean? Surely I owe you something. You towed me in and gave me a full tank of gas."

"Look," Mr. Ward said in fatherly tones. "I own this station and you are my friend. If I want to do this for you, it's O.K."

On his visits to the seminary I don't suppose Billy Graham ever met Mr. Ward. I sincerely hope he never bought an old Buick from him.

At any rate the Prayer Breakfast went well, and in a casual conversation afterward a prominent Texas businessman told Jim Wright he was sending Billy Graham down to Texas in his executive jet. The businessman couldn't go, so he invited Jim Wright to go along as company for the evangelist. The Majority Leader readily accepted. But since there was only one seat available, the boss said I should catch my commercial flight as planned and we would meet in Fort Worth. But then he answered an urgent call from his Executive Assistant, Kathy Mitchell. He called me aside.

"Marshall, Tip wants to see me this afternoon," he said. "It probably won't take long, but I don't want to delay Dr. Graham's airplane. Let's switch plans. You fly down with him and I'll come on a commercial flight right behind you."

So it was a few hours later that I found myself aboard a small jet at National Airport. There was only one other passenger on the plane. Sitting face to face with me across a small table was the best-known Christian evangelist in the world—a man who, even then, had taken the Gospel personally to more than 60 million people. His crusades had spanned the United States and reached Great Britain, North Africa, France, Germany, Italy, Switzerland, India, the Philippines, Hong Kong, Taiwan, Japan and Korea. In one 16-week crusade in Madison Square Garden, he preached to more than two million people.

As we taxied out to take off, a crew member came back to make sure Dr. Graham and I were strapped in.

"As soon as we get up to cruising altitude, I'll come back and get you something to drink," he said.

"Fine," I said, wondering what kind of drinks he would offer with the renowned Baptist evangelist on board. Having just survived a nerve-racking, rush-hour cab ride and the bedlam of National Airport, I would have loved a vodka tonic. But I wasn't sure I would be comfortable drinking one sitting face-to-face with Billy Graham.

This, after all, was no ordinary man. A one-time North Carolina farm boy and door-to-door Fuller brush salesman before answering his call to the ministry in 1938, he had gone on to become the best-known Christian evangelist in the world and a confidant of Presidents.

Even though I had expected to feel a bit intimidated, I found Dr. Graham an easy man to talk to. I recalled his visits to Southwestern Baptist Seminary (without mentioning Mr. Ward) and told him a little about my job on the Hill. He talked about some of his crusades overseas and specifically mentioned a flight to Africa in which he had unwisely remained too long in his airline seat. He suspected that experience was to blame for his having developed thrombophlebitis, a disease which involves blood clots in the leg veins, and which for a time threatened his life.

Before long a crewman emerged from the flight deck and asked if he could get us anything to drink. I felt very uncomfortable. Personally I enjoy a cocktail in the evening. Even the Bible seems to take a tolerant view of a little nip now and then.

On the other hand I clearly remembered my Baptist upbringing. The preachers in Bishop gave no quarter in their righteous condemnation of the evil liquid that defiles innocence, dethrones reason, destroys homes, creates misery and poverty and leads to the bottomless pit of degradation and despair.

And here I was, sitting three feet from the best-known Baptist in the world. Moreover, at 30,000 feet, I felt we might be close to his home office.

The crewman was waiting for my drink request.

"What all do you have?" I asked, hoping Dr. Graham, who had invited me to order first, would not detect the uncertainty in my voice.

"Almost anything you want—Cokes, Dr Peppers, fruit juice, any kind of soft drink," he said.

Seldom in my life have I heard better news. Since a vodka tonic was no longer an option, the crewman had spared me the necessity of turning it down and thus becoming a full-fledged a hypocrite. As it was now, I would be only a simple liar.

"A Coke sounds real good," I said.

As we sipped our soft drinks and our plane bored on toward the Dallas-Fort Worth area, the weather began to turn bad. Clouds increased, and a blanket of murk began to obscure the lights on the ground. As an executive aircraft, we were scheduled to land at Love Field in Dallas. Jim Wright, in a commercial plane an hour or so behind us, was due to land at Dallas/Fort Worth International Airport, which is only eight miles to the west.

As we started our landing approach, I was astonished to see that, despite the clouds hanging all around Love Field, the airport itself was as clear as a bell. Every detail of the runways and the terminal area stood out vividly. With bad weather all around, visibility right here was perfect. Our landing was a piece of cake.

On the ground, I thanked the crew and told Dr. Graham how much I enjoyed his company. Then I rented a car and drove to Fort Worth, only to discover that the weather had forced Jim Wright's commercial plane to land in Houston. The airline said it regretted this, but DFW was completely socked in.   Jim Wright should have flown with Billy Graham.

20

The Man Who Left the House Because He Loved It

For 27 years I watched Jim Wright. For most of his Congressional career I stood at his elbow. I saw him scrape Stockyards horse dung off his boots as an obscure Congressman from Fort Worth and I saw him gavel into session the historic 100th Congress of the United States. I looked over his shoulder as he talked with poor bedraggled wretches in homeless shelters and with Presidents and Prime Ministers. I saw him happy enough to float on a cloud and sad enough to cry, if he had only known how. Over these years I got to know him pretty well. Except for the times when we felt like strangling each other, I enjoyed it a lot.

On January 6, 1987, this man, Jim Wright, my boss and my friend, was sworn in as Speaker of the House of Representatives— a boyhood dream come true. He was the elect of the elect— occupying an office which had been held only by 47 other Americans in the history of our country. It was heady stuff to see the man I had come to know so well now occupying the supreme legislative office mandated by Article I of the Constitution of the richest and strongest nation on earth.

While I realized that the new Speaker had inherited this Bicentennial Congress only as a happenstance of the calendar, I hoped this was a favorable omen. Even if not, it was an opportunity to watch history being written on the first few calendar pages of our country's third century. On one of those pages maybe I could even leave an anonymous smudged fingerprint.

Even though many of us on his staff had done our best to help him reach this goal, this victory was his alone. He had paid his dues and bided his time. Impatient by nature, he had restlessly served 32 years in the House, including 10 as Majority Leader enveloped in the sizable shadow of his friend Speaker Thomas P. O'Neill.

But now this charming old pol had returned to his beloved Boston, and Jim Wright was the inheritor not only of his awesome responsibilities but also of his elegant office suite in the East Front of the Capitol. The atmosphere reeked of history.

Outside, across the plaza, towered majestic magnolias and poplars and oaks, along with a massive English elm believed to be a hundred years older than the Capitol itself. In the marble hallway in front of the Speaker's suite stood a strapping Capitol policeman, guarding the former Mayor of Weatherford, Texas, who now was second in the Constitutional line of succession to the Presidency of the United States.

Just outside the door of the new Speaker's spacious private office sat his Executive Assistant, Kathy Mitchell, working both as his scheduler and private secretary with the same quiet efficiency she had given these tasks for most of her adult life.

As Administrative Assistant and Chief of Staff to the Speaker, I had a private office with built-in bookcases, a handsome walnut desk, and a swivel chair suitable for a Supreme Court Justice. At a desk nearby worked my associate, Anne Page. She handled Air Force arrangements for official foreign trips for members. In addition to many other duties as well, she always managed to sneak me notes identifying people in my office whose names she instinctively knew I couldn't remember.

In this new, rarefied atmosphere, it was easy to feel intimidated. Having your boss ascend to the Speakership is a sobering experience, and frankly I had a few concerns about the magnitude of the job. All over Washington I knew there were fellows who would gladly have given the leftmost portion of certain highly-prized parts of their anatomy for the job I now held. Moreover, many had better educations and higher IQ's than

I, not to mention fewer candles on their birthday cakes and considerably more hair.

Ironically, many of these people—some of them good friends of mine—yearned far more than I did for prominence and power. It was nice, of course, suddenly to be addressed as Mr. Lynam by people who in the past had probably suspected I was a clerk-typist in the House stationery store. But the fact is that I always felt pretty much like what I was—a Texas newspaper reporter, hired by Jim Wright a quarter century before, who had worked for him ever since with as much diligence and loyalty as I could muster. My friend Craig Raupe always said there were two kinds of people in Congress—members and clerks—and you should damn well never forget which one you were. I was a clerk.

Soon after meeting Jim Wright for the first time back in the early 1950's, it was obvious to me that he had a mind that soaked up information faster than those paper towels sop up coffee spills on TV. Moreover, he could retrieve information like a 486 computer. At work I quickly learned the peril of giving him any information, even in casual conversation, unless you were absolutely sure what you were talking about. Once in House debate I was stunned to hear him refer to a California school controversy that I had mentioned flippantly as a passing thought several years before. I had not told him that my sole source for that information came from a couple of sentences on a radio newscast to which I was only half-listening.

Through the years, I came to admire his heart as well as his mind. In an office conversation after work one night, he mentioned having read about a psychologist who advanced an interesting theory. It held that the events which children experience in their 12th year are most decisive in shaping their feelings and values for the rest of their lives. For Jim Wright himself, I realized later, this was surely true. This formative year of his life had come during the depths of the Great Depression— and it profoundly affected the way he thought about the needs and hopes of everyday people.

Never realizing he had told the story before, he somberly recounted to me several times the pain and humiliation that befell his grandfather in those grim days. He had labored faithfully on the same job for 23 years. Yet the company abruptly fired him at age 63 to avoid paying the modest pension it had promised him at

65. The family watched in anguish as this proud man's sense of self-worth was steadily eroded away as he failed, day after day, in his desperate search to find another job. As a youngster Jim Wright didn't understand at first why his mother and father uprooted their family from their comfortable home in Weatherford and moved to Fort Worth. Later he found out they had done so for only one reason—to rent an apartment in his grandfather's house. Without this rent money to make house payments, his grandfather and grandmother would have been evicted.

Often he would recall, too, how his mother always shared their family's food with jobless men who rode freight trains from town to town, searching in vain for work. When these hungry vagabonds trudged to the back door of the Wright home, they always got a sandwich or a bowl of stew, even though his parents at one point were forced to sell the family piano to put food on their own table. It was the memory of these bleak days, embedded forever in Jim Wright's mind, that I believe provided the first defining moment of his Speakership.

It all started quietly, in the dead of night, about six weeks earlier. Driving down Constitution Avenue one morning, sleepy motorists were astonished to see a life-sized Bethlehem manger scene, the ultimate symbol of Christmas, standing prominently on the northeast corner of the pristine Capitol grounds. A contingent of Washington's homeless—the wretched refuse we prefer to have only on somebody else's teeming shore—had erected the scene during the night and now had gathered protectively around it. Mitch Snyder had struck again.

You don't remember Mitch Snyder? Well, even if future scientists finally discover how to clone human beings, they would still have a problem building a Mitch Snyder. There is no way the pieces would logically fit together. You would need a batch of genes from a quiet, selfless humanitarian like Mother Teresa, spiked with a batch of combative genes from a crafty Washington political manipulator like Dick Morris. On the surface, it would be an impossible mix. Yet in Mitch Snyder, there it was.

A former management consultant who once did a brief prison term, Snyder over the years had thrown his talent and energy into mobilizing help for the homeless people of Washington. Others had done this, too, but none with the instinctive leadership ability—or the personal daring—of Mitch Snyder.

Over the years the sight of Washington's homeless people— wretched, ragged and often mentally impaired—had become as common as the sight of the city's pigeon-splotched statues. With their plastic bags and trademark grocery carts, these forlorn men and women sleep or sit staring blankly on street corners and in city parks. Yet they seem largely invisible to most of the capital's 9 to 5 downtown business crowd as well as to the GS-8's laboring in obscurity behind the frosted glass panels in the corridors of government.

Unable to stir much interest in the White House or Congress about the plight of these people, Mitch Snyder in 1984 took a bold and dangerous step. During the President Ronald Reagan's re-election campaign, he began a one-man hunger strike, demanding that the government make available a decaying and abandoned federal building on 2nd Street NW for use as a homeless shelter. He nearly died.

The presidential campaign was in its 51st day, with the election only two days away. Mitch Snyder had withered away into a skeletal ghost of himself. Then, when word filtered out that "60 Minutes" was preparing a segment dramatizing this man's willingness to sacrifice his life in an effort to help the homeless, President Reagan capitulated. He agreed to turn the building into a "model" shelter, even though later, Mitch Snyder would have to fast twice more to get the $6 million that had been promised to refurbish the shelter.

After the success of that epic public drama, Mitch Snyder began to play the Washington press corps like Tiger Woods plays golf. Always eager to puncture official pomposity in Washington, especially on behalf of a person who seems free of devious motives, reporters gloried in Mitch Snyder's spunky attacks on the establishment and made his a household name. As an educated and forceful man, Mitch Snyder could surely could have built a comfortable and affluent life for himself in the suburbs. Yet he chose to sleep in a crowded and smelly homeless shelter, to dress in tattered jeans and to identify completely with the street people of Washington. Soon his fame spread. CBS did a movie called "Samaritan" on his good works. The press enshrined him as "Mr.

Homeless" in America and enthusiastically assisted him in high-pressuring Washington officialdom.

And then, a month and a half before Jim Wright was to become Speaker, Mitch Snyder turned his attention to Capitol Hill. With the help of his homeless group, the Community for Creative Non-Violence, he erected the Christmas manger scene on the Capitol grounds as a disquieting holiday reminder that, like many Americans today, long ago in Bethlehem, even the Christ child was homeless.

For any such display, however meritorious its cause, to be placed on House and Senate property was, of course, a violation of federal law. Fully aware of this, Mitch shrewdly organized a 24-hour vigil around the display. This guaranteed that if the Capitol police tried to remove the exhibit from government property, they would face an angry confrontation with poor, homeless people who were there to protect it. Wouldn't the 11 o'clock news love this? Wouldn't the newspapers love scenes of the Capitol police brandishing nightsticks to subdue a group of poor, hungry people defending a Christian manger scene symbolizing the plight of the homeless?

Once again, Mitch Snyder had put Washington officialdom on the spot. Christmas, a season of warmth and generosity, was approaching. The scene, with its Biblical figures, carried deep religious connotations. While most Americans surely were concerned about the homeless, most probably thought that, when you came right down to it, helping these unfortunate people was really the government's responsibility—certainly not that of individuals like themselves.

Realizing how easily they could fall into the diabolical trap Mitch Snyder had set, neither the Capitol police nor their bosses, the Sergeants at Arms of the House and Senate, made any move against the display. Not in a thousand years would any of these authorities have dared take any action unless they had direct orders from, well, uh, the Speaker.

At this point, in early December, 1986, any action to move the display would have required an order from Thomas P. (Tip) O'Neill. Since his term as Speaker would not expire until the new Congress was convened in January, the likable red-faced Irishman still held ultimate authority over the Capitol police. With Congress in recess, O'Neill was, of course, back home in Boston.

It is extremely doubtful that he ever even considered ordering police action. Even if so, his hand could have been stayed by his recollection of events like that of the United States Army attacking a rag-tag army of bonus marchers in Washington in 1932. Shown in countless television documentaries today, these old newsreel films depict a haughty General Douglas MacArthur, astride a prancing horse, directing his troops against destitute World War I veterans. Like the homeless of 1986, these Americans who fought at Saint Mihiel and Meuse-Argonne had come to the Capitol grounds seeking help from their government. Tip O'Neill, a man with a big heart, would have cringed at being remembered as a latter-day Douglas MacArthur. Besides, Tip O'Neill knew the torch was about to pass. Within a matter of days, it would be January 6, 1987.

This was the 105th anniversary of Sam Rayburn's birth, and the day Jim Wright had chosen to take his oath of office. It was a joyous, tumultuous day at the Capitol for hundreds of friends who had flown up from Texas, and for thousands of other well-wishers from the Washington area. They watched the ceremony. They celebrated. Thousands of others back in Fort Worth celebrated, too, as they watched the events over a satellite television hookup. Busy, euphoric and maybe a bit dazed, Jim Wright enjoyed probably the most gratifying day of his life. Friends who had known him since childhood swapped stories describing the disposition, the temperament and the character he would bring to this high office. None knew that within 24 hours, a tiny, unexpected incident would let Jim Wright define himself more clearly than any of us could have ever done.

Jack Russ was worried. As Sergeant of Arms for the House, he shared with a Senate counterpart the day-to-day responsibility for the Capitol Police. Realizing the Christmas manger scene on the Capitol grounds was as sensitive as an unexploded bomb, he nevertheless could bite his lip no longer. He brought his problem to the new Speaker, who was busy getting settled in his Capitol office.

As work crews moved in and out with furniture and books, Jack Russ explained that he had repeatedly warned Mitch Snyder and his followers that their display violated federal law.

"What do they say?" asked Jim Wright.

"They don't say anything. They just stand there and smirk at me," he said. Frustrated and angry over this blatant violation of a law he was sworn to enforce, he asked the new Speaker to give him permission to act. He wanted to remove the display, by force if necessary, and to subdue and arrest any of the homeless people who tried to resist.

Jim Wright walked to the window of his office. In the fading winter sunlight, he silently gazed toward the northeast corner of the Capitol grounds. His eyes were directed toward the manger scene, but I was not sure that was the only image in his mind. In a moment, he turned back to the Sergeant at Arms. "No, Jack," he said. "There's got to be a better way."

Disappointed, Jack Russ moved toward the door. As he left, Jim Wright ordered him not to undertake police action—at least not right now.

"This is one," he said quietly, "that I'm going to have to handle myself."

What happened next was vintage Jim Wright—and nobody could have been more surprised than Mitch Snyder. The moment Jack Russ left the office, Jim Wright dispatched an exceptionally able member of our staff, young, soft-spoken Steve Charnovitz, to the manger scene. "Find Mitch Snyder," he said. "Tell him the Speaker would like to talk with him, if it's convenient." Less than half an hour later, Mitch Snyder found himself sitting face to face and sipping coffee with a very unusual Washington official— one who, so far, at least, had neither scowled at him nor seemed intimidated by his presence.

You got the impression that he was far more surprised by Jim Wright's friendly welcome than he would have been by a Capitol police SWAT team attack. As he sat in his rumpled Army surplus jacket and tattered dungarees, he spoke movingly of the urgent needs of the hungry and the homeless—and how nobody in official Washington seemed even to be interested, much less willing to help.

Almost begging, he said, "If you would just come down to the shelter with me, you would understand." And then came a moment I will remember forever.

Jim Wright leaped from his chair and grabbed his topcoat. "Let's go!" he cried.

Mitch Snyder was petrified. "Not now!" he protested, shaking his head in astonishment.

Clearly unprepared for this kind of instantaneous response from anybody connected with the government, Mitch Snyder mumbled an explanation that it was nearly dark and besides, he wanted to notify the press of the Speaker's scheduled visit. Maybe it was my imagination, but in Jim Wright's eye I thought I caught a twinkle which lasted only a millisecond. In any case, the message to me was unmistakable. Even if his books had not yet been placed on the shelves, and even if his pictures had not yet been hung on the wall, the House of Representatives had a new and different kind of Speaker.

Three days later, escorted by Mitch Snyder and accompanied by a swarm of reporters and television crews, Jim Wright stepped over a cat sprawled in a worn hallway and entered the run-down shelter at 2nd and D Streets NW. Grossly overcrowded, the building housed 800 men, many of them elderly. Some were sitting or sleeping on cots lining the rooms and hallways.

"Comfortable and polite middle-income people don't like to focus on this problem," Jim Wright said. Moving from cot to cot, he talked with a few of these bedraggled and benumbed men who lived in the shadows of American life. He listened attentively to Mitch Snyder's urgent appeal. Then, before leaving, he promised to press for passage of a $500 million bill to provide help to the nation's homeless—$400 million more than the Reagan administration was asking—plus an emergency food aid bill. Quietly and without protest, Mitch Snyder and his friends moved their Christmas manger scene off the Capitol grounds.

To me, Jim Wright's success in this tiny incident seemed to be a microcosmic preview of his Speakership. Old instincts die hard, and for years as a newspaperman I had always looked for some small, telltale incident or omen that seemed to offer an insight into a larger view. In the private cocoon of my own mind, I accepted his adroit handling of the Mitch Snyder episode as exactly this sort of portent—a harbinger of successes yet to come. Undoubtedly I attached to it a symbolism far beyond its real importance. *This is it,* I wanted to believe. *This is the daring, go-it-alone, do-it-now, get-it-done* leadership style that would be Jim Wright's heritage in the history books. I knew its boldness would frighten the timid and discombobulate the orthodox. But I wanted to believe it would pave the way for one of the most dynamic and productive Congresses in history. I also thought, in my euphoria, that all Americans would cheer such forceful leadership and wish him well. Over the next 29 months, I would see how right I was on the first part, and how dead wrong on the second.

At this writing it's been almost ten years since Jim Wright stood in the well of the House and resigned both his Speakership and his seat in Congress. So tragic and unfair were some events which led to his resignation that even today, nearly a decade later, I find them painful to relate. On September 16, 1988, he went before the House Ethics Committee and addressed all the issues that had been raised against him by Congressman Newt Gingrich of Georgia. But then came a runaway "outside counsel" with burning political ambitions and a blank check to wine and dine committee members, plus swarms of right-wing political enemies and, in its instinctive zeal for piling on, the press. Day by day the accusations were stacked, one atop another, like lumber stockpiled for a gallows. And by then it was too late. Hounded and pilloried until his ability to lead the House was eroded and virtually destroyed, only one honorable course was left open to Jim Wright. To prevent further harm to the institution he loved, he must resign.

To me, this seemed a frightful penalty to extract from a man who was never charged, even by his fiercest political enemies, with having violated any law. His role as a national leader—and indeed, his whole political life—was compromised, and eventually voluntarily ended, by charges that he violated the rules of the House.

He never claimed he was entirely blameless. In his resignation speech he wondered in anguish if he himself had caused a lot of his trouble.

"Maybe I have," he said. "God, I hope I have not, but maybe I have. Have I been too partisan? Too insistent? To abrasive? Too determined to have my way? Perhaps. Maybe so."

Courageous words, these. Today they stand in sharp contrast to the efforts of other national leaders, both before and after Jim Wright's time, to blame their problems on others. Whether justified or not, this Jim Wright refused to do.

While his forceful personality surely antagonized some, I believe his troubles were rooted also in the malignant mood of ill will that began to spread through the House at least three years before he became Speaker in 1987 and continues to grip the institution even now. For most of the 1990's, the House has been stirred by deep political partisanship and even hatred. A proud and strong-willed leader became a highly inviting target for the frustration and resentments and anger that remain rampant today.

It was in 1984 that a small group of Republicans, led by Congressman Gingrich, methodically began attacking the reputations and the motives of their Democratic colleagues. Since C-SPAN covered "special order" speeches by individual members each day after the House had finished its legislative business, this group used the free cable television exposure to inveigh against the character and patriotism of Democrats, singling out many by name. Some were denounced as "dictators" and "cheaters." By policy, House television cameras had always focused tightly on the person who was speaking, rather than on the chamber at large. Thus, in 17 million homes, a person watching C-SPAN had no way of knowing these partisan speeches were going unchallenged mainly because they were being made to an empty hall.

When Democratic members complained to Tip OíNeill that they were being deprived of a chance to defend themselves, the Speaker ordered the House cameras to begin panning the chamber. For the first time viewers were able to see that these vitriolic attacks were being spewed out over a vast sea of empty seats.

On May 15 Gingrich appeared on the House floor to defend an earlier coordinated Republican attack on Democratic foreign policy statements. For Tip O'Neill, this was the last straw.

Red-faced and furious, the massive, white-maned lawmaker lumbered up the aisle and leveled an accusing finger at Gingrich. "You deliberately stood in the well of this House and took on these members when you knew they would not be here," he thundered. "It's un-American. It's the lowest thing I've heard in my 32 years here."

While O'Neill's words were surely no worse than many of the Republican attacks calling him "corrupt" and "the most partisan Speaker in history," his counterattack was indisputably harsh and was stricken from the record.

This, then, was the climate of antagonism into which Jim Wright stepped as Speaker. While it would eventually destroy his effectiveness and prompt his resignation, it would not prevent the 100th Congress from becoming one of the most productive in memory. Nowhere can this be seen more clearly than in his role in ending that despicable little war in Nicaragua.

Like millions of his generation, Jim Wright knew about war. Only days after the Japanese attacked Pearl Harbor on December 7, 1941, he dropped his studies at the University of Texas and enlisted in the Army Air Corps. He got his wings a year later and was ordered to the Pacific, where he flew B-24 combat missions and was awarded the Distinguished Flying Cross. But Jim Wright also knew about peace.

Infatuated even in his high school days with the study of history, he steeped himself in accounts of the events which shaped our country. Of these, none intrigued him more than President Woodrow Wilson's heroic but ultimately futile effort after World War I to win Senate approval for the League of Nations. While his high school pals doted on the comic strip exploits of Detective Dick Tracy, Jim Wright read with growing admiration how this ailing President whistle-stopped across the country in 1919 in an effort to bring our country into an organization fostering peace among nations. As Jim Wright sat in his room in the 1930s and burrowed into his history books, he wondered again and again why Woodrow Wilson's lonely quest for peace seemed to have been so frivolously rejected. Deep in the psyche of an impressionable red-headed teenager in Texas, a tiny seed had been planted.

Other formative ideas and questions took root, also. There was, for example, the military service he knew his father had been called upon to render in 1916 on the U.S.-Mexico border. As the captain of a National Guard unit, the elder Wright had been sent to the Rio Grande to prevent Pancho Villa's forays into the United States. To the son, it seemed incongruous that military action should ever be necessary between neighboring nations at peace. He began to dig into other books to learn more about Mexico and Latin America.

Decades later, after joining his Congressional staff, I discovered the depth of Jim Wright's bedrock belief that our hemispheric neighbors were entitled to the same respect we demanded for ourselves. His reason, repeated like a mantra in speech after speech, was simple: *No area in the world is more important to the future of the United States than Latin America.* He championed the Alliance for Progress, the Latin-American development program launched in 1961 by President John F. Kennedy. A few years later, having been appointed to the U.S.-Mexico Interparliamentary Conference, he began crawling out of bed at 5:30 to attend Spanish language classes before beginning his regular work day on Capitol Hill. As the only member of the U.S. delegation to address the Mexicans in their own language, he earned a measure of respect seldom accorded Norteamericanos. With enhanced credentials and ever-growing interest, he traveled widely and built solid friendships among Latin America's democratic leaders.

It does not seem unusual, then, that a man with these credentials would be invited to help bring peace to Nicaragua. What was astonishing was the source of this invitation. It came from President Ronald Wilson Reagan.

In his role as Majority Leader and later as Speaker, Jim Wright found Ronald Reagan a curious combination of talents and interests. He didn't know quite what to make of the man. Like millions of other Americans, Jim Wright found him to be a charming fellow—a wonderful story-teller, gracious and self-effacing. The thing that disturbed Jim Wright was that Reagan the President had demonstrated time and again in personal contacts that he didn't seem to know a damn thing about running the government. Nor did he seem particularly anxious to learn, leaving day-to-day leadership to a coterie of arch conservative advisers. And there was another curious thing.

How did Reagan come to embrace Republicanism after having been a stalwart Democratic liberal? Even as the darling of the right wing, Reagan as President offered generous praise of Franklin D. Roosevelt, Harry S. Truman and Sam Rayburn.

"I think I've got it figured out," Jim Wright mused one day. "He only likes *dead* Democrats."

It was in July, 1987, that a good friend, Tom Loeffler, came to the Speaker's office. As a four-term Republican Congressman from Texas who had left the House to make an unsuccessful race for Governor, Loeffler and Jim Wright knew and respected each other. Today Loeffler had come to the office as an emissary of the President. The Reagan White House knew, of course, that Jim Wright enjoyed widespread respect and had numerous friends throughout Central America. But the President's advisers had missed a subtle point. They didn't know about the convictions that had grown over the years from those high school history books. Tom Loeffler asked if Jim Wright would join the President in trying to bring peace to Central America.

A bipartisan peace initiative?   With Ronald Reagan? Warning flags went up in Jim Wright's mind. While he trusted Tom Loeffler, he was understandably wary of the Oliver North element in the Reagan administration. True, the Iran-Contra scandal had virtually wiped out any chance that Congress would provide further military funding to the U.S.-backed Contra forces. Yet the new Speaker was not sure the Reagan administration really had given up on the idea of using force to topple the leftist government of Nicaragua. Could this be a devious White House scheme to issue a phony call for peace which, when it failed, would be an excuse for demanding more money from Congress to pursue the war?

Many of his fellow Democrats were certain this was the case. They warned him he would be walking into a trap. The liberals were furious. They regarded it as an obvious attempt at deception on the part of the Reagan Administration and its most fanatical supporter of the Contras, Assistant Secretary of State Elliott Abrams.

It was a tough call for Jim Wright. It would be a high-wire act without a net. He would be strictly on his own. If it blew up in his face, he would look naive and foolish. There were, of course, other considerations.

The war had cost the lives of a hundred thousand people in El Salvador and Nicaragua during the past six years. There was no assurance that the Contra forces would ever prevail over the Sandanistas. Moreover, such festering violence always posed the risk that U.S. troops could eventually become involved, just as they had in Vietnam. Yet President Reagan insisted that the Sandanistas could obtain peace only by negotiating with the Contras. Daniel Ortega, the Nicaraguan leader, was demanding talks directly with the United States. For this miserable little war, there appeared to be no end in sight.

Many thoughts must have been weighed in Jim Wright's mind over these next few days. Maybe he wondered how another man, nearly seventy years before, laid his power and prestige on the line in a courageous bid for peace, only to collapse and suffer a paralytic stroke. Maybe another thought dwelled on political power which, like money, is useless if not used. Maybe yet another was the realization that if he did not act, nobody would. And maybe there echoed in his mind the words he spoke to Jack Russ. *This is one I'm going to have to handle myself.* In the end, that is exactly what he did. He sent word to the President that yes, he would cooperate in a joint call for peace.

Do it now. Get it done. With the encouragement of his longtime friend, President Oscar Arias of Costa Rica, the Speaker drafted a proposal for a six-point Reagan-Wright peace plan. To his surprise, the White House accepted it with only modest changes. The plan included an immediate cease-fire, an end to all outside military support for both sides, restoration of all civil liberties, and preparations for free elections. Then, only a few days later, as he worked to build support in Congress, Jim Wright received heartening news.

The five Central American presidents, meeting in Guatemala, had agreed on a peace plan of their own that embraced most provisions of the Reagan-Wright plan. Drafted by President Arias, the new plan differed mainly in that the cease-fire would not be immediate, but would come within ninety days. Jim Wright was elated that a peace initiative, even if not exactly his own, had come so far so fast.

Calling him "an extraordinary player in the Central American events," an editorial in *The Washington Post* added: "He's taking a large chance, but a necessary one, in helping open the way to convert the Arias plan from paper to reality."

But the Reagan people started having second thoughts. Defense Secretary Casper Weinberger called on the White House to junk the whole effort. Contra hard-liners became even more distraught when they learned the Speaker had sat in on a meeting between Nicaraguan President Daniel Ortega and the respected Catholic leader being asked to mediate the peace, Cardinal Miguel Obando y Bravo.

The nearly hysterical pro-Contra clique in the White House was chided in *The Washington Post* by columnist Philip Geyelin. "Come now," he said. "The Speaker was doing nothing inconsistent with the role that was urged upon him by the administration's top people last summer."

House Democrats were ecstatic. "He beat 'em," cried Congressman George Miller, a California liberal who had warned of a trap. "I wouldn't have given a plugged nickel for what he was thinking of doing." Republicans were considerably less complimentary.

"He's the most arrogant abuser of power I've ever seen," complained Minority Whip Trent Lott of Mississippi. Congressman Dick Cheney of Illinois, chairman of the Republican Policy Committee, got so mad at Jim Wright be began to wax nostalgic about the warmth and affection of the previous Speaker, Tip O'Neill. "There are no such feelings for Jim Wright," he sniffed. If Jim Wright winced at such observations, it may have prompted him only to work harder.

Within the first few months of his Speakership, the House had overridden two Reagan vetoes—one on clean water, the other on highways and mass transit—and passed a budget drastically re-ordering national priorities. Public opinion polls showed vigorous support for these actions.

"Wright has emerged as a political lone ranger, leading Democrats into high-risk territory often before they are ready to go," said *The Washington Post*. His "approach marks a dramatic shift in the running of the House and in the role of the House Speaker as Washington's No. 1 Democrat."

All this worried Newt Gingrich. Jim Wright already had surpassed even his highest expectations. In his book, *The Ambition and the Power*, John M. Barry quotes a Gingrich observation: *If Wright ever consolidates his power, he will be a very, very formidable man. We have to take him on early to prevent that.* Thus, like a battlefield commander stalemated by an unexpectedly strong force, Gingrich soon switched his attack to another sector—the House Ethics Committee.

His initial accusations were based on newspaper clippings, some eight to ten years old, dealing with Jim Wright's personal finances. Certain that he knowingly had done nothing wrong, the Speaker asked the committee to look into the charges. He was sure this would take no more than a couple of weeks at most and lead to complete exoneration.

But then came two unexpected events. One was that Common Cause, supposedly a non-partisan citizens' lobby, joined Gingrich in calling for an investigation of Jim Wright. This gave a measure of respectability to what up to then had been seen merely as a Gingrich political ploy. Many Democrats were infuriated. Having worked closely with Common Cause on issues like arms control and halting Contra aid, they felt betrayed. They suspected that the formerly high-minded lobby group had taken this action to raise money and to make good its claim of bipartisanship.

The other blow came when Richard J. Phelan, an ambitious Chicago lawyer, was named as outside special counsel for the investigation. The moment Phelan's name surfaced, I received an urgent call from a leading Fort Worth attorney. As a longtime friend of Jim Wright's, the local lawyer knew Phelan and warned that he would approach this crucial position as a prosecutor looking for headlines rather than an impartial set of facts. Jim Wright's attorney, William C. (Bill) Oldaker, and I were urged by our Fort Worth friend to fight for another counsel—one who would be even-handed and who entertained no personal political ambitions. In this we were unsuccessful, but our friend's fears were well founded. After observing Phelan's handling of the investigation, *Legal Times* in its issue of April 24, 1989, described his role this way:

"What began as the rather flimsy efforts of Rep. Newt Gingrich (R-Ga.) to harass Wright during an election year became, in Phelan's hands, a broad-based indictment of much of the speaker's personal dealings over decades in public office. Phelan used the original charges brought by Gingrich as a springboard into all of Wright's financial affairs."

The journal noted that Phelan regularly wined and dined committee members—the judges and jurors in the Jim Wright case—while running up $150,000 in "out-of-pocket expenses" during the investigation. Any such ex parte activity by Oldaker would have been considered unethical. To bolster his personal efforts, Phelan enlisted seven associate attorneys. The eight lawyers billed the committee for more than 6,000 hours of legal work at $125 an hour, *Legal Times* reported.

By now this wide-ranging investigation had begun to take on a life of its own.   Gingrich kept up a growing drumbeat of attacks.   Right-wing zealots became ever   more certain they could now cripple if not destroy Jim Wright.   Planted stories, many without foundation, were foisted on news organizations.   Swept up in the feeding frenzy, the press became a wolf pack, with reporters vying with each other   to come up with new accusations or horror stories about the alleged misdeeds of the Speaker.   One newspaper exhumed a story about a forty-year-old unsolved murder in which a Jim Wright opponent had been mysteriously shot to death during a race for the Texas Legislature.   Try as we would, it was tough for our staff not to take on a bunker mentality.

One day David Montgomery of the *Fort Worth Star-Telegram*—the hometown paper for which I had worked two years as a reporter—called me to say he was checking out an anonymous accusation that the Speaker's wife was illiterate.   David had talked with Betty Wright many times.   He knew she had worked on the executive staff of Hotel Texas in Fort Worth in the 1950s and later on the House Public Works Committee in Washington.

Furious, I refused even to acknowledge such a question.   "You know damn well that's not true, David!" I shouted.   "Why are you doing this?"

Jim Wright was even more infuriated than I, but he responded by trying to make a joke of the question, saying that Betty was literate in English, Spanish and shorthand.

To a few reporters, the reason for the wave of vicious rumors and dirty tricks was obvious.   "House Speaker Jim Wright has reached the top of the heap in Washington.   The proof is not in adulation, but in the amount of vitriol poured on him by frustrated Republicans," wrote columnists Jack Anderson and Dale Van Atta.

They pointed out that Jim Wright was cast as a the consummate bogeyman in Republican fund-raising literature.   One letter sent out by the Council for Inter-American Security was so vicious it caused two board members to resign.   It accused Jim Wright of "treasonous acts" because he met with Cardinal Miguel Obando y Bravo and Nicaraguan leader Daniel Ortega in a quest for Central American peace.

Even Jim Wright supporters back in Fort Worth were subjected to abuse.   Some friends were awakened by late-night telephone calls. "This is an urgent message from the Speaker of the House," cried a recorded message. Then it claimed to be a fund-raising pitch for ex-Senator Gary Hart of Colorado, whom Jim Wright had never supported.

In Washington, reporters got anonymous tips that Jim Wright had lied about his role as a flyer in World War II. Another was an utterly groundless accusation that he beat his wife so badly she had to be hospitalized. Less preposterous but equally untruthful, stories were planted that Jim Wright flew free on a corporate airplane owned by a nursing home. There was no such airplane. Another story asserted that Jim Wright was under investigation for an income tax violation. The next day an Internal Revenue Service official disavowed this falsehood.

President Reagan's top economic development official, Orson Swindle III, even flew to Fort Worth and spoke before a civic club, accusing the Speaker of wasting taxpayers' money by earmarking $11.8 million in federal grants to revitalize the Stockyards area.

In his dedicated efforts to root out every last vestige of what he considered Jim Wright's evil and nefarious deeds, Phelan focused on the Speaker's little book, *Reflections of a Public Man.*

This was a 117-page paperback consisting of short speeches, articles and essays written by Jim Wright over the years. It was printed by Carlos Moore, a longtime friend who ran a small Fort Worth printing company. Moore pointed out that his firm incurred far less overhead than big publishing houses in New York, and proposed a royalty split giving Jim Wright 60 per cent, or $3.57, of the book's sale price of $5.95.

From these book sales the Speaker made about $55,000. Some were bought as gifts for their members by labor and business organizations which supported Jim Wright. Phelan saw this as a scheme Jim Wright contrived to circumvent the House limitation on speech honoraria.

Several earlier books by Jim Wright had been published by big New York firms, and a few lonely voices in the press saw this latest publishing arrangement as somewhat less heinous than the Texas chainsaw murders. Henry Mitchell, a *Washington Post* columnist, pooh-poohed claims that this was not an honest-to-goodness book and that an author should not receive a royalty higher than the usual 10 per cent.

"Would Wright's book be judged a 'real' book if only the publishers, with their usual greedy low cunning, had raked off the profit instead of the author?   A businessman is applauded in America if he makes huge profits, but a book author is thought to be guilty of something irregular if his royalty arrangements are unusually lucrative," he wrote.

But the pendulum had swung too far.   At this point no Republican would have dared to breathe a word in Jim Wright's behalf.   Many Democrats, while proud of the House's accomplishments under his leadership in the 100th Congress, refused to venture into the whirlwind of controversy which had enveloped him.

Even at home, there was no peace for the Speaker. The press had begun its "death watch" at his home in suburban Virginia. When he woke up in the morning he would find reporters and television crews encamped on his lawn.   When he ventured outside, boom mikes were thrust in his face. "When are you going to quit, Mr. Speaker?" came the insistent shouts.

Jim Wright's only consistent comfort came from polls conducted among the people who knew him best—his constituents, the people he had served for 34 years. These polls showed 81 per cent of the people in his Texas district would vote for him again. Among Republican voters, his level of support was 72 per cent.

In those last few days, a few Congressional friends tried to negotiate some means of accommodation between Jim Wright and Phelan. Jim Wright would have no part of this. He rejected outright anything that smacked of a plea bargain.

It was not until his resignation speech, ironically, that he got an unfettered opportunity to take his side of the story fully and coherently to the public. Now, in the glare of nationwide television, he had asked for and was granted one full hour. In a dramatic speech filling ten pages of the *Congressional Record*, he cited facts and included authoritative documents disproving the charges against him in all three basic areas—that his wife Betty did no real work on a job paying $18,000 a year; that her employer, George Mallick, had a "direct interest in legislation"; and that the book was an effort to skirt the limit on speech honoraria.

Even though he felt certain of the rightness of his actions, Jim Wright realized weeks before his final speech that in truth, he could not expect to provide the dynamic leadership he believed the House deserved—the kind that had marked his first two years as Speaker. So rampant was partisan hostility in the House that, even with his innocence ultimately confirmed, he knew his Speakership had been damagingly compromised. The very spectacle of a Speaker so grievously accused by his political enemies was turning the House into a media circus and disrupting the nation's legislative business.

The Speakership was not necessary to Jim Wright's happiness. His self-respect was. If he couldn't be an effective Speaker, he didn't want to be Speaker at all.

"I do not want to be a party to tearing up this institution. I love it," he said.

"Let me give you back this job...as a propitiation for this whole season of ill will."

He urged members of House not to take retribution on each other. "All of us in both political parties must resolve to bring this period of mindless cannibalism to an end," he said. "There's been enough of it."

On May 31, 1989, Jim Wright stood alone in the well of the House, secure in his enormous sense of dignity, and spoke his final words in the historic chamber that he loved.

"I am not a bitter man. I am not going to be. I am a lucky man. God has given me the privilege of serving in this, the greatest lawmaking institution on earth, for a great many years, and I am grateful to the people of my district in Texas, and grateful to you, my colleagues, all of you. God bless this institution. God bless the United States."